Dorothea Ruggles-Brise

The minstrelsy of Ireland

200 Irish songs, adapted to their traditional airs

Dorothea Ruggles-Brise

The minstrelsy of Ireland
200 Irish songs, adapted to their traditional airs

ISBN/EAN: 9783744736497

Printed in Europe, USA, Canada, Australia, Japan

Cover: Foto ©Thomas Meinert / pixelio.de

More available books at **www.hansebooks.com**

AUGENER'S EDITION,

No. 8928.

THE

MINSTRELSY OF IRELAND

200 𝕴𝖗𝖎𝖘𝖍 𝕾𝖔𝖓𝖌𝖘,

ADAPTED TO THEIR TRADITIONAL AIRS,

ARRANGED FOR VOICE WITH PIANOFORTE ACCOMPANIMENT,

AND SUPPLEMENTED WITH HISTORICAL NOTES,

by

ALFRED MOFFAT.

"Music is the first faculty of the Irish; and scarcely anything has such power for good over them. The use of this faculty and this power publicly and constantly, to keep up their spirits, refine their tastes, warm their courage, increase their union, and renew their zeal—is the duty of every patriot."— THOMAS DAVIS.

❦ ❦ ❦

Augener & Co., London.

199, REGENT STREET, W.

City Branch—   Library and School Department—
23, Newgate Street, E.C.   81, Regent Street, W.

PREFACE.

I HAVE much pleasure in acknowledging the great kindness and courtesy which I have received from all to whom I have applied for help in the compiling of this volume of Irish folk-songs. My thanks are due to Dr. Patrick W. Joyce, Dublin; Mr. John Glen, Edinburgh; Mr. Frank Kidson, Leeds; Mr. F. C. Cronin, Limerick; Count and Countess Plunkett, Dublin; Mr. D. J. O'Donoghue, Finglas; and Mr. Francis Fahy, London. To Mr. T. L. Lyster, Principal Librarian of the National Library of Ireland, I am especially indebted for allowing me access to the valuable Joli Collection of Irish music contained in the National Library of Ireland. Owing to the kindness of Miss Dora Sigerson (Mrs. Clement Shorter), Miss Katharine Tynan (Mrs. Hinkson), Miss Rosa Mulholland (Mrs. Gilbert), Dr. George Sigerson, Mr. Michael Hogan (the Bard of Thomond), and Mr. W. B. Yeats, I have been enabled to enrich my work with many beautiful songs by these writers. My thanks are also offered to my anonymous correspondent for the interesting collection of traditional Irish airs, forwarded to me from Dublin about the beginning of the present year; also to Messrs. Pigott & Co., Dublin, for permitting me to extract some melodies from Hoffmann's *Ancient Music of Ireland.*

ALFRED MOFFAT.

March, 1897.

INDEX OF FIRST LINES.

v

INDEX OF TITLES.

A baby was sleeping, its mother was weeping.

THE ANGELS' WHISPER.

Andante.

Samuel Lover.

VOICE.

PIANO.

1. A ba - by was sleep - ing, Its
2. Her beads while she num - ber'd, The
3. "And while they are keep - ing Bright
4. The dawn of the morn - ing Saw

con Ped.

1. moth - er was weep - ing For her hus - band was far on the wild rag - ing sea, And the
2. ba - by still slum - ber'd, And smil'd in her face as she bend - ed her knee: "Oh!
3. watch o'er thy sleep - ing, Oh, pray to them soft - ly, my ba - by, with me: And
4. Der - mot re - turn - ing, And his wife wept with joy her babe's fa - ther to see, And

sf   p

rit.   p

1. tem - pest was swell - ing Round the fish - er - man's dwell - ing, And she
2. bless'd be that warn - ing, My child, thy sleep a - dorn - ing, For I
3. say thou would'st ra - ther They'd watch o'er thy fa - ther, For I
4. close - ly ca - ress - ing Her child with a bless - ing Said, "I

rit.

rit.

1. cried, "Der - mot, dar - ling, oh! come back to me!"
2. know that the An - gels are whis - p'ring with thee."
3. know that the An - gels are whis - p'ring with thee."
4. knew that the An - gels were whis - p'ring with thee!"

p   rit.

"A superstition of great beauty prevails in Ireland, that, when a child smiles in its sleep, it is talking with the Angels" (original note to song). Lover's song was published in 1840; the air, under the title of "Mary, do you fancy me?" is in Bunting's *Ancient Irish Music*, 1796, and in Holden's *Periodical Irish Melodies*, vol i., issued early in the century.

B 2

A long farewell I send to thee.

FAREWELL TO THE MAIG.

Translated from the Irish by EDWARD WALSH.

Andante.

VOICE.

PIANO.

p con espress.

poco rit.

1. A long fare -
2. Fare-well to
3. Forc'd by the

1. - well . . . I send to thee, . . . Fair Maig of corn and fruit and
2. her . . . to whom 'tis due, . . . The fair skin, gen - tle, mild-lipp'd,
3. priests . . my love to thee, . . . Fair Maig thro' life I ne'er shall

1. tree, Of state and gift, . . . and gath-'ring grand . . . Of song, ro -
2. true, For whom ex - il'd o'er the hills I go . . . . My heart's dear
3. see; And must my beau - teous bird fore-go, ... And all the

Dr. Petrie, from whose collection I have taken this air, considers, that owing to its construction, the tune may have been an English one imported into Ireland. "It would be strange if, during the last seven centuries, in which our island has been so largely planted from England, no melodies should have been introduced amongst us which had sufficient beauty to insure their perpetuation, even after they had been forgotten in the country in which they had their origin" (Petrie Collection, p. 111.) A good example of one of these imported tunes is "One Sunday after Mass," which I have shown on p. 212 to be the composition of Leveridge, and in print as early as 1719 ; the ballad, "It was an old beggarman, weary and wet." (Petrie Coll., p. 117)

1. - mance, and chief - tain bland. Uch och ón! . . . dark for - tune's
2. love what - e'er my woe. Uch och ón! . . . dark for - tune's
3. sex that wrought me woe.— Uch och ón! . . . my grief, my

1. rig - our—Wealth, ti - tle, bribe . . . of glo - rious fig - ure, Feast, gift,
2. rig - our—Wealth, ti - tle, bribe . . . of glo - rious fig - ure, Feast, gift,
3. ru - in! 'Twas drinking deep . . . and beau - ty woo - ing That caus'd thro'

1. all gone, and gone my vig - our Since thus I wan - der lone - ly.
2. all gone, and gone my vig - our Since thus I wan - der lone - ly.
3. life my whole . . . un - do - ing And left me thus wand'ring lone - ly.

is also nothing more than a modern version of the old Scotch ballad, "The Gaberlunzie Man," printed in the *Orpheus Caledonius* 1725, and *Tea Table Miscellany*, 1724, and attributed by some to James V. of Scotland; various other examples might be quoted from Petrie's Collection, and they show how necessary it is to have a knowledge of the printed folk music of the three countries in forming a true collection of any one of them. The melody given above was taken down from the singing of a country girl about 1810, to a street ballad commencing :—

"Oh! Nancy, Nancy, don't you remember
The protestations that you made to me ?"

4

Arise from thy slumbers.

Translated from the Irish by MARY BALFOUR.

Andante tranquillo.

VOICE.

PIANO.

p

con espress. e rit.

cres.

1. A - rise from thy slum - bers, oh,
2. A bed of fresh i - vy to

1. fair - est of maids! With me wilt thou wan - der to Trui-gha's green
2. rest thee I'll bring, The black - birds and thrush - es a - round us shall

cres.
sf

p

1. shades, Where sor - rel and bright . . . . . . row - an ber - ries a -
2. sing; And there with un - ceas - - - ing at - tach - ment I'll

p

cres.   *rit.*

1. bound, And nuts in rich clus - ters the branch - es have crown'd.
2. prove How sooth - ing the cares of af - fec - tion and love.

cres.   *rit.*

Air: "The Old Truigha," and given in Bunting's *Ancient Music of Ireland,* 1809, with Miss Balfour's verses headed "From
a literal translation of the original Irish." It has much affinity with "Lough Sheeling" (see p. 40), and must not be confounded
with the melody known as "Green woods of Truigha," to which Moore wrote "Silence is in our festal halls" (see p. 222). It
has also nothing in common with "The green woods of Treugh" in R. A. Smith's *Irish Minstrel,* 1825; "The green woods of
Trucha," in Mulhollan's *Irish Airs,* 1810; "The green woods of Trugh" in Murphy's *Irish Airs and Jiggs,* 1809; all of which are
distinctly different airs although bearing similar titles.

As a beam o'er the face of the waters.

THOMAS MOORE.

Andante.

VOICE.

1. As a beam o'er ... the
2. One fa - tal .... re -
3. Oh! this thought in .... the

PIANO.

p con espress.

rit.

p

1. face of the wa - ters may glow While the tide runs ... in dark - ness and
2. mem - b'rance, one sor - row that throws Its bleak shade .. a - like o'er our
3. midst of en - joy - ment will stay Like a dead leaf - less branch in the

1. cold - ness be - low, So the cheek ... may be ting'd with a warm sun - ny
2. joys and our woes, To which life .... no - thing dark - er or bright - er can
3. sum - mer's bright ray; The beams ... of the warm sun play round it in

f

1. smile,... Tho' the cold heart to ... ru - in runs dark - ly the ... while.
2. bring,... For which joy has no ... balm . . and af - flic - tion no ... sting.
3. vain, ... It may smile in his ... light . . . but it blooms not a - gain.

p con espress.

rit.

colla voce.

p

rit.

Air: "The Young Man's Dream." As shown in Appendix, this air is the progenitor of the celebrated air "The Last Rose of Summer." It is printed in Bunting's *Ancient Irish Music*, 1796, and in Hime's *Selection of the Most Admired Original Irish Airs never before Printed.* This *Selection* is undated, but is certainly not later than from 1800 to 1810: in spite of its promising title-page, it is only remarkable for not containing a single air which had not been already printed. Moore's verses are from the first number of the Melodies, 1807.

G

As beautiful Kitty.

KITTY OF COLERAINE.

EDWARD LYSAGHT.

Allegretto.

VOICE.

1. As beau - ti - ful Kit - ty one
2. I sat down be - side her, and

PIANO.

1. morn - - ing was trip - ping, With a pitch - er of milk from the
2. gen - - tly did chide her, That such a mis - for - tune should

1. fair of Cole - raine, When she saw me she stum - bled, the
2. give her such pain ; A kiss then I gave her, and

"The authorship of this song has been erroneously attributed to Edward Lysaght" (O'Donoghue) ; it was issued early in the century by Kelly of Waterford as a chap-book and is to be found in many collections of Irish songs. The air, which has nothing in common with "Kitty of Coleraine ; or, Paddy's Resource," to which Moore wrote his song, "Ill Omens," is printed in George Thompson's *Irish Airs*, vol. ii., O'Farrell's *Pocket Companion*, Bk. iv., *Musical Cabinet*, etc.

1. pitch - er it tum -bled, And all the sweet but - ter - milk wa - ter'd the plain. "Oh!
2. ero I did leave her, She vow'd for such plea -sure she'd break it a - gain. 'Twas

1. what shall I do now? 'Twas look - ing at you, now; Sure,
2. hay - mak - ing sea - son,— I can't tell the rea - son— Mis -

1. sure, such a pitch - er I'll ne'er meet a - gain, 'Twas the pride of my dai - ry! O
2. -for -tunes will nev - er come sin - gle, 'tis plain, For ver - y soon af - ter poor

1. Bar - ney Mac -Clea - ry, You're sent as a plague on the girls of Cole - raine!"
2. Kit - ty's dis - as - ter, The dev - il a pitch - er was whole in Cole - raine!

As I gaed o'er the Highland hills.

PEGGY BAWN.

Allegretto.

VOICE.

1. As

PIANO.

p

poco rit.

Ped.

1. I gaed o'er the High-land hills To a far - mer's house I
2. court - ed her the lea - lang eve, Till . . near the dawn of
3. be - ing come and break - fast To the par - lour I was
4. of - fer sir, is ve - ry good, And I thank you too," said
5. Peg - gy Bawn, thou art my own, And thy heart lies in my

1. came, The night be - ing dark and some - thing wet, I . . .
2. day, When frank - ly she to me did say "A -
3. ta'en, The gude - man . . kind - ly ask - ed me If I'd
4. I; "But the' I can - not be your son - in - law, And I'll
5. breast, And tho' we . . at a dis - tance are, Yet I

The Air "Peggy Bawn," or "Fair Peggy," seems to have been a great favourite about a century ago. In 1788 Shield introduced it in his opera *Marion*, the book of which was written by Mrs. Brooke. It is also to be found in O'Farrell's *Irish Music for the Union Pipes*, circa 1797–1800, Aird's Collection, vol. v., 1797, Holden's *Periodical Irish Melodies* and other works. A somewhat curious setting is to be seen in "James Warwick's MS.," 1807, a little MS. collection of tunes now in the "James Walker Collection " in the Aberdeen Public Library; it is there entitled "Peggy Bawn, thou art my dear." I have been unable to discover the author of the ballad given above; it was very popular during the first half of the century.

1. ven - tur'd in - to the same, Where I was kind - ly
2. - lang wi' thee I'll gae; For Ire - - land is a
3. mar - ry his daugh-ter Jane; "Five hun - - dred merks I'll
4. tell you the rea - son why; My bus - - 'ness call - eth
5. love thee still the best; Al - - though we at a

1. treat - ed, And a pret - - ty girl I spied, . . Who
2. fine coun - try, And the Scots to you are kin, . . So
3. give her Be - side a piece of lan'," . . But
4. me in haste; I . . . am the king's servant bound . . . And
5. dis - tance are, And the seas be - tween us roar, . . . Yet

1. ask'd me if I had a wife? But mar - riage I de -
2. I will gang a - lang wi' thee, My for - tune to be -
3. scarce - ly had he spoke the word, Than I thought of Peg - gy
4. I must gang a - wa' this day Straight to E - din - burgh
5. I'll be con - stant, Peg - gy Bawn, To thee for ev - er -

Vers s 1 to 4. | **Last time.**

1. - nied.   2. I   5. - more
2. - gin."   3. Day
3. Bawn.   4. "Your
4. - town."   5. Oh,

_p_

poco rit.

As I went a-walking one morning in spring.

I'M A POOR STRANGER AND FAR FROM MY OWN.

For Note to the above song see Appendix.
* Verse 3 adapted from a broadside ballad in the British Museum Library.

As when the softly blushing rose.

MILD MABEL KELLY.

Andante molto espressione.   Translated from the Irish by CHARLOTTE BROOKE.

1. As when the soft - - ly blush-ing
2. The tim - id lus - - tre of thine
3. The po - ets of . . . I - er - ne's
4. Since the fam'd fair . . of an - cient

1. rose   Close by some neigh - b'ring li - ly grows,   Such is the glow   thy cheeks dif -
2. eye   With na-ture's pur - est tints can   vie;   With the sweet blue - - bell's a - zure
3. plains   To thee de - vote . . their choic-est strains, And oft their harps   for thee are
4. days   Whom bards and worlds . con-spir'd to praise, Not one like thee   has since ap -

1. - fuse, . . . And such their   bright . . . and blend - ed   hues.
2. - gem, . . .   That droops up - on . . . . its mod - est   stem.
3. strung, . .   And oft thy   match - - less charms are   sung.
4. - pear'd, . . Like thee, to   ev - - - 'ry heart   en - dear'd.

rit.

pp espress.

This air is from the Petrie Collection, 1855, where it is designated "Donnell O'Graedh"; it was taken from a MS. collection of tunes which belonged to James Hardman, author of *Irish Minstrelsy; or, Bardic Remains of Ireland*, 2 vols., 1831. Dr. Petrie considers "Donnel O'Graedh" to be a setting of "Molly Bán" in Bunting's Collection, 1840; an examination of the two airs will show that their affinity is but slight. The original Irish verses are attributed to Carolan. The air called "Mild Mabel O'Kelly," different settings of which are printed in Bunting's Collection, 1809, and Mulhollan's *Irish Airs*, 1810 may possibly be the original tune composed by Carolan for his song: but these versions are probably very different from the bard's composition; they are certainly of no use for *vocal* purposes.

As Jack the jolly ploughboy.

THE JOLLY PLOUGHBOY.

VOICE.

PIANO.

1. As
2. For
3. I've
4. For

1. Jack the jol - ly plough-boy Was plough-ing o'er his land, He cried un - to his
2. Jack's a jol - ly plough-boy Whose life is free from care, His heart, so light, re -
3. heard of ma - ny won - ders That are in ci - ties seen, And I my-self to
4. when the work is o - ver He to his cot - tage goes, And al - ways finds a

1. hors - es And bold - ly bid them stand; Then down up - on his plough he sat
2. joic - es To breathe the sweet spring air; The birds a - round are sing - ing now, Their
3. Lim' - rick Some months a - go have been, But tho' it is a wond'rous sight The
4. wel - come, No sad - ness there, or woes, So give to me a ploughman's life From

"The Jolly Ploughman" was obtained by Bunting from Duncan the harper in 1792, but first published by him in his collection of 1840. It bears striking resemblance with the tune "Moll Roone," and is the original of Samuel Lover's "Lowbacked Car." Bunting's remark that it is "very ancient" is absurd; the form of the melody shows it to be of modern growth. The song is founded upon the verse printed in Bunting's book.

1. mer - ry song to sing, . . And Jack he sang his song so sweet That
2. songs of joy a - gain, . So join - ing then with glad - some shout, He
3. streets and folk to see, . I'd ra - ther live a plough -man's life A -
4. cares and sor - rows free : . . And o'er the fur - row'd land to sing A

rit. . . . . . . *Chorus.*

1. all the val - leys ring, . . ⎫
2. chants his clear re - frain, . . ⎬ With a too - ra - nan nan - ty na ! Sing
3. -mid the mea - dows free, . . ⎭
4. song right mer - ri - ly, . .

colla voce.

too - ra - nan nan - ty na ! . While the e - choes pro - long The sweet

notes of his song, And his too - ra - nan nan - ty na ! . . .

Mr. Chappell claims this lively air as English, and informs us that it occurs in a manuscript of about 1770 belonging to Dr. Rimbault, as "The girl I left behind me; or, Brighton Camp." Mr. Chappell considers that this refers to the encampments along the coast in 1758-9 when Admirals Hawke and Rodney were watching the French fleet. All this may be true enough, but by no means proves that the air was not originally imported from Ireland. It has a decidedly Irish flavour about it, and in

1. that dear isle 'twas leav — — ing; So loath we part from
2. faint, so sad, there beam — — ing; While mem' - ry brings us
3. nought but love is want — — ing; We think how great had
4. faint be - hind them glow — — ing; So, when the close of

1. all we love, From all the links that bind us, So
2. back a - gain Each ear - ly tie that twin'd us, Oh,
3. been our bliss, If heav'n had but as - sign'd us, To
4. plea - sure's day To gloom has near con - sign'd us, We

1. turn our heads wher - e'er we rove To those we left be - hind us.
2. sweet's the cup that cir - cles then To those we left be - hind us.
3. live and die in scenes like this, With some we've left be - hind us.
4. turn'd to catch one fad - ing ray Of joy that's left be - hind us.

many ways greatly resembles that undoubtedly Irish melody, known as "The Rose tree in full bearing." Moore's verses were written in the autumn of 1817, and published in the following year in the seventh number of the *Melodies*; his version of the air is singularly incorrect. Bunting's setting, given in his work of 1840, and which he informs us was obtained from "A. O'Niel, harper" in 1800, is a mere parody on the genuine air.

C

At early dawn.

THE DAWNING OF THE DAY.

EDWARD WALSH.

In *Ancient Irish Music* Dr. Joyce gives the above air as sung in the South of Ireland. The same melody was originally printed by Alexander Campbell in *Albyn's Anthology*, 1816, as a Border air; it was obtained from the singing of James Hogg, "The Ettrick Shepherd." I am inclined to think that the Scottish Borders produced the tune which, while it has very little Irish character, has a great deal of similarity with the airs peculiar to the counties constituting the Borders of England and Scotland; it is also to be observed that the traditional verses given in *Albyn's Anthology* are distinctly purer than those recovered by Dr. Joyce; I append the two first verses for the reader's perusal.

> O once my *Thyme* was young,
> It flourish'd night and day;
> But by there cam' a false young man,
> And he stole my *thyme* away.

> Within my garden gay
> The rose and lily grew;
> But the pride o' my garden is wither'd away
> And it's a' grown o'er wi' *rue*.

The "Thyme and the Rue" was a favourite refrain in Scottish ballads; for instance :—

> Hey, and the rue grows bonnie wi' thyme
>   And the thyme it is wither'd, and the rue is in prime,

is the burden of the old ballad called "Kellyburnbraes," an improved version of which was supplied by Burns to the fourth volume of the *Scots Musical Museum*, 1792; a traditional version was printed in Cromek's *Remains of Nithsdale and Galloway Song*, 1810. The verses given above are from *Irish Popular Songs*, 1847.

p   *rit.*   *p*

1. glow, ... The lamp of light to glow; As
2. o'er, ... That swept the tall grass o'er; With
3. said, ... "Dear maid," I gent - - ly said; A

1. on by bow'r, and town, and tow'r, And wide - spread fields I
2. milk - ing pail she sought the vale, And bright her charms dis -
3. blush o'er - spread her li - ly cheek, She rose and sprang a -

1. stray, . . . I meet a maid in the green - wood shade, At the
2. play, . . . Out - shin - ing far the morn - ing star, At the
3. way, . . . The sun's first light pur - sued her flight At the

rit.

1. dawn - ing of the day, . . . At the dawn - ing of the day. . . .
2. dawn - ing of the day, . . . At the dawn - ing of the day. . . .
3. dawn - ing of the day, . . . At the dawn - ing of the day. . . .

rit.

c 2

At the yellow boreen.

Translated from the Irish by Dr. GEORGE PETRIE.

1. At the yel - low bo - reen Is my heart's se - cret queen, A-
2. Should my love with me come, I would build her a home, The

1. -lone on her soft bed a - sleep - - - ing; Each tress of her hair, Than the
2. fin - est e'er told of in E - - - - rin; And 'tis then she would shine, And her

George Petrie obtained this air from the singing of a County of Clare peasant named Thade Mac Mahon, whose memory was a rich depository of the fine tunes of his native country. Dr. Petrie considers it to be a good example both in its structure and in its tone of sentiment of a class of tunes which are very abundant in the county of Clare. "Boreen" is the diminutive of *Bothair*, "a road," and means "a little road" or "lane."

1. King's gold more fair, The dew from the grass might be sweep - - ing; I'm a
2. fame ne'er de - cline, For boun - ty o'er all the palm bear - - ing; For in

1. man of Teige's race, Who has watch'd her fair face, And a -
2. your bo - som bright Shines the pure sun - ny light, As

1. -way from her ev - er I'm sigh - - ing, And, oh, my heart's store, Be not
2. in your smooth brow grate-ful ev - - - er; And, oh, could I say You're my

1. griev'd ev - er - more That for you a young man should be dy - - ing.
2. own from this day, Death's con - test would fright - en me nev - - er.

Avenging and bright.

Thomas Moore.

Con spirito.

VOICE.

PIANO.

1. A - veng-ing and
2. By the red cloud that
3. We swear to re -
4. Yes, mon -arch! tho'

1. bright fall the swift sword of E - rin On him who the brave sons of Us - na be -
2. hung o - ver Con - or's dark dwelling When Ul - ad's three cham-pions lay sleep-ing in
3. -venge them! no joy shall be tast - ed, The harp shall be si - lent, the mai-den un -
4. sweet are our home re - col - lec-tions, Tho' sweet are the tears that from ten - der -ness

1. -tray'd; For ev' - ry fond eye which he wa - ken'd a tear in, A drop from his
2. gore, By the bil -lows of war, which so of - ten high swell-ing, Have waft - ed these
3. wed, Our halls shall be mute, and our fields shall lie wast - ed Till ven -geance is
4. fall, Tho' sweet are our friendships, our hopes, our af - fec -tions Re - venge on a

rit.

1. heart wounds shall weep o'er her blade.
2. he - roes to vic - to - ry's shore;
3. wreak'd on the mur - der - er's head!
4. ty - rant is sweet-est of all!

rit.   *f*   *dim.*

Moore's song, which was suggested by the well-known Irish story of "Deirdri," was written for the fourth number of the *Melodies* published Nov. 1811. He obtained the air from Holden's *Irish Airs*, vol. ii., 1806, where it is printed as "Crookaun a Venée" (*Cruachan na Finne*, or "Mount of the Fennians"). In Panorma's *National Airs* it is called "Bryan Borne."

Beauing, belleing, dancing, drinking.

THE RAKES OF MALLOW.

Con spirito.

VOICE.

PIANO.

1. Beau - ing, belle - ing,
2. One time nought but
3. Rack - ing ten - ants,

1. danc-ing, drink-ing, Breaking win-dows, swearing, sink - ing, Ev - er rak-ing, ne - ver think-ing,
2. clar - et drink-ing, Then like po - li - ti-cians, think-ing, Rais-ing funds when funds are sink-ing,
3. stew-ards teas - ing, Swift-ly spend-ing, slow-ly rais - ing, Wish-ing thus to spend their days in

1. Live the Rakes of Mal - low; Spend-ing fast - er than it comes, Beat - ing wait-ers,
2. Live the Rakes of Mal - low; Liv - ing short but mer - ry lives; Go - ing where the
3. Rak - ing as at Mal - low; Then to end this rak-ing life They get so - ber,

1. bai - liffs, duns, Bac - chus' true - be - got-ten sons, Live the Rakes of Mal - low.
2. De - vil drives, Hav - ing sweethearts, but no wives, Live the Rakes of Mal - low.
3. take a wife, Ev - er af - ter live in strife, And wish a - gain for Mal - low.

As "Rakes of Mallow" this air occurs in Burk Thumoth's *Twelve English and twelve Irish airs, London, circa* 1747-50, and as "The Rakes of London" in Johnson's *Two Hundred Country Dances,* vol. vi., London, 1751. In the latter publisher's *Compleat Tutor for the Guittar, circa* 1755, it is styled "Rakes of Marlow," and in Aird's *Selection of Scotch, English, Irish and Foreign Airs,* vol. ii., Glasgow, 1782, "The Rakes of Mall." Arnold has made good use of the tune in his opera, "Auld Robin Gray," 1794. The "Rakes" were the young gentlemen of last century who frequented the "waters" of Mallow. The author of the song is unknown; Collins suggests Lysaght, but this is hardly possible because that poet was born in 1763, and we have seen that the title at least of the song existed in print as far back as 1750.

𝔅eautiful and wide are the green fields of 𝔈rin.

THE FAIR HILLS OF HOLY IRELAND.

EDWARD WALSH.

Adagio.

VOICE.

PIANO.

p

con espress.

rit.

p

con Ped.

1. Beau - ti - ful and wide are the
2. How clus - t'ring his ring - lets, how

1. green fields of E - rin, Ul - lach - an dhuv, O! With
2. left - y his bear - ing, Ul - lach - an dhuv, O! Each

1. life - giv - ing grain in the corn there - in, . . . Ul - lach - an dhuv, O! And
2. war - rior leav - ing the broad bays of E - rin, Ul - lach - an dhuv, O! Would

"*Ullachan dubh* O is an expression of lamentation something like the English 'alack and well-a-day.' Accordingly Moore in his *Irish Melodies* calls the air 'The song of sorrow,' which is sufficiently correct." (P. W. Joyce, Irish Music and Song). The air was introduced in Shield's opera *The Poor Soldier*, 1782; it is sung as a serenade by the character Dermot, to verses beginning, "Sleep on, my Kathleen dear." After this its popularity became very great, and we find it included in the collections of Mulhollan, O'Farrell, Bunting, Murphy, John Lee, and many others. It is one of the airs cited in Walker's *Irish Bards*, 1786. Numerous translations of the old song associated with this melody have been made by Mangan, Furlong, Ferguson, etc.; the verses adopted here are from Walsh's *Irish Popular Songs, Dublin*, 1847; the original song was said to have been composed by an Irish student in Paris. An inspection of any of the older printed versions of *Ullachan dubh* O will show the reader that Professor Stanford's assertion that "Moore has much altered the air, especially in the seventh line" is incorrect; hardly two settings of the melody are to be found which are exactly alike.

1. hon - ey in the woods of the mist - wreaths deep, And in sum - mer by the paths the
2. hea - ven grant the hope - in my bo - som swell-ing, I'd seek that land of joy in life's

1. bright streams leap; At burn - ing noon, rich sparkling dew the fair flow'rs steep On the
2. gifts ex - cel-ling, Be - yond your rich re - wards I'd choose a lone - ly dwell-ing, On the

1. fair hills of E - rin, O !
2. fair hills of E - rin, O !

p con espress.　　*rit.*

con Ped.

3. Gain - ful and large are the corn - stacks of E - rin, Ul - lach - an dhuv,

p

O!   Yel-low cream and   but - ter a - bound   e - ver there - in,

Ul - lach - an dhuv,   O!   And sor - rel soft and   cress - es where

bright streams stray, And speak-ing cuc-koos fill   the   grove the live-long day,   The

lit - tle thrush so no - ble of sweetest sounding lay, On the   fair hills of E - rin,   O!

Before the sun rose at yester dawn.

PULSE OF MY HEART.

Translated from the Irish by EDWARD WALSH.

Andantino.

VOICE.

PIANO.

p

con Ped.

rit.

con sempre. Ped.

1. Be - fore the sun rose at
2. Her beau - ti -ful voice more

1. yes - ter dawn, I met a fair maid a - down the lawn: The
2. hearts hath won, Than Or - phe - us' lyre of old had done; Her

1. ber - ry and snow to her cheek gave its glow, And her brow was as fair as the
2. ripe eyes of blue were crys - tals of dew, On the grass of the lawn, be -

con espress.

1. sail - - ing swan— Then pulse of my heart! what gloom is thine?
2. -fore the sun— And, pulse of my heart! what gloom is thine?

Dr. Petrie gives two versions of this air in his *Ancient Music of Ireland*, 1855, the one noted from the singing of a Clare peasant, the other, which may be regarded as the Connaught form of the air, obtained from a Cork musician of the name of William Ford, who made a tour in the western counties in 1846-7 for the purpose of collecting Irish melodies. I have adopted the Clare version as being the best. Alluding to this tune Dr. P. W. Joyce observes in *Irish Music and Song*, 1888, that it is well known among the peasantry in every part of the country, and that in disturbed times it was very generally selected as the air of the Whiteboys or Ribbonmen songs—or "treason songs," as they were called. Dr. Joyce remembers hearing in his youth fragments of several of them. I have taken the verses from Walsh's *Irish Popular Songs*, 1847; they are translated from an Irish song which Petrie considers to have been written to the air.

Bright fairies by Glengariff's bay.

THE INVOCATION.

THOMAS DAVIS.

Allegretto.

VOICE.

1. Bright
2. Her
3. Old

PIANO.

rit.

1. fair - ies by Glen - gar - iff's bay, Soft woods that o'er Kil -
2. eyes are dark - er than Dun -loe, Her soul is whi - ter
3. Man - ger - ton! thine ea - gle's plume, Dear In - - nis - fal - len!

1. -lar - ney sway, Bold e - choes born in Céim - an - eich, Your
2. than the snow, Her tress - es, like Ar - bu - tus flow, Her
3. bright - er bloom, And, Mu - cruss! whis - per thro' the gloom Quaint

As "Planxty Power" this air is printed in Miss Owenson's *Twelve Hibernian Melodies*, 1805, and as "Fanny Power" in Bunting's *Ancient Music of Ireland*, 1840. I do not know on what ground the air received the title; in *A Favourite Collection of the so much admired Old Irish Tunes, The Original and Genuine Composition of Carolan, Dublin*, 1780, it is called "Mrs. Trench." Walsh prints

1. kins - man's greet - ing hear! . . . . He asks you, by old
2. step like fright - ed deer. . . . . . Then, still thy waves, ca -
3. le - gends to her ear. . . . . . Till strong as ash - tree

cres.   *f*

1. friend - ship's name, By all the rights that min - strels claim, For
2. -pri - cious lake: And cease - less, soft winds round her wake, Yet
3. in its pride, And gay as sun - beam on the tide, We

cres.

1. E - rin's joy and Des - mond's fame, Be kind to Fan - ny dear! . . .
2. nev - er bring a cloud to break The smile of Fan - ny dear! . . .
3. wel - come back to Lif - fey's side Our bright - est Fan - ny dear! . . .

f

an air in his *Compleat Country Dancing Master*, 1718, called "The Whim," which bears some resemblance to "Mrs. Trench" in the first phrase. Davis's poem, marked to be sung to "Fanny Power," is included in the edition of his collected songs and ballads published in Dublin in 1846.

Bright red is the sun on the waves of Lough Sheelin.

THE FLOWER OF FINÆ.

THOMAS DAVIS.

VOICE.

Andante.

1. Bright
2. Her
3. But
4. Lord
5. In the

PIANO.

p   *poco rit.*

1. red   is   the   sun . .   on . . the   waves   of   Lough
2. hair   is   like   night . .   and   her   eyes   like   grey
3. who   down   the   hill - side than   red   deer   runs
4. Clare   on   the   field   of .   Ram - - i   lies is
5. clois - ters   of   Y - pres   a   ban - ner   is . .

1. Shee - lin,   A . .   cool   gen - - tle   breeze   from   the
2. morn - ing,   She . . trips   on   the   hea - ther as . .
3. fleet - er,   And . . who   on   the   lake - side is . .
4. charg - ing,   Be - - fore   him   the   Sas - san - ach . .
5. sway - ing,   And . . by   it   a   pale   weep - ing . .

This air, called "Do you remember that night," was contributed with two additional settings to the Petrie Collection, vol. ii., by Dr. P. W. Joyce. In reprinting it in his *Ancient Irish Music*, 1873, Dr. Joyce remarks that he noted it down from the singing of a farmer living in Coolfree, on the borders of Cork and Limerick. He also took down some stanzas of a sad Irish song which he says to it, said to have been composed by a young widowed bride, whose husband had been drowned in conveying her relations in a boat across the Shannon, after the wedding : one of these verses is printed in Petrie's Collection, vol. ii., p. 3. The minor setting of the air will be found in the present work, set to Mangan's song, "Oh Amber Hair'd Nora."

1. moun - tain is steal - ing, While . . . fair round its
2. if its touch scorn - ing, Yet her heart and her
3. hast - 'ning to greet her? Who but Fer - gus O' -
4. squad - rons en - larg - ing, Be - hind him the
5. maid - en is pray - ing; That . . . . flag's the sole

1. is - lets the small rip - ples play, . . . But
2. lips are as mild as May - day Sweet
3. Far - rel, the fier - y and gay, . . . The
4. Cra - vats their sec - tions dis - play, . . . Be -
5. tro - phy of Ram - i - lies fray, . . . This

1. fair - er than all is the . . . Flow'r of Fin - av.
2. Ei - ly Mac - Mah - on, the . . . Flow'r of Fin - av.
3. dar - ling and pride of the . . . Flow'r of Fin - av.
4. -hind him rides Fer - gus and . . . shouts for Fin - av.
5. nun is poor Ei - ly, the . . . Flow'r of Fin - av.

Bright sun! before whose glorious ray.

IRISH WAR-SONG.

EDWARD WALSH.

1. Bright sun! be - fore whose glo - rious ray Our pa - - gan fa - thers bent the knee; Whose pil - - lar al - tars yet can say, When time was young our
2. The eldir - seach wild, whose trem - bling string Had long the "song of sor - row" spoke, Shall bid the wild Rosg - Ca ta sing, The curse and crime of
3. Send the loud war - cry o'er the main; Your sun - burst to the breez - es spread: That slo - gan rends the heav'n in twain, The earth reels back be -

Walsh's song is marked in the *Spirit of the Nation*, 1846, to be sung to an air called "The world's turn'd upside down." I have adapted it to the above magnificent air, preserved in Bunting's *Ancient Irish Music*, 1840, as "The Merchant's Daughter." Bunting has marked the air to be played "briskly," which is obviously a mistake; the whole character of the melody is too majestic. I have also extracted the spurious accidentals in the second and seventh bars of Bunting's setting.

1. sires were free; Who see'st how fall'n their off - springs be, Our
2. Sax - on yoke. And, by each heart his bond - age broke, Each
3. -neath your tread. Ye Sax - on des - pots, hear, and dread! Your

1. ma - tron's tears, our pa - triot's gore; We swear, be - fore high
2. ex - ile's sigh on dis - tant shore, Each mar - tyr 'neath the
3. march o'er pa - triot hearts is o'er; That shout hath told, that

rit.

1. heav'n and thee, The Sax - on holds us slaves no more!
2. heads-man's stroke, The Sax - on holds us slaves no more!
3. tramp hath said, Our coun-try's sons are slaves no more!

D

By the Feal's wave benighted.

DESMOND'S SONG.

Thomas Moore.

Andante maestoso.

1. By the Feal's wave be -night - ed, Not a star in the skies, To thy door by love light - ed I first saw those eyes; Some
2. Love came and brought sor - row Too soon in its train; Yet so sweet . . that to - mor - row 'Twere wel - come a - gain; Tho'
3. You who call it dis - hon - our To bow to this flame, If you've eyes . . look but on her, And blush while you blame; Hath the
4. No man for his glo - ry To an - - ces - - try flies; But wo - man's bright sto - ry Is told in her eyes; While the

From the *Melodies*, Pt. ix., 1824, where the air is marked "unknown." In the summer of 1823, Moore visited Ireland, and was received everywhere with great enthusiasm : in a letter written during this tour to Power, his music publisher, the Poet remarks, "I have not, I am sorry to say, added to my stock of Irish melodies, but I have, however, laid in a few recollections and feelings about Ireland which will not fail to show themselves in whatever else I may do upon the subject." That this was true is proved by the contents of the ninth number of the *Melodies* which appeared in the following year. Of the twelve songs it contains, nine have reference to local feelings or traditions, or to circumstances which arose out of the Poet's visit to his native country. "Desmond's Song" is founded on a romantic anecdote in the history of the Geraldines.

1. voice whis - per'd o'er me As thy thres - hold I should
2. mis - e - ry's full mea - sure My por - tion should
3. pearl . . . less white - ness Be - cause of its
4. mon - arch but tra - ces Thro' mor - tals his

1. cross'd, There was ru - in be - - fore me, If I
2. be, I would drain it with plea - sure If
3. birth? Hath the vio - - let less bright - ness For
4. line, Beau - ty, born . . . of the Gra - ces Ranks

1. loved, I was lost.
2. pour'd out by thee.
3. grow - ing near earth?
4. next to di - vine!

f

Ped. Ped. Ped.

Come, buy my nice fresh ivy.

THE HOLLY AND IVY GIRL.

JOHN KEEGAN.

Andante.

VOICE.

PIANO. { *p con espress.* *rit.*

Ped.

1. "Come,
2. "Ah!
3. The

mf

con Ped.

1. buy   my   nice   fresh   i - vy,   And   my   hol - - ly - sprigs so
2. won't you   buy   my   i - vy?   The   lov - - li - est   e'er
3. pale   sing - er still sang   on, . . .   But   no   one   came   to

1. green;   I   have   the   fin - est   branch - es   That
2. seen!   Ah!   won't   you   buy   my   hol - ly?   All
3. buy;   The   crowd passed to   and   fro, . . .   But

sf

The name of this beautiful melody is "The fair maid of Wicklow"; it is in R. A. Smith's *Irish Minstrel, Edinburgh, 1825*, set to a song by the Scotch poet Tannahill, entitled "The Dirge of Carolan." John Keegan, the author of the verses given above, was born about 1809, and died 1849; he was the most popular of Irish peasant poets. "His life was not a very happy one, as he

1. ev - - er yet were seen. Come, buy from me, good
2. you who love the green! Do take a lit - tle
3. did not heed her cry. She ut - - ter'd one low

1. Chris - tians, And let me home, I pray, And I'll
2. branch of each, And on my knees I'll pray, That
3. pierc - ing moan, Then cast her boughs a - way, And

dim.

1. wish 'Mer - ry Christ-mas Time,' . . . And a 'Hap - py New Year's Day.'"
2. God may bless your Christ - mas, And be with your New Year's Day."
3. smi - - ling cried, "I'll rest with God Be - fore the New Year's Day."

dim.

sempre Ped.

contracted an unfortunate marriage, according to his own account, and suffered much misery in consequence" (O'Donoghue, Diet. Poets of Ireland). I ought to mention that it was in Mr. Graves' *Irish Song Book*, that I found Keegan's verses adapted to this air.

Come in the evening.

THE WELCOME.

Poco appassionata.

mf   THOMAS DAVIS.

VOICE.

PIANO.

mf   *f sf*   *mf*

1. Come in the
2. I'll pull you sweet
3. We'll look thro' the
4. So come in the

1. ev-'ning or come in the morn-ing, Come when you're look'd for, or
2. flow-ers to wear if you choose them. Or, af-ter you've kiss'd them, they'll
3. trees at the cliff and the ey-rie, We'll tread round the rath on the
4. ev-'ning or come in the morn-ing, Come when you're look'd for, or

p   *cres.*

1. come with-out warn-ing, Kiss-es and wel-come you'll find here be-
2. lie on my bo-som; I'll fetch from the moun-tain its breeze to re-
3. track of the fai-ry, We'll look on the stars and we'll list to the
4. come with-out warn-ing, Kiss-es and wel-come you'll find here be-

p   *cres.*

mf   *f*

1. -fore you, And the oft-'ner you come here, the more I'll a-dore you.
2. -store you; I'll fetch from my fan-cy a tale that won't tire you. Oh! your
3. ri-ver: Till you ask of your dar-ling what gift you can give her. Oh!
4. -fore you, And the oft-'ner you come here, the more I'll a-dore you.

mf   *f*

Air: *Astoreen Machree*, or, "O Treasure of my heart," preserved in Dr. Joyce's *Ancient Irish Music*, 1873 : it was noted in 1852 from the whistling of a native of Crossmolina in the county of Mayo. Davis's song is adapted to a jig-tune called *An Buachalin bui ih*, or, "The Yellow Boy," in the *Spirit of the Nation*, 1846. As this air is not only quite unsuited to the passionate sentiment of the song, but also employs the compass of one octave and a half, I have adapted *Astoreen Machree* instead, which in every way admirably suits Davis's beautiful poem.

1. Light is my heart since the days we were plight - ed,
2. step's like the rain to the sum - mer vex'd farm - er, Or
3. she'll whis - per you, "Love, as un - change - ab -ly beam - ing, And
4. Light is my heart since the days we were plight - ed,

1. Red is my cheek that they told me was blight - ed; The green of the
2. sa - bre and shield to a knight with - out ar - mour: I'll sing you sweet
3. trust, when in se - cret, most tune - ful - ly stream-ing, Till the star - light of
4. Red is my cheek that they told me was blight - ed; The green of the

1. trees . . looks green - er than ev - er, And the lin - nets are sing - ing, "true
2. songs . . till the stars rise a - bove me, Then wan - d'ring I'll wish you, in
3. hea - ven a - bove us shall quiv - er, As our souls flow in one down e -
4. trees . . looks green - er than ev - er, And the lin - nets are sing - ing, "true

1. lov - ers! don't sev - er!"
2. si - lence, to love me.
3. -ter - ni - ty's riv - er."
4. lov - ers, don't sev - er!"

dim.   sf

Come o'er the sea.

Thomas Moore.

1. Come o'er the sea,
2. Was not the sea

1. Maid-en! with me, Mine thro' sun - shine, storm and snows! Sea -sons may roll,
2. Made for the free, Land for courts and chains a - lone? Here we are slaves,

1. But the true soul Burns the same wher - e'er it goes; Let for - tune frown, so we
2. But on the waves, Love and li - ber-ty's all our own; No eye to watch, and no

"Come o'er the sea," with the air "Cuishla ma chree," or "Pulse of My Heart," is the opening song in the sixth number of Moore's *Irish Melodies*, 1815. The following verse is a fragment of the original words associated with the melody ; it is from the first edition of the *Melodies*, and was probably obtained from the person who communicated the air.

Cuishlih ma chree,
Did you but see
How, the rogue, he did serve me :—(*bis*)
He broke my pitcher, he spilt my water,
He kiss'd my wife, and he married my daughter !
O Cuishlih ma chree, etc.

The composition of "Come o'er the sea" seems to have cost the poet some trouble ; in a letter of August, 1814, to his music publisher, "honest James Power," we find him remarking, "I write now merely to say that I have done 'Cuishlah ma chree' after many trials." The melody, which Stevenson has marked to be sung "with impassioned melancholy," is singularly beautiful ; I have considered it advisable, however, to extract the absurd and obviously incorrect F♯ in the twelfth bar in Moore's version.

1. love, and part not; 'Tis life where *thou* art, 'tis death where thou art not : Then come o'er the sea,
2. tongue to wound us, All earth for - got, and all hea - ven a-round us. Then come o'er the sea,

colla voce.

1. Maid-en! with me, Come wher-ev - er the wild wind blows; Sea -sons may roll,
2. Maid-en! with me, Mine thro' sun - shine, storm and snows; Sea -sons may roll,

1st *time.*

1. But the true soul Burns the same wher - e'er it goes.
2. But the true soul Burns the same wher - e'er it goes.

p

2nd *time.*

molto rit.

Come, rest on this bosom.

THOMAS MOORE.

As " Lough Sheeling" this air is in Holden's Collection. vol. ii., 1806, and again in the same author's *Periodical Irish Melodies*, printed a few years later. Dr. George Petrie claims to have supplied this and other melodies "To my young friend the late Francis Holden, Mus. Doc., and which were printed in his collections" (Petrie Collection, p. viii.). The works to which

1. home is still here; Here still is the
2. glo - - ry and shame? I know not, I
3. hor - - rors of this; Thro' the fur - - nace un - -

1. smile that no cloud can o'er - cast, And the heart and the
2. ask not, if guilt's in that heart, I but know that I
3. - shrink - ing thy steps to pur - sue, And shield thee and

1. hand all thy own to the last!
2. love thee what - ev - - er thou art,
3. save thee, or per - - ish there too.

Dr. Petrie refers are the collections mentioned above; they were published by Smollett Holden, the father of Dr. Petrie's friend. Dr. Petrie also informs us that the air was generally known as *Gradh geal mo chroidhe*, or "Bright Love of my Heart." Other forms of the air "The Old Truigha" (see p. 4), and "Thy Fair Bosom" in Bunting's Collection, 1809, and in Holden's *Old Established Irish Tunes*, vol. ii., 1806.

Dear Erin, how sweetly.

JOHN PHILPOT CURRAN.

1. E - rin, how sweet - ly thy green bo - som ris - es, An em - er - ald
2. sons . . they are brave, but the bat - tle once o - ver, In bro - ther - ly

1. set in the ring of the sea; Each blade of thy mea - dows my
2. peace with their foes they a - gree; And the ros - e - ate checks of thy

1. faith - ful heart priz - es, Thou queen of the west! the world's cush - la - ma-
2. daugh-ters dis - cov - er The soul - speak-ing blush that says, "cush - la - ma-

I have heard Curran's song sung to various Irish airs, such as "Paistheen Fuen," "Dermot O'Dowd," "The Bank of Green Rushes," and others; the original setting was probably the old air, "Paistheen Fuen," of which the above melody seems to be a form. I have taken it from Henderson's little collection of Irish songs and airs published at Belfast in 1847.

1. - chree! Thy gates o - pen wide to the poor and the stran - ger; There
2. - chree!" Then flour - ish for ev - er, my dear na - tive E - rin, While

1. smiles hos - pi - tal - i - ty, hear - ty and free! Thy friend - ship is
2. sad - ly I wan - der an ex - ile from thee; And firm as thy

cres.

1. seen in the mo - ment of dan - ger; And the wan - - d'rer is
2. moun - tains, no in - - ju - ry fear - ing, May hea - ven de -

cres.

dim. rit.

1. wel - com'd with cush - la - ma - chree.
2. fend its own cush - la - ma - chree!

sf *p*

dim. rit.

Dear harp of my Country.

Thomas Moore.

1. Dear harp of my Coun-try! in
2. Dear harp of my Coun-try! fare-

1. dark-ness I found thee, The cold chain of si-lence had hung o'er thee long, When
2. -well to thy num-bers, This sweet wreath of song is the last we shall twine! Go,

1. proud-ly, my own Is-land Harp, I un-bound thee, And
2. sleep with the sun-shine of Fame on thy slum-bers, Till

This air has been called "*New Langolee*" to distinguish it from an older melody of the same name. It is to be found in Charles and Samuel Thompson's *Twenty-four Country Dances for 1775*, Aird's *Scotch, English, Irish, and Foreign Airs*, vol. i., 1782, and in the collection of Irish Tunes by Mulhollan, Hoblen, Murphy, and others. "Dear Harp of my Country" is the closing song of the sixth part of the *Irish Melodies*, 1815, with which number the series was supposed to finish. "Thus" (to quote from Mr. T. W. Lyster's *Select Poetry*) "Moore claims with joy that he had released the lyric genius of Ireland from the chains of cold, dark silence, and that he had brought her to light, freedom, and song. Now he bids farewell to this field of endeavour, while with eager, generous modesty he disclaims all personal merit; the inspiration of his songs has been that of the national music; he, the poet, has been merely as the wind passing over the harp strings."

1. gave all thy chords to light, free - dom and song! The
2. touch'd by some hand less un - worth - y than mine. If the

1. warm lay of love, and the light notes of glad - ness Have
2. pulse of the pa - tri - ot, sol - dier, or lov - er, Have

1. wa - ken'd thy fond - est, thy live - li - est thrill; But so oft hast thou e - choed the
2. throbb'd at our lay, 'tis thy glo - ry a - lone; I was but as the wind pass - ing

1. deep sigh of sad - ness, That ev'n in thy mirth it will steal from thee still.
2. heed - less - ly o - ver, And all the wild sweet - ness I wak'd was thy own.

Did you hear of the Widow Malone?

THE WIDOW MALONE.

Charles Lever.

Allegretto.

Voice.

mf

1. Did you
2. Of
3. But so
4. Till one
5. And the

Piano.

p

rit. . . . .

1. hear of the Wid - ow Ma - lone, O - hone! Who liv'd in the town of Ath -
2. lov - ers she had a full score, Or more; And for - tunes they all had ga -
3. mod - est was Mis - tress Ma - lone, 'Twas known, No one ev - er could see her a -
4. Mis - ter O' - Bri - en from Clare, How quare! It's lit - tle for blush - ing they
5. wid - ow they all thought so shy, My eye! Ne'er thought of a whim - per or

mf

1. -lone, O - hone! Oh! she melt - ed the hearts Of the swains in these parts, So
2. -lore, In store! From the min - is - ter down To the clerk of the crown, All were
3. -lone, O - hone! Let them o - gle and sigh, They could ne'er catch her eye, So
4. care, Down there! Put his arm round her waist, Gave ten kiss - es at laste, "Oh," says
5. sigh, For why? But, "Lu - ci - us," says she, "Since you've made now so free, You may

1. love -ly the Wid - ow Ma - lone, O -hone! So love -ly the Wid-ow Ma - lone. . . .
2. court-ing the Wid -ow Ma - lone, O -hone! All were courting the Wid-ow Ma - lone. . . .
3. bash-ful the Wid -ow Ma - lone, O -hone! So bash - ful the Wid-ow Ma - lone. . . .
4. he, "you're my Mol - ly Ma - lone, My own! Oh," says he, "you're my Mol - ly Ma - lone." . . .
5. mar -ry your Ma -ry Ma - lone, O -hone! You may mar-ry your Ma - ry Ma - lone." . . .

colla voce.

For note to this song see Appendix.

Down by the sally gardens.

The air to which I have adapted Mr. Yeats's beautiful song is called, "Far beyond yon mountains"; it is one of those traditional airs collected by George Petric, and published after his death by F. Hoffmann in the work entitled, *Ancient Music of Ireland, from the Petric Collection*, 1876. I am indebted to Messrs. Pigot & Co., Dublin, for permission to reprint the air.

E

Droop all the flowers in my garden.

MY ROSE.

Dora Sigerson.

Air. "Black-eyed Susan." This is one of the traditional melodies collected by Dr. Petrie and published in 1879 in that interesting volume of Irish music issued by Messrs. Pigot and Co., Dublin, entitled, *Ancient Music of Ireland from the Petrie Collection, arranged for the Pianoforte by F. Hoffmann*. A reference to the Appendix No. I. will show that it is merely an Irish form of Leveridge's air of the same name ; it must be admitted, however, that a century's residence in the Emerald Isle has by no means proved a drawback to it ; on the contrary, the Irish form appears to me to be infinitely finer than the original English composition, and for this reason merits a place in this volume. I may observe that Hoffmann's Collection teems with English and Scotish airs, picked up by Dr. Petrie in Ireland. Had Dr. Petrie lived to continue the publication of the *Ancient Music of Ireland*, we may be sure that these 'foreign' tunes would have not received a place in the work. Leveridge's air was sung in *The Village Opera*, 1729, *The Chambermaid*, 1730, *The Devil to Pay*, 1731, etc. Miss Dora Sigerson (Mrs. Clement Shorter) is one of the best known of the younger Irish poetesses. She is the daughter of Dr. George Sigerson, M.D., the well-known author and poet. The beautiful song, "My Rose," to which I have adapted the air "Black-eyed Susan," is from the volume of collected poems entitled *Verses*. By Dora Sigerson. London, 1893.

1. fair - est com - pan - ion Ne'er a - gain will they know. Bring me no
2. walls of my gar - den, What save the world's cold breath? Then bring no

1. flow - ers for wear - ing, Take these strange buds a - way, . . . For I
2. flow - ers for wear - ing, Take these strange buds a - way, . . . Since I

1. can - not now have the fair - est; My rose that has died to - day.
2. can - not now have the sweet - est; My rose that has died to - day.

E 2

Erin! the tear and the smile in thine eyes.

THOMAS MOORE.

Andante affettuoso.

VOICE.

PIANO.

p poco rit.

con Ped.

1. E - rin! the tear and the smile in thine eyes,
2. E - rin! thy si - lent tear nev - er shall cease,

As almost all which has been written about this Queen of folk airs is to be traced to Bunting's *Ancient Irish Music*, 1840, I shall briefly review that author's statements. (1) The air is ancient, author and date unknown. (2) Gerald O'Daly, harper, is reputed to have composed it, but probably only adapted Irish words to it. (3) It is undoubtedly pure Irish, but not in the form usually given. (4) Was sung by Leoni in Dublin about 1780 to words commencing "Ducea tu non vaoatu Eithlin a Ruin," in which setting the music was altered to suit the Italian taste. (5) Bunting's setting taken from Hempson's performance as arranged by Lyons, the harper, who wrote variations to the air which evince very graceful and original genius : air restored to its original simplicity. To believe the air ancient is to repudiate the theory that it was composed by O'Daly ; nevertheless we find this harper alluded to in Grove's Dictionary, vol. ii., p. 19, as "the composer of 'Aileen-a-Roon.'" Possibly Leoni sang the air as described, but as early as *circa* 1740 the same setting was printed by Walsh, of London, as a sheet song, the title of which is, *Aileen aroon, an Irish Ballad. Sung by Mrs. Clive at ye Theatre Royal* (see Appendix No. II.). Kitty Clive, *née* Raftor, the Irish soprano vocalist, was born in 1711. She sang at Drury Lane from 1728, married 1732, died 1786. We see, therefore, that this setting was not only in existence before Leoni's time, but that it was actually introduced by an Irish singer ; and what more likely than that Kitty Clive should sing the songs of her native land ?—especially at a period when simple ballads were so popular. The best proof we have of statements No. 5 is to be found in Bunting's own volume, for the absurd setting which he publishes as the "air restored to its original simplicity" is very possibly one of these identical variations alluded to ; the "very graceful and elegant genius evinced" is, however, doubtful. In short, the general idea which has been deduced from Bunting's statements, is that same harper—Lyons or Hempson—introduced the air into Scotland and England, and that an Italian singer is responsible for the singularity of the version so popular last century ; also, while a feeling exists that Moore's setting of the air is not pure, no one knows exactly why it is not, and where it came from. The earliest printed copy of "Aileen a Roon" which I have been able to find is in Coffey's *Beggar's Wedding*, 1729 [1728?]. This work was "first performed at Dublin with indifferent success, but being afterwards reduced into one act, and played in London under the title of *Phebe* in 1729, it pleased so well as to obtain a run of thirty nights" (Baodon, Theat. Dict. 1792). That the work was welcomed in its original state in England is proved by its having passed through at least four editions ; I have only seen the second edition of 1729, without music, and the fourth edition of 1731—exactly the same as the second edition but with the airs added. Now this work contains what is probably the first printed setting of "Aileen a Roon" ; see Appendix, No. III., and it is my opinion that the melody obtained a footing in England with the introduction of the *Beggar's Wedding* in 1729. It is possible that it was played in England by some Irish harper at an earlier date, but that it became popular before the appearance of Coffey's opera is hardly improbable. After this date, then, "Aileen a Roon" became a great favourite, and we find Walsh issuing the sheet already mentioned, and Burk Thumoth (including it in his *Scotch and Irish Airs*, Bk. i., c. 1745-50 ; it will be seen by a reference to the Appendix, No. IV., that his version differs but slightly from that published by Walsh. In fact, the "Kitty Clive"

1. Blend like the rain - bow that hangs in thy skies! Shin - ing thro'
2. E - rin! thy lan - guid smile ne'er shall in - crease! Till, like the

1. sor - row's stream, Sad - d'ning thro' plea - sure's beam, Thy suns, with
2. rain - bow's light Thy var - ious tints u - nite, And form in

1. doubt - ful gleam, Weep while they rise!
2. Hea - ven's sight One arch of peace!

version of the air held ground and became an especial favourite in Scotland until the close of the century. It is to be found in Oswald's *Pocket Companion*, Bk. v., c. 1750; Johnson's Guittar Tutor, c. 1755; Bremner's Guittar Tutor, c. 1758-9; McLean's Collection, 1772; Clarke's *Flores Musicæ*, 1773; Shield's *Mountains of Wicklow*, 1798, and many other works. This, then, takes us up to the present version, as used by Tom Moore and now sung all over the civilized world. That it was known in Scotland, and that it was there associated with a number of old songs is evident; "You're Welcome to Paxton Town, Robin Adair," with the air exactly as adopted by Moore, is printed in the *Edinburgh Musical Miscellany*, vol. ii., 1793; it is alluded to by Burns in Cromek's *Reliques*, 1808, in a footnote to the "Address to General Dumourier, a parody on 'Robin Adair.'" The real ballad of "Robin Adair," beginning "What's this dull town to me," does not appear to have been written until later; the version of the air containing the so-called "Scotch snap" was apparently introduced by Braham the singer, and in Bryson's *Complete Repository*, Edinburgh, c. 1820, (not earlier than 1819, nor later than 1821) we find it entitled "Robin Adair. New Sett sung by Mr. Braham"; in the *London Minstrel*, 1823, the ballad and the air are published. I will not enter into the well-known traditional story of Adair and Lady Catharine Keppel, because, although possibly the foundation of the modern ballad, it has no direct bearing upon the version of the air in question. In 1805, George Thomson republished the setting from the *Edinburgh Miscellany*, with piano accompaniment by Joseph Haydn, and it was probably from this then fashionable work that Moore obtained the air to which he wrote his immortal song "Erin, the tear and the smile in thine eye," for the first number of the *Melodies*, 1807. By whom this so-called "Robin Adair" version was composed it is impossible to say; but no one will venture to deny its infinite superiority over the old florid setting used by Mistress Clive. From time to time we hear of traditional settings of "Aileen a Roon" being discovered in "secluded spots"; these are generally obtained from the singing of "old women," and are announced as "pure," "ancient," "original," and so on. But when we come to consider how almost impossible it is for an air to be handed about from mouth to mouth, and from generation to generation, without undergoing immense changes, the importance of these "traditional" settings diminishes. Considering that the present air, with Tom Moore's song, has been popular in every field and cabin in Ireland for almost a century, it stands to reason that all existing versions of the melody must have been more or less influenced by it.

Fairest! put on awhile.

Thomas Moore.

Allegretto tranquillo.

VOICE.

PIANO.

p

con Ped.

sempre con Ped.

1. Fair - est! put on a - while These
2. Fields where the spring de - lays, And
3. Is - lets so fresh - ly fair, That
4. Lakes where the pearl lies hid, And
5. Then if while scenes so grand, So

1. pin - ions of light I bring thee, And o'er thine own green isle In
2. fear - less - ly meets the ar - dour Of the warm sun - mer's gaze With
3. nev - er hath bird come nigh them, But from his course through the air, He
4. caves where the gem is sleep - ing, Bright as the tears thy lid Lets
5. beau - ti - ful, shine be - fore thee, Pride for thy own dear land Should

1. fan - cy let me wing thee. Nev-er did A - riel's plume, At gold - en sun - set, hov - er
2. on - ly her tears to guard her. Rocks thro' myr - tle boughs, In grace, ma - jes - tic frown - ing,
3. hath been won down by them. Types, sweet maid, of thee, Whose look, whose blush in - vit - ing
4. fall in lone - ly weep - ing. Glens, where O - cean comes To 'scape the wild wind's ran - cour,
5. hap - ly be steal - ing o'er thee, Oh, let grief come first, O'er pride it - self vic - to - rious,

1. O'er such scenes of bloom, As I shall waft thee o - ver.
2. Like some bold war-ri - or's brows That Love hath just been crown - ing.
3. Nev - er did Love yet see, From heav'n, with - out a - light - ing.
4. Har - bours, worth - i - est homes, Where Free-dom's fleet can an - chor.
5. Thinking how man hath curst What heav'n hath made so glo - rious.

For note to this song see Appendix.

Forget not the field.

THOMAS MOORE.

Andante.

VOICE.

PIANO.

con Ped.

1. For -
2. Oh!
3. But 'tis

1. -get not the field where they per - ish'd, The tru - est— the
2. could we from death but re - cov - er Those hearts, as they
3. past— and tho' bla - zon'd in sto - ry The name of our

1. last of the brave— All gone! and the bright hopes we
2. bound - ed be - fore, In the face of high heav'n to fight
3. Vic - tor may be, Ac - curst is the march of that

dim. rit.

1. cher - ish'd, Gone with them and quench'd in their grave!
2. o - ver That com - bat for Free - dom once more.
3. glo - ry Which treads o'er the hearts of the free.

dim. rit.

For note to this song see Appendix.

Farewell!—but whenever you welcome the hour.

THOMAS MOORE.

Andante.

VOICE.

PIANO.

1. Fare - well!—but when - ev - er you
2. And still, on that even-ing, when
3. Let Fate do her worst; there are

1. wel - come the hour Which a - wak - ens the night - song of mirth in your bow'r, Then
2. plea - sure fills up To the high - est top spar - kle each heart and each cup, Wher-
3. re - lies of joy, Bright dreams of the past, which she can - not de -stroy, Which

1. think of the friend who once wel - com'd it too, And for - got his own griefs to be
2. - e'er my path lies, be it gloom - y or bright, My soul, hap-py friends shall be
3. come in the night -time of sor - row and care, And bring back the fea - tures that

The earliest printed version of this air is probably that entitled "To Rodner we will go," in Aird's *Selection of Scotch, English, Irish, and Foreign Airs,* vol. vii., 1788, p. 160 (see Appendix No. V.). As "Moll Roone," the air, with Moore's "Farewell! but whenever you welcome the hour," was published in the fifth number of the *Melodies,* Dec. 1813.

1. hap - py with you.   His   griefs may re - turn,—not a   hope   may re -main   Of   the
2. with   you that night;   Shall   join   in your re - vels, your   sports   and your wiles, And   re -
3. joy   used to wear.   Long,   long   be my heart with such   mem - o - ries fill'd,   Like   the

dim.   *rit . . a tempo.*

1. few   that have brighten'd his   path - way of pain,   But   he   ne'er will for - get   the short
2. turn   to me beam-ing   all   o'er with your smiles,   Too   blest, if it   tells   me that,
3. vase   in which ro - ses   have   once been dis - till'd :   You may   break, you may shat - ter the

f   dim.

rit . . . .   a tempo. mf

1. vis - ion that   threw   Its en - chant - ment a - round him while   lin - g'ring with you!
2. mid the gay   cheer,   Some   kind   voice had mur-mur'd " I   wish   he were here!"
3. vase, if you   will,   But the   scent   of the ro - ses will   hang   round it still.

Farewell! for I must leave thee.

THE WEARING OF THE GREEN.

Moderato.

VOICE.

PIANO.

mf *sf*

sf

1. Oh, Pad - dy dear, and
2. Then since the col - our
3. But if at last our

1. did you hear the news that's go - ing round? The sham -rock is for - bid by law to
2. we must wear is Eng -land's cru - el red, Sure Ire -land's sons will ne'er for - get the
3. col - our should be torn from Ire-land's heart, Her sons, with shame and sor - row from their

1. grow on Ir - ish ground, Saint Pa - trick's Day no more we'll keep, his col - ours can't be
2. blood that they have shed. You may take the sham-rock from your hat, and cast it on the
3. dear old isle will part; I've heard a whis - per of a coun -try that lies be-yond the

mf

In one of those excellent articles entitled "The Native Music of Ireland" (Citizen Magazine, Jan. 1841), W. E. Hudson remarks that this air, with the old song, was the solace of every peasant in the years which followed 1798, of every heart, gentle or simple, who felt for the sorrows of his distressed country. There are many versions of the old song; the following is the first verse of what may be considered the oldest :

I met with Buonaparte, he took me by the hand,
Saying, "How is old Ireland, and how does she stand ?"
'Tis the most distressed country that ever I have seen.
They are hanging men and women for the wearing of the green.

Some versions substitute "Napier Tandy" for "Buonaparte." The air is evidently modern and there is strong reason to believe that it is an adaptation from a composition by James Oswald, the Scottish composer and music seller of last century. The air in question appears as "The Tulip" in *Airs for the Spring. By James Oswald* (see Appendix No. VI.). There is a licence from George II. attached to this work dated 1747 ; but the date of the issue of the book was probably ten years later. It is from Oswald's "Tulip" that the Scottish air "Sae will we yet" is derived.

1. seen, For there's a cru - el law a - gainst the wear - ing of the green, I
2. sod, But 'twill take root and flour - ish there, tho' un - der-foot 'tis trod. When
3. sea, Where rich and poor stand e - qual in the light of free-dom's day. Oh,

1. met with Nap-per Tan - dy, and he took me by the hand, And he said, "How's poor old
2. law can stop the blades of grass from grow-ing as they grow, And when the leaves in
3. E - rin! must we leave you driv-en by a ty - rant's hand? Must we ask a mo-ther's

1. Ire - land, and how does she stand?" She's the most dis-tress - ful coun - try that
2. sum-mer-time their ver - dure dare not show, Then I will change the co - lour that I
3. bless-ing from a strange and dis - tant land? Where the cru - el cross of Eng-land shall

1. ev - er yet was seen, They are hang - ing men and wo-men for the wear - ing of the green.
2. wear in my cau-been, But till that day, please God, I'll stick to wear - ing of the green.
3. nev - er-more be seen, And where, please God, we'll live and die still wear - ing of the green.

Far in the mountains with you.

ROBERT D. JOYCE, M.D., M.R.I.A.

1. Far in the moun-tains with
2. There on my rock - - y
3. Deep - ly in broad Kil -
4. Then come a - way, a -

1. you, my E - ve - leen, I would be lov - ing and true, my
2. throne, my E - ve - leen, Ev - - er, ev - er a - lone, my
3. -more, my E - ve - leen, Down by the wild stream's shore, my
4. -way, my E - ve - leen, We will spend each day, my

1. E - ve - leen; Then climb the moun - tains with me!
2. E - ve - leen; I sit. . . . dream - ing of thee;
3. E - ve - leen; I've made a sweet house for thee;
4. E - ve - leen; Bliss - - - - ful and lov - ing and free;

I have Dr. P. W. Joyce's permission to use the above air and song, the latter, the composition of Robert D. Joyce, M.D., M.R.I.A., and from that poet's *Ballads of Irish Chivalry*. Dublin: James Duffy. Dr. Joyce learned the melody from his father and inserted it in his collection of traditional Irish tunes published in 1873.

1. Long have I dwelt by the for - - est riv - er - side, Where the
2. High on the fern - - clad rocks re - clin - ing there, Though the
3. Yel - low and bright thy long, long flow - ing hair, Flow'rs the
4. Come to the woods where the streams are pour - ing blue, Which the

1. bright rip - ples flash and quiv - er wide, There the fleet hours shall
2. wild birds their songs are twin - ing fair, Then, I hear, and I
3. fair - est are ev - - - er blow - ing there, Fair - - er still with thy
4. ea - gle is ev - - - er soar - ing through; I'll grow fond - er each

1. bliss - - ful ev - er glide O'er us, sweet Gra - gal Ma - chree!
2. see thy shin - ing hair, Still, still, sweet Gra - gal Ma - chree!
3. clear eyes glow - ing there, Fond - - ly, sweet Gra - gal Ma - chree!
4. day a - dor - ing you, There, there, sweet Gra - gal Ma - chree!

Fill the bumper fair.

Thomas Moore.

Allegro con spirito.

VOICE.

mf

1. Fill the bum - per fair!
2. Sa - ges can, they say,
3. It chanc'd up - on that day,
4. Some drops were in that bowl, Re -

PIANO.

mf   f   mf

1. Ev - - 'ry drop we sprin - kle O'er the brow of Care
2. Grasp the light - ning's pin - ions, And bring down its ray
3. When, as bards in - form us, Pro - me - - theus stole a - way The
4. - mains of last night's plea - sure With which the sparks of soul

1. Smooths a - way a wrin - kle. Wit's e - lec - tric flame
2. From the starr'd do - min - ions; So we, Sa - ges, sit,
3. liv - ing fires that warm us: The care - less youth, when up, To
4. Mix'd their burn - ing trea - sure; Hence the gob - let's show'r

p   cres.

p   cres.

As "Bob and Joan," a setting of this fine air was printed by Nathaniel Gow in his *Complete Repository, Part ii., Edinburgh,* 1802. The following extract from a letter written by Moore to his music publisher, James Power, in March, 1815, seems to suggest that the version of "Bob and Joan" supplied by the poet underwent some alteration. "The new setting of 'Fill the bumper' will do—but Stevenson seems to have resolved upon doing it tastelessly" (Suppressed Letters, p. 41). Moore's song is in the 6th number of the Melodies, 1815.

1. Ne'er so swift - ly pass - es As when thro' the frame It
2. And 'mid bum - pers bright - 'ning From the heav'n of Wit,
3. Glo - ry's fount as - pir - ing Took nor urn nor cup To
4. Hath such spells to win us, Hence its migh - ty pow'r

1. shoots from brimming glass - es; Fill the bum - per fair! Ev - 'ry drop we sprin-kle
2. Draw down all its light-ning; Would'st thou know what first Made our souls in - her - it
3. hide the pil - fer'd fire in, But oh! his joy when round The halls of heav - en spy - ing, A
4. O'er the flame with-in us; Fill the bum - per fair! Ev - 'ry drop we sprin-kle

Last time.

1. O'er the brow of Care Smooths a - way a wrin - kle.
2. This en - no - bling thirst For wine's ce - les - tial spi - rit?
3. -mong the stars he found A bowl of Bac - chus ly - ing.
4. O'er the brow of Care Smooths a - way a wrin - kle.

Fly not yet.

THOMAS MOORE.

1. Fly not yet, 'tis just the hour When plea - sure, like the mid - night flow'r, That
2. Fly not yet, the fount that play'd In times of old through Am - mon's shade, Though

1. scorns the eye of vul - gar light, Be - gins to bloom for sons of night, And maids who love the
2. i - cy cold by day it ran, Yet still, like souls of mirth, be - gan To burn when night was

1. moon! . . 'Twas but to bless these hours of shade, That beau -ty and the moon were made; 'Tis
2. near. . . And thus should wo-man's heart and looks At noon be cold as win - ter brooks, Nor

Air: "Planxty Kelly," from Bunting's *Ancient Irish Music*, 1796, and on whose authority it is stated to be the composition of Carolan. Moore adopted the same version of the air as John Mulholland in his *Collection of Ancient Irish Airs, Belfast*, 1810. The song "Fly not yet," which was published in the first number of the *Melodies*, 1807, was one of the songs cited in the action Power versus Walker, to recover damages for literary piracy.

1. then, their soft at - trac-tions glow - ing Set the tides and gob -lets flow -ing. Oh! stay,—
2. kin - dle till the night re -turn -ing Brings their ge - nial hour for burn-ing. Oh! stay,—

1. Oh! stay,— Joy so sel - dom weaves a chain Like this to-night, that, oh! 'tis pain To
2. Oh! stay,— When did morn -ing ev - er break And find such beam-ing eyes a -wake As

1. break its links so soon. . . Oh! stay,— Oh! stay,— Joy so sel - dom
2. those that spar - kle here? . . Oh! stay,— Oh! stay,— When did morn -ing

1. weaves a chain Like this to-night, that, oh! 'tis pain To break its link so soon.
2. ev - er break And find such beam-ing eyes a -wake As those which spar -kle here?

Go where glory waits thee.

THOMAS MOORE.

As "The Maid of the Valley" this air is in Bunting's first Collection, 1796. The original Irish name for it is *Bean dubh an ghleanna*, or, "The Dark Maiden of the Valley"; Dr. Petrie says that it should be *Moll*, or *Poll dubh an ghleanna*. Under the same title a totally different air is given in O'Daly's *Poets of Munster*, 1849, p. 185, but this evidently arises from some error on

1. Oth - er arms may press thee, Dear - er friends ca - ress thee, All the joys that bless thee,
2. Oft as sum -mer clos - es, When thine eye re - pos - es, On its lin -g'ring ros - es,
3. Then should mu-sic, steal - ing All the soul of feel - ing To thy heart ap - peal - ing,

1. Sweet - er far may be, But when friends are near - est, And when joys are dear - est,
2. Once so lov'd by thee, Think of her who wove them, Her who made thee love them,
3. Draw one tear from thee; Then let mem - 'ry bring thee Strains I used to sing thee,

1. Oh! then, re-member me. . .
2. Oh! then, re-member me. . .
3. Oh! then, re-member me. . .

the part of the editor of that work. I do not know who superintended the musical portion of the first series of the *Poets and Poetry of Munster*, but for the most part the versions of the airs are remarkably poor and unvocal, and the editorial observations display a singular ignorance of some well-known facts regarding the printed history of the melodies.

Had you seen my sweet Coolin.

THE COOLIN

THOMAS FURLONG.

The composition of this beautiful air, known as "Molly St. George," has been attributed to Carolan by James Hardiman, and to Connallon by Bunting. The probability is that it was in existence long before these bards tuned their harps. It was sung in Coffey's opera *The Beggar's Wedding*, 1729, to verses beginning, "In thy arms, my dear Tib, will I end all debate" (see p. 50 for a description of this work); it is also to be found in Burk Thumoth's *Twelve English and Twelve Irish Airs*, c. 1745, and it is satisfactory to note that these two versions differ but slightly. The setting given above is from *The Beggar's Wedding*; the reading of the sixth and fifteenth bars is, however, from Thumoth's work. Bunting inserted "Molly St. George" in his Collection of "Unpublished" Airs, 1796; the setting in the *Farmer and O'Reilly MS.*, c. 1817, and printed in the *Citizen Magazine*, June, 1841, has been evidently copied from Bunting's volume. I have adapted Furlong's translation of "The Coolin" to "Molly St. George," and I hope this proceeding will receive approbation; I have done so because the air of "The Coolin" is already inserted in this work, set to Moore's beautiful song, "Tho' the last glimpse of Erin."

1. smile, She's the fair - est of the flow'rs of our green - bo-som'd isle. In
2. shown, Still! still, my sweet Cool - in, that heart is thine own. Thou

1. Be - lan - a - gar dwells the bright bloom-ing maid Re - tir'd like the
2. light of all beau - ty, be true still to me, For - sake not thy

1. prim - rose that blows in the shade; Still dear to the eye that fair
2. swain, love, tho' poor he may be; For rich in af - fec - tion, in

1. prim-rose may be, But dear - er and sweet - er is my Cool - in to me.
2. con - stan - cy tried, We may look down on wealth in its pomp and its pride.

rit.

Has sorrow thy young days shaded.

Thomas Moore.

Andante.

Voice.

Piano.

1. Has
2. Has
3. Has
4. If

1. sor - row thy young days shad - ed, As clouds o'er the morn - ing
2. love to thy soul so ten - der Been like a La - ge - nian
3. Hope like the bird in the sto - ry, That flit - ted from tree to
4. thus the young hours have fleet - ed, When sor - row it - self look'd

1. fleet ? . . . . Too fast have those young days fad - - ed, That
2. mine, ... Where spar - kles of gold - en splen - dour All
3. tree, ... With the tal - is - man's glit - ter - ing glo - - ry— Has
4. bright; . . . If thus the fair hope hath cheat - - ed, That

Air : "Sly Patrick." This is merely another version of "The Old Head of Dennis" ; see p. 265. It is singular that the origin of the air did not occur to Petrie, whom we find discussing it at length on p. 176 of the *Ancient Music of Ireland*. On p. 48 of *Letters of Thomas Moore to his music publisher, James Power, New York*, 1854, the publication of which was suppressed in London,

mf   *cres.*

1. ev - en in sor - row were sweet? . . . .   Does Time with his cold wing
2. o - ver the sur - face shine? . . . .   But if in pur - suit we go
3. Hope been that bird to thee? . . . .   On branch af - ter branch a -
4. led thee a - long so light; . . . .   If thus the cold world now

mf   *cres.*

1. with - er Each feel - ing that once was dear? . . .   Then
2. deep - er, Al - lur'd by the gleam that shone, . . .   Ah!
3. -light - ing, The gem did she still dis - play, . . .   And, when
4. with - er Each feel - ing that once was dear: . . .   Come,

p

rit.

1. child of mis - for - tune, come hith - er, I'll weep with thee, tear for tear! . . .
2. false as the dream of the sleep - er, Like Love, the bright ore is gone. . . .
3. dear - est and most in - vit - ing, Then waft the fair gem a - way? . . .
4. child of mis - for - tune, come hith - er, I'll weep with thee, tear for tear! . . .

p   *rit.*

we see from whom "Sir Patrick" came. "Pray, let Mr. Denison correct the spelling of *Cuishlah ma chree* according to Dr. Kelly, and likewise procure the name of ' Has sorrow thy young days,' as I have just hunted through all my music for Kelly's book and cannot find it." This letter is undated, but was probably written early in 1815. Vol. vi. of the *Melodies* appeared in March of the same year, and it includes "Sly Patrick."

Have you been at Carrick?

EDWARD WALSH.

Andantino.

VOICE.

PIANO.

p

poco rit.

con Ped.

1. Have
2. Oh!
3. When
4. Lo!

1. you been at Car - 'rick, and saw you my true. . . . love . .
2. I've been at Car - rick, and saw thy own true. . . . love . .
3. seek - ing to slum - ber, my bo - som is rent . . . . with . .
4. yon - der the maid - en, il - - lus - tri - ous, queen - - - like, . .

sempre con Ped.

1. there? And saw you her fea - tures all beau - ti - ful,
2. there, And saw, too, her fea - tures all beau - ti - ful,
3. sighs, I toss on my pil - low till morn - ing's blest
4. high, With long flow - ing tress - es a - down to her

A poor version of this air is given in O'Daly's *Poets and Poetry of Munster*, Series ii., 1860. The one adopted here is from Dr. Joyce's *Irish Music and Song*, 1888; it is given by the author of that work in the form known to him in his earliest days, and as he has heard it sung hundreds of times by the old people of Munster. "Were you at Carrick" is truly a lovely melody, and has all the appearance of considerable antiquity. Walsh's verses were published in his *Irish Popular Songs with English Metrical Translations*, Dublin, 1847.

1. bright and fair? Saw you the most fra - - grant
2. bright, and fair; And saw the most fra - - grant
3. beams a - rise; No aid, bright be - lov - ed! can
4. san - dal - tie— Swan, fair as the li - ly, de -

1. flow'r - ing, sweet ap - ple - tree; Oh! saw you my . . .
2. flow'r - ing, sweet ap - ple - tree; Oh! I saw thy . . .
3. reach me save God a - bove, For a blood - lake is . . . .
4. - scend - ed of high de - gree, A my - riad of . . . .

poco rit.

1. lov'd one,— and pines she in grief like me?
2. lov'd one,— she pines not in grief, like thee!
3. form'd of the light of my eyes with love!
4. wel - comes, dear maid of my heart, to thee!

poco rit.

Have you gazed at Shane Glas.

SHANE GLAS.

Translated from the Irish of Turlogh O'Carolan,
by Thomas Furlong.

Moderato. *mf*

VOICE.

1. Have you gaz'd at Shane Glas as he
2. With-out vers - es no po - et can
3. Have you chanc'd on your way hand-some

PIANO.

p   *poco rit.*   *mf*

1. went to the fair, How live - ly his step, and how care - less his air, With his
2. boast of the name; With-out mu - sic no harp - er the ti - tle can claim— No
3. Sal - ly to meet, With her gown snowy white, and her nice lit - tle feet, When she's

f

mf

1. breast full of fav - ours from ma - ny a lass; Oh! there's not a sweet girl that ap-
2. lov - er, thro' life, with - out quar - rels can pass; The gal - lant, whose head is not
3. bound to the fair, or re - turn - ing from Mass? With her smile so be - witch - ing, her

mf

For this air I beg to thank my anonymous correspondent in Dublin who has so kindly forwarded me several "traditional melodies not in printed books." My correspondent names it "After dark, my love and I. Limerick air," and as it seems to suit Furlong's translation of the song called "Shane Glas," attributed to Carolan, and printed in Hardiman's *Irish Minstrelsy*, vol. i., 1831, I have adapted it accordingly. I greatly regret that my correspondent did not give me any further information re-

1. - pears on the green, But simpers and blush-es wher - ev - er he's seen; They
2. smash'd for the fair, Is a boast - er un - wor - thy their fa - vours to share. Then
3. glanc-es so bright, And her soft cheeks so tempt-ing - ly fair to the sight. Oh!

1. cry, he's the boy, our darling and joy, Still rea - dy to sport, or to court, or to toy, Then
2. Shaue is the lad that his bruises has had, For the girls and drinking have made him half mad, Then
3. might I but find the sweet girl to my mind In yon-der green hol-ly-wood gent-ly re-clin'd, What

1. maids of the moun-tain, there's for you Shane Glas!
2. maids of the moun-tain, there's for you Shane Glas!
3. joy would it bring to the heart of Shane Glas!

garding this tune, the age of which I cannot for one moment doubt. By a reference to the tune "The Irish Lady, or Anniseed-water-Robin," which I give in the Appendix No. VII., it will be seen that we have the original before us. This air is from that wonderfully scarce work entitled *The English Dancing-Master, or Plaine and easie Rules for the Dancing of Country-Dances, with the Tune to each Dance.* London. Printed by John Playford at his Shop in the Inner Temple neere the Church doore, 1651. The same melody occurs in the fifth edition of this work, 1675,—a fine copy of which the present writer is fortunate enough to possess.

Ibe came from tbe Morth.

THE MAN OF THE NORTH COUNTRIE.

THOMAS D'ARCY McGEE.

Allegretto.

1. He   came from the
2. Oh,   Gar   -   ry -
3. But there's not—   I
4. I   wish   that in

1. North, and his   words   were   few,   But his   voice . . .   was   kind, and   his
2. -ow - en may   be   more   gay,   Than   this . . . qui-et   street   of
3. say   it with   joy   and   pride—   Bet-ter   man . . .   than   mine   in
4. Mun - ster they   on - ly   knew   The   kind, . . kind   neigh-bours I

1. heart . . . was   true;   And I knew   by   his   eyes . . .   no   guile   had
2. Bal - li - bay;   And I knew   the   sun . . . shines   soft - ly
3. Mun - ster   wide;   And Lim - er - ick   Town   has no   hap - pi - er
4. came . . . un - to;   Small   hate   or   scorn . . would   ev - er

1. he,   So I mar - ried   the   man   of   the   North . . . Coun - trie.
2. down   On the ri - ver   that   pass - es   my   na - tive   town.
3. hearth Than   mine . . . . has   been   with   my   man   of   the   North.
4. be   Be - tween . . . . the   South and the   North . . . Coun - trie.

The earliest printed setting of this pretty melody which I have seen, is that published in Daniel Wright's *Aria di Camera*, being a *Choice Collection of Scotch, Irish and Welsh Airs for the Violin and German Flute; c.* 1730. It is there designated "The Dangling of the Irish Bearns," and although, as far as I know, not attributed to Carolan, it bears considerable resemblance to the graceful compositions of our favourite bard. Thomas D'Arcy McGee was born in Carlingford, Co. Louth, in 1825; in his youth he was a strong member of the young Ireland party; a change in his political views, and his hostility towards the Fenians caused him to be considered a traitor, and he was assassinated in the streets of Ottawa in 1868.

Hear me but once.

Andante molto.

THOMAS MOORE.

PIANO.

p con espress.

rit.

p

rit.

p

1. Hear me but once, while o'er the grave In
2. Who could have thought the smile he wore When

1. which our love lies cold and dead I count each flat - t'ring
2. first we met would fade a - way? Or that a chill would

rit.

1. hope he gave, Of joys, now lost, and charms, now fled!
2. e'er come o'er Those eyes so bright, thro' man - y a day?

rit.

As "The Mountains of Wicklow " this pretty little melody occurs in R. A. Smith's *Irish Minstrel*, a work published about 1825, but suppressed by the action of Power, Moore's publisher, for infringement of copyright.

Her hair was like the beaten gold,

Andante.

VOICE.

PIANO.

mf *dim. rit.* *con Ped.*

1. Her hair was like the
2. The dew-y a - zure

1. bea-ten gold, or like the spi - der spin-ning; It was in her you might be-hold my
2. of her eyes was like a sun - beam glanc-ing; It thrill'd my soul with ten-der love to

1. joys and woes be - gin-ning. Her eyes were like the diamond bright, Her form was like—was
2. see her smile en - tranc-ing. A - las! in-con - stant as the breeze That kiss-es ev - 'ry,

cres.

1. like the fai - ry, That flits a - cross the woods at night, And such was gen - tle Ma-ry.
2. ev - 'ry flow - er, She frown'd on me, and now I dare Not e'en ap-proach her bow-er.

p *poco rit.*

Air: *An Graidhear duilleach,* or. " The Rejected Lover," printed in Bunting's and Horncastle's collections. Bunting gives the first four lines of the song, and Horncastle the entire verse. The expression of " beaten gold" seems to have been a favourite with old Irish poets; we also find it in the ancient Scottish ballad, " O saw ye my father," preserved in Herd's *Scots Songs,* vol. ii., 1776.

Flee, flee up, my bonny grey cock
And craw when it is day ;
Your neck shall be like the bonny beaten gold,
And your wings of the silver grey.

How sweet the answer Echo makes.

ECHO.

THOMAS MOORE.

1. How sweet the an - swer
2. Yet Love hath e - choes
3. 'Tis when the sigh, in

1. E - cho makes To mu - sic at night, When, rous'd by lute or
2. tru - er far, And far more sweet, Than e'er be - neath the
3. youth sin -cere, And on - ly then— The sigh that's breath'd for

1. horn, she wakes, She start - ing wakes, And far a - way, o'er
2. moon - light's star, The moon - light's star, Of horn, or lute, or
3. one to hear,— For one to hear Is by that one, that

1. lawns and lakes, Goes answering light!
2. soft gui-tar, The songs re-peat.
3. on - ly Dear, Breath'd back a -gain!

For note to this song see Appendix.

There we dwell.

LOVE AND THE NOVICE.

THOMAS MOORE.

Andantino.

VOICE.

PIANO.

f *sf*   *sf*   *p* > *poco rit.* . . . . .

1. "Here we dwell in ho - li - est bow - ers, Where An - gels of light o'er our
2. Love stood near the Nov - ice and lis - ten'd, And Love is no nov - ice in
3. Love now warms thee wak - ing and sleep - ing, Young No - vice, to him all thy

p

1. o - ri - sous bend, Where sighs of de - vo - tion and
2. tak - ing a hint; His laugh - ing blue eyes soon with
3. o - ri - sous rise, He tin - ges the hea - ven - ly

The following is Professor Stanford's note to this air in his edition of Moore's *Melodies* "restored": "In spite of Bunting's authority (in the preface to his second edition) Moore has adopted the spurious form of this air in the minor key, besides making numerous alterations for the worse in the melody. I have restored the form given by Bunting." I do not know what Professor Stanford means by "second edition," but in the third collection of 1840 we find Bunting dogmatising upon the subject : "This ancient air has hitherto been improperly set in a minor instead of a major key. A slight examination will prove that the setting now adopted bears in itself strong marks of originality." He then alludes to this "improper setting" being in Neale's and Thumoth's collections, but because he has heard his major version sung by the "peasantry of to-day," presumes that it must be the correct one ! Bunting's remarks are hardly worth criticising : it is enough to point out that while the peasant's setting "of to-day" remains unknown, the real *Coan dubh deelish*—the genuinely ancient melody—continues to be

1. breath - ing of flow - ers To Hea - ven in min - gled o - dours as - cend!
2. pi - e - ty glis - ten'd; His ro - sy wing turn'd to hea - ven's own tint.
3. fount with his weep - ing, He bright - ens the cen - ser's flame with his sighs.

1. Do not dis - turb our calm, O Love! So like is thy form to the
2. "Who would have thought," the ur - - chin cries, "That Love could so well, so
3. Love is the saint en - shrin'd in thy breast, And an - gels them-selves would ad -

1. cher - ubs a - bove, It well might de - ceive such hearts as ours!"
2. grave - ly dis - guise His wan - der - ing wings and wound - ing eyes?"
3. - mit such a guest If he came to them cloth'd in Pi - e - ty's vest.

poco rit.

sung and to give delight to all who hear it. When I draw my readers' attention to the fact that Tom Moore's song, with the air, appeared in the fourth number of the *Melodies*, published in 1811, just twenty-nine years before the publication of Bunting's major air and opinion thereon, they will agree with me, I think, in considering Professor Stanford's remark, "in spite of Bunting's authority," etc., to be somewhat inconsistent, to say the least of it. Moore's setting of the air is undoubtedly good, as a comparison with the many printed versions of *Cuan dubh devlish* will show. His omission of a part of it, acknowledged in a foot-note, appears to me to show good judgment, because the omitted part is evidently an instrumental addition by some harper or violin player. Smollett Holden, whose knowledge of Irish folk-music was great, appends a note to *Cuan dubh devlish*, which I think Bunting must have overlooked. "The Editor has selected this Copy of the Melody as being generally considered the best set. 'Tis sung differently in every province in Ireland." Versions of the air are given in Playford's *Dancing-Master*, vol. ii., 1728, as "Irish Round; or, Kinington-Wells," and in Thumoth's *Twelve Scotch and Twelve Irish Airs*, c. 1745-50, as "Curri Koun Dilich."

His kiss is sweet, his word is kind.

THE BOATMAN OF KINSALE.

Thomas Davis.

Moderato.

1. His kiss . . . is sweet, his
2. The wind . . . that round the
3. His hook - - er's in the

1. word is kind, His love is rich to me; I
2. Fast - net sweeps Is not a whit more pure— The
3. Seil - ly van, When seines are in the foam; But

1. could . . . not in a pa - lace find A true - er heart than
2. goat . . . that down Cnoc Shee - hy leaps Has not a foot more
3. mon - - - ey nev - er made the man, Nor wealth a hap - py

I have taken Davis's song from the volume of his poems issued in Dublin in 1846; it is marked to be sung to the air *An Cota Caol*. *An Cota Caol*, or the slender or threadbare coat, is published in Bunting's *Music of Ireland*, 1809.

1. he.   The ea - gle shel - ters not his nest From
2. sure.   No firm - er hand, nor free - er eye E'er
3. home.   So blest with love and li - ber - ty, While

1. hur - ri - cane and hail   More brave - ly than he
2. fac'd an ... au - tumn gale—   De Cour - cy's heart is
3. he can .. trim a sail   He'll trust .... in God and

1. guards my breast,—The Boat - man of Kin - sale.
2. not so high,—The Boat - man of Kin - sale.
3. cling to me,—The Boat - man of Kin - sale.

82

How dear to me the hour.

THOMAS MOORE.

Air: "The Twisting of the Rope," from Bunting's Collection, 1796. Moore's song was written for the second number of the Melodies, 1807. The original Irish song to the air is printed in Hardiman's Irish Minstrelsy, vol. i., 1831. In giving a translation of it in Irish Popular Songs, 1847, Edward Walsh appends the following note: "This is said to be the original song composed in that delightful inne, 'The Twisting of the Rope.' Tradition thus speaks of its origin. A Connacht harper, having put up at the residence of a rich farmer, began to pay such attentions to the young woman of the house as greatly displeased her mother, who instantly conceived a plan for the summary ejectment of the minstrel. She provided some hay, and requested the harper to twist the rope which she was making. As the work progressed and the rope lengthened, the harper of course retired backward, till he went beyond the door of the dwelling, when the crafty matron suddenly shut the door in his face, and then threw his harp out at the window."

How dimm'd is the glory that circled the Gael.

LAMENT FOR IRELAND.

Translated from the Irish by J. J. CALLANAN.

1. How dimm'd is the glory that cir - cled the Gael, And fall'n the high peo - ple of green In - nis - fail! The . . sword of the Sax - on is red . . . with their gore, And the migh - ty of . . na - tions is migh - ty no more!

2. Oh! where is the beau - ty that beam'd on thy brow? Strong hand in the bat - tle, how weak art thou now! That . . heart is now bro - ken that nev - er would quail, And thy songs are now turn'd in - to weep - ing and wail.

3. We know not our coun - try, so strange is her face; Her sons, once her glo - ry, are now her dis - grace; Gone, . . gone is the beau - ty of fair . . In - nis - fail, For the stran - ger now . . rules in the land of the Gael.

For note to this song see Appendix.

Hush, baby mine, and weep no more.

LULLABY.

Translated from the Irish by EDWARD WALSH.

VOICE.

PIANO.

1. Hush, ba - by mine, and weep no more, Each
2. The steed of gold - en hous - ings rare, Be -
3. Brian's gold - en - hilt - ed sword of light, That
4. And dain - ty rich and beoir I'll bring, And

1. gem thy re - gal fa - thers wore When E - rin, E-iner - ald Isle, was free, Thy
2. -strode, by glo - rious Fal - vey Fair, The chief who at the Boyne did shroud, In
3. flash'd de - spair on foe -man's flight; And Mur -cha's fierce, far - shoot-ing bow, That
4. rai - ment meet for chief and king; But gift and song shall yield to joy— Thy

1. po - et sire be-queaths to thee!)
2. blood-y wave, the sea-kings proud!
3. at Clon-tarf laid he-roes low.
4. mo -ther comes to greet her boy!

Hush! ba -by dear, and weep no more; Hush, ba -by mine, my

treas-ur'd store; My heart-wrung sigh, my grief, my groan, Thy tear -ful eye, thy hun-ger's moan!

This air is interesting as being a singular version of the Scotch tune "The White Cockade," or "O, an ye were died, guidman," which probably crept into Ireland about 1745. O'Daly has a barbarized piper's version of it in the *Poets and Poetry of Munster*, 1849, the first half of which, however, is a variation of another Scotch air known as "Twine weel the Plaiden." As far back as 1687 we find Playford printing an early version of "The White Cockade" as a Scots tune in *Apollo's Banquet*; he calls it "The Duke of Buccleugh's Tune." In Walsh's *Compleat Country Dancing-Master*, 1718, vol. i., the entire air is given as "Fidler's Morris," and in *Oswald's Caledonian Pocket Companion*, book iv., c. 1748, it is called "I wish that you were dead, goodman," which is the first line of the old Scotch song associated with the air, preserved in Herd's *Scots Songs*, vol. ii., 1776.

I groan as I put my nets away.

SONG OF AN ISLAND FISHERMAN.

KATHARINE TYNAN.

Adagio.

VOICE.

1. Why
2. Her
3. You

PIANO.

mf

poco rit.

con Ped.

mf

1. groan as I put out my nets up - on the say, To hear the lit - tle gir - shas shout a -
2. would you go so fast with him you nev er knew? In all the throu-ble that is past I
3. lone-some grave I keep from all the cold world wide, But you in life and death will sleep the
4. will not run a - gain laugh - in' to see me land, Oh, what was pain and throu-ble then, hold-

mf

1. dance a - mong the spray, Och - one! the chil - der pass a - way, and
2. nev - er frown'd on you. The light of my old eyes you are! the
3. straug - er still be - side. Och - one! my thoughts are dark and wild; but
4. - in' your lit - tle hand? Or when your dar - lin' head let fall its

p

p

1. lave us to our grief; The stran-ger took my lit - tle lass at fall-ing of the leaf.
2. com - fort o' my heart! Wait - in' for me your moth - er lies in bless-ed In - nis-hart.
3. lit - tle blame I say; An ould man hung-g'rin' for his child, a - work the live-long day.
4. soft curls on my breast? Why do the chil - der grow at all to love the stran-ger best?

This singular "Lamentation Air" is from Dr. Joyce's collection of traditional Irish tunes published in 1873. Mrs. Hinkson's beautiful song, which she has kindly allowed me to insert in this work, was printed with the air in Mr. Graves' excellent little *Irish Song Book*, second edition, 1895.

I am a wand'ring minstrel man.

BRIDEEN BAN MO STORE.

EDWARD WALSH.

Poco allegretto.

VOICE.

1. I
2. My
3. It

PIANO.

mf   *p rit.*

1. am a wan-d'ring min - strel man, And Love my on - ly
2. girl hath ring - lets rich and rare, By Na - ture's fin - gers
3. is not that thy smile is sweet, And soft thy voice of

p

1. theme; I've stray'd be - side the plea - sant Bann, And
2. wove— Loch Cur - ra's swan is not so fair As
3. song— It is not that thou fleest to meet My

This is one of the melodies attributed to Carolan. In the work entitled *A Favourite Collection of the so much admired Old Irish Tunes, The Original and Genuine Compositions of Carolan, the celebrated Irish Bard, Dublin*, 1780, it is entitled "Honble. Thos. Burk"; Burk Thumoth calls it simply "Thomas Burk" in his *Twelve English and Twelve Irish Airs, c.* 1745. As "My Love's a Bonny Naithing" Oswald included it in his *Pocket Companion*, book viii, *c.* 1755. In the little oblong MS. collection of tunes noted about 1735, and to which I have alluded on p. 128, an excellent version of the air is given, and shows in how pure a state the air

1. cke   the   Shan - non's   stream ;   I've   pip'd   and   play'd   to
2. is   her   breast   of   love.   And   when   she   moves   in
3. com - ings   lone   and   long!   But   that   be - neath   thy

1. wife   and   maid   By   Bar - row,   Suir,   and   Nore,   But
2. Sun - day   sheen   Be - yond   our   cot - tage   door,   I'd
3. breast   doth   rest   A   heart   of   pur - est   core,   Whose

1. nev - er   met   a   maid - en   yet   Like   *Bri - deen   ban   mo   store.*
2. scorn   the   high - born   Sax - on   queen   For   *Bri - deen   ban   mo   store.*
3. pulse   is   known   to   me   a - lone,   My   *Bri - deen   ban   mo   store.*

has come down to us. In printing "Thomas Burk" in his *Ancient Music of Ireland* as an air "never before published," Bunting gives us another example of his superficial knowledge of the history of printed Irish music. And "Thomas Burk" is by no means the only example of an air printed long prior to Bunting's volume but given by him as "unpublished"; such airs as "Molly St. George," "Have you seen my Valentine?" "Gracy Nugent," and many others, were all in print many years before 1796.

I dream of you in the flowering time.

A SUMMER LOVE DREAM.

MICHAEL HOGAN (The Bard of Thomond).

Andante molto.

VOICE.

PIANO.

p con espressione.

con Ped.

1. I
2. I
3. I'm
4. Thank

1. dream of you in the flow'r - ing time, When the sum - mer is all a -
2. dream of you when the moon - light dew Lies white on the glist - n'ing
3. ev - er in love, for my heart is fresh With the dews of e the - re - al
4. God! who gave my soul a wing To fly where the ea - gle

1. -glow, . . . And the king - ly sun flings his heav'n - ly fire On the
2. mead,. . . . And the world with si - - lent won-der looks up At her
3. spring, . . . And my heart is dark with the mag - ic wine Of each
4. flies, ... And fresh-en'd the blos - som of my heart With the

This pleasing air, which I have adapted to Mr. Michael Hogan's song, is named "The Little Red Lark." I have taken it from Hoffmann's Collection, 1877, and am indebted to Messrs. Pigot & Co., Dublin, for their kind permission to do so. Want of space has unwillingly forced me to omit two verses of the Bard of Thomond's beautiful song.

1. blos-soms that laugh be - low, . . . When the fai - - ry birds like
2. beau - ti - ful sis - ters ar - ray'd, . . And a hon - ey - drop from the
3. beau - te - ous bril - liant thing, . . And my ban - quet - hall is the
4. dews of its ho - ly skies, . . . And with the de - sert

sempre Ped.

1. liv - ing harps Give a voice to the wood - land wide; . . . Then I
2. an - gel's feast Seems in my soul to glide; . . . Then I
3. dark green wood With its bloom on the sun - beams dyed; . . . Oh,
4. hon-ey of song Has sweet-en'd my life's dark void; . . . And

poco rit.

1. dream of you as I walk a -long, And I wish you were by my side. . . . .
2. dream of you at that love - ly hour, And wish you were by my side. . . . .
3. liv - ing rose of my charm-ed soul, I wish you were by my side. . . . .
4. sent me one of his an-gels of love To sit at my poor hearth side. . . . .

poco rit.

I grieve when I think on the dear happy days.

DRAHERIN O MACHREE.

MICHAEL HOGAN (Bard of Thomond).

Andantino.

VOICE.

PIANO.

mf

1. I
2. To -
3. Oh!
4. He
5. Now I'm

mf   *rit.*   *sf*   *p*

1. grieve when I   think on the dear hap - py days of
2. - ge - ther we   lay in the sweet - scent - ed mea - dows to
3. sweet were his words as the hon - ey that falls in the
4. went to the wars when proud Eng - land u - ni - ted with
5. left to weep like the sor - row - ful bird of the

mf

cres.

1. youth, When all the bright dreams of this faith - less
2. rest, To - - ge - ther we watch'd the gay lark as he
3. night, And his young smil - ing face like the May - bloom was
4. France; His regi - ment was first in the red bat - tle
5. night, This earth and its plea - sures no more shall af -

cres.

3

I am indebted to Dr. P. W. Joyce for this lovely melody, in whose collection of traditional Irish tunes it appears. It is well known all over the south of Ireland, and the song *Drahareen-O-Machree* ("Little Brother of my Heart"), which has given it a name, is heard everywhere among the people (*Ancient Irish Music*, 1873, p. 39). The airs printed in Holden's Collection as

cres.

1. world seem'd truth; When I stray'd thro' the wood - land, as
2. sung o'er his nest, To - - geth - er we pluck'd the red
3. fresh and as bright; His eyes were like dew on the
4. charge to ad - vance; But when night drew its veil o'er the
5. - ford me de - light; The dark nar - row grave is the

f   *dim.*

1. gay as a mid - sum - mer bee, In bro - ther - ly
2. fruit of the fra - - grant haw - tree, And I lov'd, as a
3. flow'r of the sweet ap - ple - tree; My heart's spring and
4. go - - ry and life - - wast - ing fray, Pale, bleed - ing and
5. on - - ly sad re - - fuge for me, Since I lost my heart's

poco rit.

1. love with my Dra - her - in O Ma - chree!
2. sweet - heart, my Dra - her - in O Ma - chree!
3. sum - mer was Dra - her - in O Ma - chree!
4. cold lay my Dra - her - in O Ma - chree!
5. dar - ling— my Dra - her - in O ' Ma - chree!

I knew by the smoke that so gracefully curl'd.

THE WOODPECKER.

Moderato.

THOMAS MOORE.

VOICE.

1. I
2. "And
3. "By the

PIANO.

p   >   *sf rit.*   *p*

1. knew by the smoke that so grace - ful - ly curl'd . . A -
2. here in this lone lit - tle wood," I ex - claim'd, . . "With a
3. shade of yon su - mach, whose red ber - ry dips . . . In the

cres.

1. -love the green elms that a cot - tage was near, And I
2. maid that was love - ly to soul and to eye, Who would
3. gush of the foun - tain, how sweet to re - cline, And to

cres

I have Dr. Joyce's kind permission to take this pretty air from his *Ancient Irish Music comprising one hundred Irish airs hitherto unpublished.* Dublin, 1873. The verses are from the pen of Thomas Moore, and were published as "Ballad Stanzas" in his *Epistles, Odes, and other Poems.* London, 1806. At one time they were very popular, and musical settings to them were written by Kelly, Stevenson, and others. The following quotation from a letter dated April, 1813, (from Moore to his publisher, James Power,) shows that the poet's estimation of his song was not very high: "I think the Wood-pecker a very poor thing indeed, but it seems to take wonderfully. I wish I could write such popular things for you, my dear sir—with all my heart I do wish it, and I *must* try—perhaps I may succeed" (Suppressed Letters, p. 11).

1. said, "If there's peace to be found in this world, . . . A
2. blush when I prais'd her, and weep if I blam'd, . . How
3. know that I've sigh'd up - on in - no - cent lips, ... Which

1. heart that is hum - ble might hope for it there."
2. blest I could live and how calm I could die!" Ev' - ry
3. ne'er had been sigh'd on by an - y but mine."

leaf was at rest, and I heard not a sound . . . But a

wood - peck - er tap - ping the hol - low beech - tree.

I love my love in the morning.

Gerald Griffin.

Moderato.

VOICE.

PIANO.

mf

mf < *sf*   *dim.*   *p*   *poco rit.*

1. I
2. I
3. I

1. love my love in the morn - - ing, For she, like morn, is
2. love my love in the morn - - ing, I love my love at
3. love my love in the morn - - ing, I love my love at

mf sf   *p*

1. fair, Her blush - ing cheek, its crim - son streak, Its clouds, her gold - en
2. noon: For she is bright as the lord of light, Yet mild as au - tumn's
3. ev'n: Her smile's soft play is like the ray That lights the west - ern

mf

p

Air: "The Mountains High," from John Mulholland's *Ancient Irish Airs.* Belfast, 1810. I have heard Griffin's song sung to the air "The girl I've left behind me": I think it will be admitted that "The Mountains High" is more suited to the sentiment of the poem. Another version of the melody was recovered by Dr. Joyce: it is preserved, with one of the old verses of the song associated with the air, in *Ancient Irish Music*, 1873, p. 21.

1. hair; Her glance, its beam, so soft and kind, Her
2. moon: Her beau - ty is my bo - som's sun, Her
3. heav'n: I lov'd her when the sun was high, I

1. tears, its dew - y show'rs; And her voice, the ten - der
2. faith my fos - t'ring shade, And I will love my
3. lov'd her when he rose, But best of all when

poco rit.

1. whis - p'ring wind That stirs the ear - ly bow'rs.
2. dar - ling one Till ev'n the sun shall fade.
3. ev'n - ing's sigh Was mur - m'ring at its close.

molto rit.

H

I love to wander when the day is o'er.

Andante molto sostenuto.

VOICE.

PIANO.

con Ped.

1. I love . . . to
2. In dream - - y
3. I see . . . their

1. wan - der when the day is o'er, . . . And hear . . . the waves . . that
2. thought . . my ear - ly friends ap - pear, . . . And all . . . . I lov'd . . on
3. smile . . . as oft it beam'd be - fore, . . . I hear . . . their voice . . a-

1. break up - on the shore, Their heav - ing breasts . . re - flect each star - ry
2. earth a - gain are near, As oft . . . with me . . . . they watch'd the bil - lows
3. -mid the o - cean's roar; And half . . . for - get . . . . while gaz - ing on the

1. ray, . . . And seem . . . to speak . . . of years long past a - way . . . .
2. foam . . . That roll'd . . . so wild - ly round our is - land home. . . . .
3. waves . . That all . . . I lov'd . . . are sleep - ing in their graves. . . . .

Last time.

Both air and verses are from "The Native Music of Ireland" in the *Citizen Magazine*, Dublin, Feb., 1841, the author of which tells us that he obtained the tune from the Farmer and O'Reilly MS. Collection of Irish Airs. The Irish name signifies "The sound of the waves." I have not seen the MS. referred to, but Hudson states that Edward Farmer was a country schoolmaster who settled in Dublin early in the century; he earned a livelihood by teaching the Irish language. O'Reilly was the author of an Irish-English dictionary, and he and Farmer seem to have formed the MS. collection of tunes for their amusement. This was about 1817.

I once lov'd a boy.

Dr. George Petrie obtained this beautiful air from Miss Holden, the daughter of Smollett Holden, the editor of the valuable collection of Irish airs published in 1806, to which I have so often referred in this work. The melody was originally noted from the singing of a servant girl. The song is an old street ballad, and seems to have been at one time very popular in Dublin. It was issued as a broad-sheet by Bartle Corcoran, the great Dublin ballad-monger.

H 2

I once was a guest at a nobleman's wedding.

Moderato.

VOICE.

1. I once was a guest at a no - ble-man's wedding.
2. Cloth'd like a min - strel, her form - er true lov - er Has
3. "Oh! here is the to - ken of gold that was broken; Thro'
4. Oh, car - ry her soft - ly, the grave is made rea - dy; At

PIANO.

p   *rit.* *a tempo.*

cres.

1. Fair was the Bride, but she scarce had been kind, And now, in our mirth, she had
2. ta - ken his harp up, and tuned all the strings; Then a - mong stran - gers his
3. sev - en long years it was kept for your sake; You gave it to me as a
4. head and at foot, plant a lau-rel - bush green; For she was a young and a

cres.

p   *rit.*

1. tears nigh the shed-ding; For thoughts of her true love still run in her mind.
2. grief to dis - cov - er, A fair maid-en's false - hood he bit - ter - ly sings.
3. true lov - er's to - ken; No long - er I'll wear it a - sleep or a - wake."
4. sweet no - ble la - dy; The fair - est young bride that I ev - er have seen.

p   *rit.*

Air: "The Nobleman's Wedding." Dr. George Petrie gives three versions of this air in his collection of traditional Irish tunes. The setting adopted here was obtained from the son of the celebrated John Philpot Curran. The ballad was written for Petrie's work by William Allingham, and is founded on fragments of the original Irish song to the air.

I'd mourn the hopes that leave me.

THOMAS MOORE.

Moderato.

VOICE.

1. I'd
2. 'Tis
3. And
4. Thus

PIANO.

1. mourn the hopes that leave me If thy smiles had left me too, I'd weep when friends de-ceive me, If
2. not in fate to harm me While fate leaves thy love to me, 'Tis not in joy to charm me, Un-
3. tho' the hope be gone, love, That long spar-kled o'er our way, Oh! we shall jour-ney on, love, More
4. when the lamp that light-ed The trav'l-ler at first goes out, He feels a-while be-night-ed, And

cres.

1. thou wert like them un-true. But while I've thee be-fore me, With heart so warm, and eye so bright, No
2. -less joy be shar'd with thee. One minute's dream about thee Were worth a long and endless year Of
3. safe-ly with-out its ray. Far bet-ter lights shall win me A-long the path I've yet to roam—The
4. looks a-round in fear and doubt. But soon the prospect clear-ing, By cloudless starlight on he treads, And

cres.

1. clouds can lin-ger o'er me, That smile turns them all to light!
2. wak-ing bliss with-out thee, My own love, my on-ly dear!
3. mind that burns with-in me, And pure smiles from thee at home.
4. thinks no lamp so cheer-ing As that light which hea-ven sheds.

rit.

For note to this song see Appendix.

I saw from the beach.

Thomas Moore.

Andantino.

VOICE.

1. I saw from the beach, when the morn-ing was shining, A
2. Ah! such is the fate of our life's ear-ly promise, So
3. Ne'er tell me of glo-ries, se-rene-ly a-dorn-ing The

PIANO.

1. bark o'er the wa-ters move glo-rious-ly on; I came when the sun o'er that
2. pass-ing the spring-tide of joy we have known; Each wave that we danc'd on at
3. close of our day, the calm eve of our night;—Give me back, give me back the

1. beach was de-clin-ing, The bark was still there, but the wa-ters were gone!
2. morn-ing ebbs from us, And leaves us at eve, on the bleak shore a-lone. Each
3. fresh-ness of morn-ing, Her clouds and her tears are worth even-ing's best light. Give me

1. came when the sun o'er that beach was de-clin-ing, The bark was still there, but the wa-ters were gone!
2. wave that we danc'd on at morn-ing ebbs from us, And leaves us at eve on the bleak shore a-lone.
3. back, give me back the wild fresh-ness of morn-ing, Her clouds and her tears are worth evening's best light.

"I saw from the beach," Air: "Miss Molly," was printed in the *Melodies*, No. vi., 1815. Prior to this date the air is to be found in Fitzsimon's *Irish Minstrelsy*, 1814, as "Miss Molly, my dear, I'll go," and on a sheet published by Nathaniel Gow of Edinburgh in 1805 as "The Mole Catcher's Daughter." Later on Gow inserted it under the same title in his collection of airs called *The Beauties of Niel Gow*, book iii., and in a note remarks that it was one of his father's favourite Irish airs. Nathaniel was the fourth son of the celebrated Scotch violin player Niel Gow.

I've come unto my home again.

THE WANDERER'S RETURN.

GERALD GRIFFIN.

Molto adagio.

VOICE.

PIANO.

p *pp.*

con Ped.

1. I've come un-to my home a-gain, and
2. My love lies in the blush-ing west, drest
3. And when I lift my voice and sing un-
4. Oh! I have seen the maid-en of my

1. find my-self a - lone— The friends I left in qui-et there are per-ish'd all and gone— My
2. in a robe of green—And plea-sant wa - ters sing to her and know her for their queen. The
3. - to thy si-lent shades—And e-cho wa-kens mer-ri - ly in all thy drowsy shades, There's
4. bo - som pine and die— And I have seen my bo-som friend look on me doubting-ly, And

1. fa - ther's house is ten-ant-less, my ear - ly love lies low— But
2. wild winds fan her face that o'er the dis - tant bil - lows come— She
3. not a rill,—a vale,—a hill, a wild wood, or still grove, But
4. long— oh, long have all my young af fec - tions found a tomb— Yet

sf *p*

rit.

1. one re - mains of all that made my youth-ful spi - rit glow.
2. is my last re - main-ing love, my own, my is - land home!
3. gives a - gain the burst-ing strain, and yields me love for love.
4. thou art all in all to me, my own, my is - land home.

sf

rit.

For note to this song see Appendix.

I saw thy form.

Thomas Moore.

1. I saw ... thy form in
2. As streams that run o'er
3. If souls .. could al - ways

1. youth - ful prime, Nor thought the pale .. de - cay . . . . . Would
2. gold - en mines With mod - est mur - mur glide, ... Nor
3. dwell a - bove, Thou ne'er had'st left .. that sphere, ... Or,

1. steal ... be - fore the steps of time, And waste its bloom a -
2. seem ... to know the wealth that shines With - in their gen - tle
3. could ... we keep the souls we love, We ne'er had lost thee

cres.

cres.

This air, as "Donald," is published in Geo. Thomson's _Original Scottish Airs_, 1799, set to Burns' song "From thee, Eliza, I must go"; an asterisk is prefixed to it in the index to denote that the Editor considered it to be Irish. Arnold introduced it in his opera _Zorinski_, 1795, and in 1800 it was republished in Butler's _Scottish Airs_. I do not think that the tune is either Scotch or Irish but has a distinct flavour of the Anglo-Scottish style of melody so much in vogue in London during the latter half of last

1. - way, . . . Ma-ry! Yet still thy fea - tures wore that light . . Which
2. tide, . . . Ma-ry! So, veil'd be-neath a sim - ple guise . . Thy
3. here, . . . Ma-ry! Tho' many a gift - ed mind we meet, . . Tho'

1. fleets not with . . . the breath; . . . And life . . . ne'er look'd more
2. ra - diant ge - - - nius shone. . . . And that . . . which charm'd all
3. fair - est forms . . . we see . . . . . To live . . . with them is

1. pure - ly bright Than in thy smile of death, . . . Ma-ry!
2. oth - er eyes Seem'd worth - less in thy own, . . . Ma-ry!
3. far less sweet Than to re - mem - ber thee, . . . Ma-ry!

century, and which was cultivated by Hook, Shield, Arnold and other English operatic composers. Moore's song, with the air designated "Domhnall," was published in the fourth number of the *Melodies*, 1811. Professor Stanford's statement that a much more characteristic version of the air is to be found in the Petrie Collection, p. 152, is incorrect. Petrie's air, which he names *Donnel O'Greadh*, has no affinity whatever with "Domhnall."

I wish I were on yonder hill.

SHULE ARUN.

Moderato.

VOICE.

PIANO.

p

con Ped.

1. I
2. I'll
3. I
4. But

1. wish I were on yon - - der hill, 'Tis there I'd sit and
2. sell my rock, I'll sell my reel, I'll sell my on - ly
3. wish, I wish, I wish in vain, I wish I had my
4. now my love has gone to France, To try his for - tunes

p

con Ped.

1. cry my fill, And ev' - ry tear would turn a mill, Is go
2. spin - ning-wheel, To buy my love a sword of steel, Is go
3. heart a -gain, And vain - ly think I'd not com - plain, Is go
4. to ad-vance; If he e'er come back 'tis but a chance, Is go

Moore's song, "I wish I were by that dim lake" (*Melodies*, No. ix., 1824), was written to this melody, designated by him "I wish I were on yonder hill," from the first line of the old ballad associated with the air; another setting, sung to the same poet's "Shule Agra," has received the name of "Come, my love," from the chorus of the same ballad. Gavan Duffy places the date of the verses as early in the eighteenth century. It is interesting to note that one of the verses seems to have been incorporated in the old Scottish song called "Rantin' roarin' laddie," preserved in David Herd's *Scottish Songs*, vol. ii., 1776.

I'll sell my rock, my reel, my tow,
My gude grey mare and hacket cow,
To buy my love a tartan plaid,
Because he is a roving blade.

The version of the air adopted here is from Horncastle's *Music of Ireland*, pt. iii., 1844.

I would not give my Irish wife.

THOMAS D'ARCY M'GEE.

Spiritoso.

VOICE.

PIANO.   *f con forza.*

1. I
2. O
3. My
4. I

1. would not give my I - rish wife For all the dames of the
2. what would be this home of mine? A ru - in'd her - mit
3. I - rish wife has clear blue eyes, My heav'n by day, my
4. would not give my I - rish wife For all the dames of the

mf   *sf*

cres.

1. Sax - on land; I would not give my I - rish wife . . .
2. haunt - ed place, But for the light that night - ly shines Up -
3. stars by night, And twin - like, truth and fond - ness lie With -
4. Sax - on land; I would not give my I - rish wife . . .

sf   *cres.*

In including this air in the *Ancient Music of Ireland*, 1855, as an unpublished melody, Dr. Petrie was evidently not aware that it had been printed in a little tutor for the Irish pipes published by O'Farrell about 1797—1800. It is to be found in that interesting little work, as "We'll all take coach and trip away" (see Appendix No. IX.). Dr. Petrie's setting was

1. For . . the Queen of Fran - ce's hand. For she to me is
2. -on . . its walls from Kath - leen's face. What com - fort in a
3. -in . . her lov - ing bo - som white. My I - rish wife has
4. For . . the Queen of Fran - ce's hand. For she to me is

1. dear - er far Than cas - tles strong, or lands, or life, An
2. mine of gold, What plea - sure in a roy - al life, If the
3. gold - en hair— A - pol - lo's harp had once such strings— A
4. dear - er far Than cas - tles strong, or lands, or life, In

1. out - law— so I'm near . . her, To love . . till death my I - rish wife!
2. heart with - in lay dead and cold, If I could not wed my I - rish wife?
3. pol - lo's self might pause to hear Her bird - like ca - rol when she sings.
4. death I would be near . . her, And rise . . be - side my I - rish wife!

obtained from a MS. music book written about the middle of last century; he considers that it may be fairly regarded as
the composition of Carolan. It is hardly necessary to state that the air entitled "All Alive" in the *Dancing Master*, vol. ii., 1728,
has nothing in common with the Irish air given above.

I'll not reveal my true love's name.

Edward Walsh.

Moderato.

VOICE.

PIANO.

1. I'll
2. His
3. No
4. Wake

1. not re - veal my true love's name, Be - times 'twill swell the voice of fame; But,
2. glanc-ing eye I may com -pare To dia - mond dews on rose - buds rare; And
3. cuc - koo's note by fell or flood, No hunt - er's cry thro' ha - zel - wood, Nor
4. wake the wild harp's wild - est sound, Send spark -ling flag - ons flow - ing round, Fill

1. oh! may heav'n, my grief to quell, Re - store the he - ro safe and well, But,
2. love and val - our bright - en o'er The fea - tures of my bo - som's store, And
3. mist - wrapt val - ley yields me joy, Since cross'd the seas my roy - al boy, Nor
4. high the wine - cup's tide of joy — This health to thee, my roy - al boy, Fill

Dr. P. W. Joyce obtained this air in 1854, in the county of Limerick. The song was published in *Reliques of Irish Jacobite Poetry with metrical translations* by Edward Walsh, pt. i., 1844. It is entitled "The Lady of Albany's Lament for King Charlie."

1. oh! may heav'n, my grief to quell, Re - store the he - ro .. safe and well.
2. love and val - our bright - en o'er The fea - tures of my .. bo - som's store.
3. mist - wrapt val - ley yields me joy, Since cross'd the seas my .. roy - al boy.
4. high the wine -cup's tide of joy,—This health to thee, my .. roy - al boy.

My

he - ro brave, ma ghi - le m'fhear, My kin - dred love, ma ghi - le m'fhear; What
(pronounced: ma gil - li mar)

wring - ing woes my bo - som knows Since cross'd the sea ma ghi - le m'fhear; What

wring - ing woes my bo - som knows, Since cross'd the sea ma .. gli - le m'fhear.

I'll put you myself, my baby! to slumber.

IRISH LULLABY.

Translated from the Irish by GEORGE SIGERSON, M.D.

Andante tranquillo.

VOICE.

1. I'll
2. I'll
3.
4.

PIANO.

p molto legato e con espress.

con Ped.

1. put   you   my - self,   my   ba - by! to   slum - ber,
2. put   you   my - self,   my   ba - by! to   slum - ber, On
3. Slum - ber,   my   babe!   May   the   sweet   sleep   woo   you, And
4. Slum - ber,   my   babe!   May   the   sweet   sleep   woo   you, And

con sempre Ped.

poco rit. . . . .

1. Not   as is done   by the clown - ish   num - ber—A yel - low blan - ket and
2. sun - ni-est days of the plea - sant   sum - mer; Your gold - en   cra - dle on
3. from your slum - bers may health come   to   you! May all   dis - eas - es now
4. from your slum - bers may health come   to   you! May bright dreams come, and

poco rit. . . . .

Dr. W. P. Joyce supplied the Petrie Collection, 1855, with this beautiful "Nurse-tune;" it was obtained in 1854, from the singing of a woman in the county of Limerick. The original Irish verses sung to it were obtained from various individuals and are published in Petrie's work. Dr. Sigerson, Dublin, has kindly allowed me the use of his fine translation; it is also printed in Mr. Sparling's book of Irish songs and ballads entitled *Irish Minstrelsy.*

1. coarse sheet bringing, But in gold - en cra - dle that's soft - ly swing - ing.
2. smooth lawn lay-ing, 'Neath mur - muring boughs, that the winds are sway - ing.
3. flee and fear you; May sick - ness and sor - row nev - er come near you!
4. come no oth - er, And I be nev - er a child - less mo - ther.

To and fro, lul - la lo, To and fro, my

bon - nie ba - by! To and fro, lul - la lo,

To and fro, my own sweet ba - by!

I'll sing my children's death-song.

Translated from the Irish by J. J. CALLANAN.

Poco adagio.

VOICE.

PIANO.

p con espress.

poco rit.

1. I'll
2. Mute

1. sing my chil - dren's death - song, though My voice is faint and
2. are the tongues that sung for me In joy - ful har - mo -

1. low, . . Mine is the heart that's de - so - late, 'Tis
2. - ny; . . Cold are the lips whose wel - come kiss To

Air: "O thou of the beautiful hair," from the Petrie Collection, 1855: it was noted by Dr. P. W. Joyce in 1854, from the singing of a peasant in the parish of Ardpatrick, Co. Limerick: two stanzas of the old song associated with the melody are printed in Petrie's work. The song adopted here is a translation from the Irish by Callanan; it was published in Bolster's *Quarterly Magazine*, vol. i., Cork, 1826. The song expresses the feelings of Felix McCarthy who, during a period of disturbance

1. I . . . will mourn their fate. I'll . . sing their death - song,
2. me . . were heav'n - ly bliss. Oh ! . . but for Him whose

1. though the dart Is rank - ling . . in my heart: . . . No
2. head was bow'd 'Mid Cal - va - ry's mock - ing crowd, . . Soon

1. friend is here my pangs to soothe, In this deep sol - i - tude.
2. would I fly the pain - ful day, And fol - low in their way.

and persecution had been compelled to fly to the mountainous regions in the western part of the County of Cork. He was accompanied by his wife and four children, and found an asylum in a lonely and secluded glen, where he constructed a rude habitation as a temporary residence. One night, during the absence of his wife and himself, this ill-contrived structure gave way and buried the four children, who were asleep at the time, in its ruins. I have given four verses of this long "Lament."

I've a secret to tell thee.

Thomas Moore.

Andantino.

VOICE.

1. I've a se - cret to tell thee, but
2. There 'mid the deep si - lence

PIANO.

p

poco rit.

p

Ped. Ped. con Ped.

pp

p

1. hush! not here, Oh! not where the world its vi - gil keeps: I'll
2. of that hour, When stars can be heard in o - cean's dip, Thy-

p

1. seek, to whis - per it in thine ear, Some shore where the spi - rit of
2. -self shall, un - der some ro - sy bow'r, Sit mute, with thy fin - ger

p

p

Moore's song, "I've a secret to tell," air "Oh, Southern Breeze," was published in the tenth and last number of the *Melodies*, 1834. Bunting published the air as "Oh, Southern Breeze" in his collection of 1809, and again in a more extended form as "Why should not poor folk," in his work of 1840. He makes no remark in the latter work as to his having already printed the air, but merely remarks that he obtained it in 1792, from an old man well known by the *soubriquet* of "Poor Folk," who formerly perambulated the northern counties playing on a tin fiddle. It is an example of Bunting's carelessness that elsewhere in the

1. si - - lence sleeps, Where sum - mer's wave un - mur - m'ring dies, Nor
2. on thy lip: Like him, the boy, who born a - mong The

1. fay can hear the foun - tain's gush; Where, if one note her
2. flow'rs that on the Nile - stream blush, Sits ev - er thus,— his

1. night - bird sighs, The Rose saith, child - ing, "Hush, sweet, hush!"
2. on - - ly song, To earth, to hea - ven, "Hush, all hush!"

same work he states that he obtained the melody from "Poor Folk" in 1807. I am inclined to think that "Oh, Southern Breeze" has some affinity with an old melody called "Jack's Health," printed in Playford's *Dancing-master*, seventh edition, 1686, and used later on in the *Village Opera*, 1729, etc. I give this air in the Appendix, No. X., and shall allow my readers to judge for themselves. It must not be forgotten, however, that a tune can greatly alter its form in passing about from mouth to mouth during a period of more than a century; this has been incontestably proved in the air, "One Sunday after Mass."

116

If thou'lt be mine.

Thomas Moore.

Poco allegro.

VOICE.

PIANO.

mf

mf

rit.

1. If
2. Bright
3. And
4. All

mf

1. thou'lt	be	mine,	the	trea-sures	of	air,	Of earth and sea	shall
2. flow'rs	shall bloom	wher	ev - er	we	rove,	A	voice di - vine	shall
3. thoughts	whose source	is	hid - den	and	high,	Like	streams that come	from
4. this	and more	the	Spi - rit	of	Love	Can	breathe o'er them	who

1. lie at thy feet;	What	ev - er in	Fan - cy's	eye	looks fair,	Or in
2. talk in each stream,	The	stars shall look	like	worlds	of love,	And this
3. hea-ven-ward hills,	Shall	keep our hearts,	like	meads	that lie	To be
4. feel his spells;	That	heav'n, which forms	his	home	a - bove,	He can

ten. poco rit.

f

1. Hope's sweet mu-sic sounds	most sweet,	Shall be	ours,	if thou wilt be	mine,	love!
2. earth be all	one beau-ti-ful dream	In our	eyes,	if thou wilt be	mine,	love!
3. bath'd by those o - ter - nai rills,	Ev - er	green,	if thou wilt be	mine,	love!
4. make on earth, wher - ev - er he dwells,	As thou'lt own,	if thou wilt be	mine,	love!

colla voce.

Air: *Cailéach Ròin*, or, "The winnowing sheet," preserved in Bunting's second Collection, 1809; another melody with the same name is in Hoffmann's Collection, 1877. Moore's song was published in the seventh number of the *Melodies*, 1818. As there must be many who have never had an opportunity of seeing Irish women winnowing corn, I will briefly describe the process. The grain, having been thrashed with the flail, is, on a breezy day, heaped into sieves and then gently shaken into a large sheet spread upon the sward; the wind carries the chaff away and the corn is caught in the winnowing sheet.

In a cradle bright and golden.

LULLABY.

Dr. P. W. Joyce has kindly allowed me to extract this beautiful *Suantraidhe* (pronounced Soontree) or Lullaby from his volume of *Ancient Irish Music*, 1873.

In a shady nook one moonlight night.

THE LEPREHAUN.

Dr. P. W. JOYCE.

Allegretto.

VOICE.

PIANO.

1. In a
2. With
3. As

1. sha - dy nook one moon - light night, A Le - pre - haun I
2. tip - toe step and beat - ing heart, Quite soft - ly I drew
3. quick as thought I seiz'd the elf, "Your - fai ry purse!" I

1. spied; . . With scar - let cap and coat of green; A
2. nigh; . . There was mis - chief in his mer - ry face;— A
3. cried; . . "The purse!" he said— "'tis in your hand— That

Dr. Joyce obtained this air from the singing of a native of the county of Limerick in 1853. With reference to the ballad, I cannot do better than quote Dr. Joyce's note to the song on p. 100 of his collection of traditional Irish tunes. "It may be necessary to state, for the information of those who are not acquainted with Irish fairies, that the Leprehaun is a very tricky little fellow, usually dressed in a green coat, red cap and knee-breeches, and silver shoe-buckles, whom you may sometimes see in the shades of evening, or by moonlight, under a bush; and he is generally making or mending a shoe: moreover, like almost all fairies, he would give the world for *poitheen*. If you catch him and hold him, he will, after a little threatening, show you where

1. cruis - keen by his side. . . . 'Twas tick, tack, tick, his ham - mer went Up -
2. twin - kle in his eye. . . . He hammered and sang with ti - ny voice, And
3. la - dy at your side!" . . I turn'd to look: the elf was off! Then

1. - on a wee - ny shoe; And I laugh'd to think of a
2. drank his moun - tain dew; And I laugh'd to think he was
3. what was I to do? O, I laugh'd to think what a

1. purse of gold; But the fai - ry was laugh - ing too! . . .
2. caught at last, But the fai - ry was laugh - ing too! . . .
3. fool I'd been; And the fai - ry was laugh - ing too! . . .

treasure is hid, or give you a purse in which you will always find money. But if you once take your eyes off him, he is gone in an instant; and he is very ingenious in devising tricks to induce you to look round. It is very hard to catch a Leprehaun, and still harder to hold him. I never heard of any man, who succeeded in getting treasure from him, except one, a lucky young fellow named MacCarthy, who, according to the peasantry, built the Castle of Carrigadrohid, near Macroom in Cork, with the money. Every Irishman understands well the terms *cruiskeen* and *mountain dew*, some indeed a little too well; but for the benefit of the rest of the world, I think it better to state that a *cruiskeen* is a small jar, and that *mountain dew* is *potheen* or illicit whiskey."

120

In a valley far away.

Thomas Davis.

Andantino.

Voice.

p

1. In a
2. Oh! her
3. There are

Piano.

p

poco rit.

1. val - ley, far a - way, With my Máí - re bhán a stóir, Short would
2. sire is ver - y proud, And her mo - ther cold as stone, But her
3. lands where man - ly toil Sure - ly reaps the crop it sows, Glo - rious

p

1. be the sum - mer day, Ev - er lov - ing ev - er - more. Win - ter
2. bro - ther brave - ly vow'd She should be my bride a - lone; For he
3. woods and teem - ing soil, Where the broad Mis - sou - ri flows. Thro' the

From the *Ancient Music of Ireland*, 1855. Dr. Petrie gives the following verse from the old street-ballad connected with the air:

I wish the French would take them
That sent my love away,
And send their boats a-sinking
To the bottom of the say [sea].

The air was noted about the beginning of the present century.

1. days would all grow long, With the light her heart would pour, With her
2. knew I lov'd her well, And he knew she lov'd me too, So he
3. trees the smoke shall rise From our hearth with *maith go leōr,* There shall

1. kiss-es and her song, And her lov-ing *maith go leōr.* Fond is
2. sought their pride to quell, But 'twas all in vain to sue. True is
3. shine the hap-py eyes Of my *Māi - re bhán a stóir.* Mild is

1. *Māi - re bhán a stóir,* Fair is *Māi - re bhán a stóir,* Sweet as
2. *Māi - re bhán a stóir,* Tried is *Māi - re bhán a stóir,* Had I
3. *Māi - re bhán a stóir,* Mine is *Māi - re bhán a stóir,* Saints will

1. rip-ple on the shore, Sings my *Māi - re bhán a stóir.*
2. wings I'd nev-er soar From my *Māi - re bhán a stóir.*
3. watch a-bout the door Of my *Māi - re bhán a stóir.*

In holiday gown.

I'D WED, IF I WERE NOT TOO YOUNG.

John Cunningham.

Poco allegro.

VOICE.

PIANO.

mf

1. In
2. He
3. The

1. hol - i - day gown and my new-fan-gled hat, Last Mon-day I tript to the fair; . . . I
2. whisper'd such soft pret-ty things in mine ear; He flat-ter'd, he pro-mis'd, and swore! . . Such
3. sun was just set-ting, 'Twas time to re - tire (Our cot - tage was dis - tant a mile); I

1. held up my head, and I'll tell you for what, Brisk Ro - ger I guess'd would be
2. trin - kets he gave me, such la - ces and gear, That trust me,—my pock - ets ran
3. rose to be gone,—Ro - ger bow'd like a squire, And hand - ed me o - ver the

The original of this air is to be found in Thompson's *Country Dances for 1770* under the title of "Peggy Band." The version adopted here was sent to me from Dublin as "The road she went." In Mulholland's *Ancient Irish Airs*, Belfast, 1810, there is a tune called "That's the road she went," but it has nothing in common with "Peggy Band." John Cunningham, the author of

1. there. . He woos me to mar - ry when - ev - er we meet, There's
2. o'er. . Such bal - lads he bought me—the best he could find— And
3. stile. . His arm he threw round me—Love laugh'd in his eye— He

1. hon - ey, sure, dwells on his tongue; . . He hugs me so close, and he
2. sweet - ly their bur - then he sung; . . . Good faith, he's so hand - some, so
3. led me the mea - dows a - mong; . . . There press'd me so close, I a-

1. kiss - es so sweet, I'd wed— if I were not too young. . . .
2. wit - ty and kind, I'd wed— if I were not too young. . . .
3. -greed, with a sigh, To wed— for I was not too young. . . .

the beautiful verses which I have adapted to this air, was the son of a wine merchant : he was born in Dublin in 1729, and died at Newcastle in 1773 ; his farce, "Love in a mist," was written at the age of seventeen years. Several editions of his poems have been published.

124

In this calm sheltered villa.

Largo.

VOICE.

1. In this
2. Then

PIANO.

p con espressione.

rit.

con Ped.

1. calm shel-ter'd vil - la my fair one re - mains— The flow'r of all flow'-rets, the
2. smile, my be-lov - èd, let this cold-ness de - part— Oh! come till I press thee in

sempre con Ped.

1. pride of the plains; This my heart's hoard-ed trea - sure, my soul's sole de - light, . . In
2. bliss to my heart; Nay! nay— then I'm doom'd for thy loss to re - pine, . . I

As "The Irish Hautboy," this air is published in Longman and Broderick's *Second Collection of the most favourite Country Dances*, issued not later than 1781, in Aird's *Scotch, English, Irish and Foreign Airs*, vol. i., 1782, and in Thompson's *Hibernian Muse*, c. 1786; it bears considerable resemblance to the old Scotch melody, "The Lowlands of Holland," printed in Urbani's *Scots Songs*, 1794. A curious version of "The Irish Hautboy" is given in six-eight measure in Kinloch's *One Hundred Airs (Principally Irish)*,

1. win - ter she's my sum - mer, my sun - shine at night. Oh! thou my soul's dar - ling! most
2. die, dear-est maid - en, the blame shall be thine: Nay, call me not sense - less—nay,

1. love - ly, most dear, There's nought can bring plea - sure if thou art not near; Our
2. deem me not vain, Nor think that of pangs all un - felt I complain; Tho'

1. trust thro' the fu - ture in kind heav'n shall be,. . I'll long not for wealth, love, if bless'd but with thee.
2. low - ly my kin-dred, and scan - ty my store, Oh! why wilt thou tell me to love thee no more?

vol. ii., Newcastle, c. 1815, as "Farewell to Kilkloe." In introducing the setting adopted here in his *Ancient Music of Ireland*, Dr. Petrie remarks that the old words associated with the melody were rude and objectionable. Furlong's translation is published in Hardiman's *Irish Minstrelsy*, vol. i., 1831; the original Irish song was at one time sung to the well known air, "The Coolun."

It chanced when I was walking.

Adapted from an Old Broadside Ballad.

Moderato.

VOICE.

PIANO.

1. It
2. And
3. Oh,

1. chanc'd when I was walk - - - ing Down by the ri - ver -
2. when I gent - ly ask'd her If she would go with
3. were my love a rose - - - bud, And in the gar - den

1. -side, ... A - - mid the scent - ed bush - - - es, An
2. me, ... She laugh - ing - ly re - spond - - ed, "Good
3. grew, ... And I the hap - py gard - - - 'ner, To

This air is from the Petrie Collection, and entitled "This time twelve months I married"; it was obtained in 1854 from the singing of a Clare peasant. I have adapted the verses given above from an old broadside ballad of about 1780, of which a number of versions exist, and can be seen in the British Museum Library. The version published by Skillern beginning "Abroad as I was walking, close by the Shannon's side" is very amusing; it shows a strange cure for a love-sick swain:

One night as on my bed I lay, both sick and bad was I,
I called for a napkin strait, around my head to tye.

cres.

1. Ir - ish girl I spied; .... Her cheeks were bright and
2. sir, but I'm not free; . . . . . For Den - nis is my
3. her I would be true. . . . . . There's not a month through-

poco rit.   *a*

1. ro - - - sy, And yel - - low was her hair, ... And
2. hus - - band, And tho' he's aged and old, ... I
3. -out the year, But I'd my love re - new, ... With

poco rit.   *a*

tempo.

1. grace - ful was the green robe My Ir - ish girl did wear. . . . .
2. will not lose my good name For all your love and gold." . . . .
3. li - lies I would gar - nish her,—Sweet Wil - liam, thyme, and rue . . . . .

tempo.

K

July the first in Oldbridge Town.

THE BATTLE OF THE BOYNE.

Spiritoso.

VOICE.

PIANO.

1. Ju - ly the first, in
2. When we the Boyne be -
3. Then stout-ly we the

1. Old - bridge Town There was a griev - ous bat - - tle, Where
2. - gan to cross The en - e - my they de - - scend - ed; But
3. Boyne did cross, To give the en - e - my bat - - tle, Our

1. ma - ny a man lay on the ground By can - nons that did
2. few of our brave men were lost, So stout - ly we de -
3. can - non, to our foes' great cost, Like thun - d'ring claps did

The earliest printed version which I have been able to find of the air "Boyne Water" is in the fifth volume of Tom D'Urfey's *Pills to Purge Melancholy*, 1719 (see Appendix No. XL) where it is merely entitled "A Song." A good version of it occurs in a thick little oblong manuscript collection of tunes, chiefly Scottish, in my possession, written about 1730-5 (see Appendix No. XII). It requires much knowledge to decide the exact period in which so many old undated MSS. were written; my friend, Mr. Frank Kidson, of Leeds, who possesses much knowledge on the subject, has kindly assisted me to ascertain the date of this interesting collection of folk-airs. The following are a few of the different settings of "Boyne Water"; it will be seen that the air has been long known in Scotland. "When the King came o'er the Water" (M'Gibbon's *Scots Tunes*, iii., 1759); "The Bottom of

1. rat - tle. King James he pitch'd his tents be - tween The
2. -feud - ed; The - horse was the first that march - èd o'er, The
3. rat - tle. In ma - jes - tic mien our prince rode o'er, His

mf

1. lines for to re - tire; . . But King Wil - liam threw his
2. foot soon fol - lowed af - ter; But brave Duke Schom - berg
3. men soon fol - lowed af - ter, With blow and shout put our

f

1. bomb - shells in, And set them all on fire. . .
2. was no more, By cross - ing o - ver the wa - ter.
3. foes to rout The day we crossed the wa - ter.

the Punch Bowl" (Oswald's *Caledonian Pocket Companion*, Bk. i., *c*. 1743) : " Wha the de'il hae we gotten for a King" (*Scots Musical Museum*, vol. v., No. 464, 1796). In Aird's *Selection of Scotch, English and Irish Airs*, vol. ii., 1782, the air is designated "Boyne Water," and in Bunting's *Ancient Music of Ireland*, 1809, "The Cavalcade of the Boyne." The celebrated Leyden MS. contains a tune written in tablature for the Lyra-viol called "The Watter of Boyne." Like many of the airs in this MS., this one has been so carelessly transcribed as to be almost indecipherable. The "barring" throughout is incorrect, and signs to denote the rhythm are entirely absent. It is, however, quite clear that the tune has nothing in common with the one known now as "Boyne Water." (See Appendix, No. XIIα).

Lay his sword by his side.

THOMAS MOORE.

Andante poco maestoso.

VOICE.

1. Lay his sword by his side,— it hath
2. " Yet pause, for in fan - cy a
3. "Should some a - lien un-worth - y such

PIANO.

1. serv'd him too well Not to rest near his pil - low be - low; To the
2. still voice I hear, As if breath'd from his brave heart's re - mains; Faint
3. weap - on to wield, Dare to touch thee, my own gal - lant sword, Then

1. last moment true, from his hand ere it fell, Its point still was turn'd to a
2. e - cho of that which in Sla - ve - ry's ear, Once sound - ed the war - word,
3. rest in thy sheath, like a tal - is - man seal'd, Or re - turn'd to the grave of thy

The singularity of the title of this fine air, "If all the Sea were Ink," first printed in Holden's Collection, vol. ii. 1806, is only equalled by that of the old English melody in Playford's *English Dancing-Master*, 1651. "If all the World were Paper"; it is however, hardly necessary to remark that the airs have nothing in common with each other. Crosby also used "If all the Sea were Ink" in his *Irish Repository*, 1808, set to verses beginning "The moon throws her shadowy light on the hill." Moore's song was written for the tenth and concluding number of the *Melodies*, published 1834.

cres.

1. fly - ing foe. Fel - low lab' - rers in life, let them slum - ber in death Side by
2. "Burst your chains." And it cries, from the grave where the he - ro lies deep, "Tho' the
3. chain - less lord. But if grasp'd by a hand that hath known the bright use Of a

cres.

mf

1. side, as be - comes the re - pos - ing brave; The sword which he loved, still un-
2. day of your chief - tain for ev - er hath set, Oh! leave not his sword thus in-
3. fal - chion like thee, on the bat - tle plain,—Then, at Li - ber - ty's sum - mons, like

mf

1. -broke in his sheath, And him - self un - sub - dued in his grave.
2. -glo - rious to sleep, It hath vic - to - ry's life in it yet!"
3. light - ning let loose, Leap forth from thy dark sheath a - gain."

Lesbia hath a beaming eye.

Thomas Moore.

Allegretto.

Piano.

1. Les - bia hath a beam - ing eye, But no one knows for whom it beam - eth,
2. Les - bia wears a robe of gold, But all so close the nymph has lac.d it,
3. Les - bia has a wit re - fined, But, when its points are gleam - ing round us,

1. Right and left its ar - rows fly, But what they aim at no one dream - eth!
2. Not a charm of beau - ty's mould Pre - sumes to stay where na - ture placed it!
3. Who can tell if they're de - sign'd To daz - zle mere - ly or to wound us?

1. Sweet - er 'tis to gaze up - on My No - ra's lid that sel - dom ris - 'es;
2. Oh! my No - ra's gown for me, That floats as wild as moun - tain breez - es,
3. I'll - low'd on my No - ra's heart In sa - fer slum - ber love re - pos - es;—

Moore wrote the above charming song to the air, "Nora Creina" (*Nora Crioxa*, or "Wise Nora") for the fourth number of the *Melodies*, 1811. Prior to this date the air was published in Holden's Collection, vol. i., 1806—a curious version in minor—and in O'Farrell's *Pocket Companion for the Irish Piper*, vol. i., c. 1805. But in neither of these works is the air so good as Moore's version of it. A capital setting for dancing is in Murphy's *Irish Airs and Jigs*, 1809, as "Norah's Jigg." The following is the first verse of an amusing song set to the air "Nora Creina" in Henderson's little collection of Irish Tunes, Belfast, 1847:—

Who are you that walks this way, so like the Empress Deidamia?
Is it true what people say, that you're the famous Shibme rah?
Or are you the great Pompey? Or Britain's queen, bold Tiburcena?
Or are you Dido, or Doctor Magee? Oh, no, says she, I'm Nora Creina.
I'm the girl that makes the stir, from Cork along to Skibbereena:
All day long we drink strong tea,—and whiskey, too, says Nora Creina.

1. Few her looks, but ev' - ry one Like un - ex - pect - ed light sur - pris - es:
2. Leav - ing ev' - ry beau - ty free To sink or swell as heav - en pleas - es!
3. Bed of peace! whose rough - est part Is but the crum - pling of the ros - es!

1. Oh, my No - ra Crei - na dear! My gen - tle, bash - ful No - ra Crei - na!
2. Yes, my No - ra Crei - na dear! My sim - ple, grace - ful No - ra Crei - na!
3. Oh, my No - ra Crei - na dear! My mild, my art - less No - ra Crei - na!

1. Beau - ty lies in ma - ny eyes, But love in yours, my No - ra Crei - na!
2. Na - ture's dress is love - li - ness, The dress you wear, my No - ra Crei - na!
3. Wit, tho' bright, has not the light That warms your eyes, my No - ra Crei - na!

Let Erin remember the days of old.

Thomas Moore.

Air: "The Red Fox." In his edition of Moore's Melodies "restored," Professor Stanford accuses Moore of having altered Bunting's dance-setting of this tune in two-four time, "by halving the speed into a march." To show the inconsistency of this statement it is sufficient to point out that Moore's air was published in the second number of the Melodies, 1807, and that the version of the air which Bunting publishes in his third Collection, 1840, was obtained by him from Dr. Petrie in 1839—i.e., just

1. -va - - der; When her kings, with stand - ard of green un - furl'd, Led the
2. shin - - ing! Thus shall mem' - ry of - ten in dreams sub - lime Catch a

sempre f

1. Red-Branch knights to dan - ger, Ere the em' - rald gem of the west - ern world Was
2. glimpse of the days that are o - ver; Thus, sigh - ing, look thro' the waves of Time For the

1. set in the crown of a stran - ger.
2. long - fad - ed glo - ries they cov - er!

ff

thirty-two years after the publication of Tom Moore's "Let Erin remember the days of old." An inspection of the two slightly
different versions of the air given in Holden's Collection, vol. ii., 1806, as "The Red Dog or Fox," will show that Moore's setting
of the air is not only pure, but was evidently the accepted version at the time. It may be mentioned that "The Red Fox"
bears some resemblance to the well-known old English air, "Robin Hood and Little John, they both are gone to the Fair, O."

Let the farmer praise his grounds.

THE CRUISKEEN LAWN.

Spiritoso.

VOICE.

PIANO.

f   *poco rit.*

1. Let the farm-er praise his grounds, Let the
2. Im - - mor-tal and di - vine, Great
3. And when grim Death ap-pears, In a

cres.

1. sportsman praise his hounds, The shep - herd his sweet - scent-ed lawn; But
2. Bac-chus, God of Wine, Cre - ate me by a - dop - tion your son: In
3. few but plea-sant years, To tell me that my glass has run; I'll

cres.   *f*

1. I, more blest than they, Spend each hap - py night and day With my charm-ing lit - tle cruis-keen
2. hope that you'll comply, That my glass shall ne'er run dry, Nor my smil-ing lit - tle cruis'-keen
3. say, "Be-gone, you knave, For bold Bac-chus gave me leave To take an-oth - er cruis - keen

The air "The Cruiskeen Lawn" is the Irish form of the ancient Scottish melody "John Anderson, my jo," which is preserved in the celebrated Skene MS., pt. vii., written c. 1615-20. Mr. Chappell would fain have us believe that it is derived from an old English air, printed in Playford's *Dancing Master*, first edition, 1651, as "Paul's Steeple," and in order to prove his case, ingeniously ascribes the date of the Skene MS. to a later period—about 1700. I can only say that Mr. Chappell displays singular obstinacy upon this point. The MS. is in the Advocates Library in Edinburgh, and those interested in the matter can inspect it for their own satisfaction. It is sufficient to remark that such authorities as Dauney, Farquhar Graham and others, were quite as capable of forming an estimate regarding the age of ancient musical MSS. as Mr. Chappell, whose opinion was by no means always of

1. lawn, lawn,   lawn,   Oh! my   charm-ing lit - tle cruis - keen   lawn.
2. lawn, lawn,   lawn,   Oh! my   charm -ing lit - tle cruis - keen   lawn.
3. lawn, lawn,   lawn,   To   take   an -oth - er cruis - keen   lawn."

CHORUS.

'sGra - ma-chree ma cruis - keen, Shlan-the gal ma - vour - neen, 'sGra -ma-chree a   cool - een

bawn, bawn, bawn,   O! 's Gra - ma-chree a   cool - een   bawn.

an unbiassed description. His remark that "Moore appropriated the air under the name of 'The Cruiskeen Lawn'" is certainly amusing. Poor Tom Moore! He has been accused of "ruthlessly altering" melodies, and now of appropriating them! Let us look into facts: Moore's "Song of the Battle Eve: air, Cruiskeen Lawn," was published in the tenth number of the *Melodies*, 1834. Just twenty-eight years prior to that date, Smollett Holden printed the identical air in his *Old Established Irish Tunes* as "The Cruiskeen Lawn." But it probably did not suit Mr. Chappell to know of this fact. Again I say, poor Tom Moore! In the *Dancing Master*, vol. ii., 1728, we find John Young printing a version of the tune as "Put in all" (see Appendix No. XIII.) which bears considerable resemblance to the Irish setting. The earliest *printed* version of "The Cruiskeen Lawn" which I have been able to trace as being directly connected with Ireland, is "There was a pretty girl," air iii, in the third act of Charles Coffey's opera *The Beggar's Wedding : a New Opera as it is acted at the Theatre Royal in Dublin with great applause*, 1729 (see Appendix No. XIV.) The first edition of this work contains no music, but mentions the names of the airs. In the fourth edition, 1731, the airs are attached, otherwise it is the same as the edition of 1729. A revised version of Coffey's opera was performed at Drury Lane in 1729, with new tunes to suit the London audience; it was entitled *Phebe, or the Beggar's Wedding*. There is every reason to believe that the air has been known in Ireland and Scotland for many centuries. The theory that it is a Danish folk-air seems to have no foundation; it is evidently purely Celtic. The song, "Let the farmer praise his grounds," has been attributed to O'Keefe, but upon what authority I do not know.

Like the bright lamp.

ERIN! OH, ERIN.

Thomas Moore.

Moore's song was published in the third number of the *Melodies*, 1810. The air is named "Thamma Hulla" in Holden's Collection, vol. ii., 1806, and "I am asleep, don't waken me" in Mulholland's *Irish Airs*, 1810, and Bunting's third Collection, 1840. All these versions, or settings, of the air differ considerably, and Bunting, from whom, as Dr. Petrie remarks, more accuracy might have been expected, has unknowingly printed another setting in the same volume, as "Soft mild morning"; both versions were obtained from Hempson, the harper,—one in 1792 and the other in 1796. In including the Gaelic version of "I am asleep" as *Sha mi mo chadel* in his *Airs peculiar to the Highlands of Scotland*, 1815, Captain Fraser remarks: "It is claimed both by the Irish and the Lowland Scotch. There being very ancient Gaelic words to it, the Highlands have as well-founded a claim to it as either,

1. vain Whose spi - rit out - lives them, un - fad - ing and warm.
2. hung, The full noon of Free - dom shall beam round thee yet.
3. -bind, And day - light and li - ber - ty bless the young flow'r.

1. E - rin! Oh, E - rin! thus bright thro' the tears Of a
2. E - rin! Oh, E - rin! tho' long in the shade, Thy
3. E - rin! Oh, E - rin! thy win - ter is past, And the

1. long night of bond - age thy spi - rit ap - pears.
2. star will shine out when the proud - est shall fade.
3. hope that lived thro' it shall blos - som at last.

which the Editor is bound to assert." That the air has been long known in Scotland is proved by the fact that under the title of *Csami mi i cicittie* it was published in 1725-6 in a little work entitled *Musick for Allan Ramsay's Collection of Scots Songs, Set by Alexr. Stewart & Engraved by R. Cooper. Vol. First. Edinr. Printed & sold by Allan Ramsay.* Bk. iii., p. 62 (see Appendix No. XV.). That the air was in print at such an early date under the original Irish title will be news to most students of Irish folk music. The work, of which I have given the full title, is one of great rarity ; it is a small square 12mo. oblong, very roughly printed and full of errors ; it is divided into six parts, or books, and no second volume was issued ; it contains sixty-eight tunes with basses. "I am asleep, don't waken me" was also introduced in Coffey's *Beggar's Wedding,* 1731, as " Past one a clock in a cold frosty morning " (see Appendix No. XVI.) and in the opera *Flora,* 1732, as " At past twelve o'clock on a fine summer's morning " (see Appendix No. XVII.). Burk Thumoth included a version of it in his *Twelve Scotch and Twelve Irish Airs, c.* 1745, as " Past one o'clock " (see Appendix No. XVIII.) As I have already remarked, scarcely two of the many printed versions of this melody are to be found which do not vary. I do not know from whom Moore obtained his setting, but an examination of it with the older printed forms proves that it is not only good, but that Professor Stanford's statement in his edition of Moore's *Melodies* "restored," "there is scarcely a passage right in Moore's version," is entirely without foundation. Moore's setting, printed in 1810, is practically the same as the setting given by Holden four years earlier, but without the slightly varied repetition of the second phrase ; a reference to the Appendix No. XIX. will prove this.

Long, long have I wandered in search of my love.

THE DARK FAIRY RATH.

Translated from the Irish of GEORGE ROBERTS
by JAMES CLARENCE MANGAN.

Andantino.

VOICE.

PIANO.

p   *rit.*

1. Long, long have I
2. One bright sum-mer
3. And I said to my-
4. Then I twin'd round her

1. wan-der'd in search of my love, O'er moor-land and moun-tain, thro'
2. even-ing a-lone on my path, My steps led me on to the
3. -self, as I thought on her charms, "O, how fond-ly I'd lock this young
4. waist my arms as a zone, As I fond-ly em-braced her to

1. green-wood and grove, From the banks of the Maig un-to Fin - glas's
2. Dark Fai-ry's Rath; And seat-ed a-near it, my fair one I . .
3. lass in my arms; How I'd love her deep eyes, full of ra-diance and . .
4. make her my own; But when I glanc'd up, be-hold! nought could I

1. flood, I have ne'er seen the peer of this Child of the Wood.
2. found, With her long gold - en locks trail - ing down to the ground.
3. mirth, Like new ris - en stars that shine down up - on earth."
4. see, She had fled from my sight like the bird from the tree!

For note to this song see Appendix.

My bonny Cuckoo.

VOICE.

Allegretto.

1. My
2. The

PIANO.

1. bon - ny Cuc - koo, I tell thee true, That through the groves I'll rove with you: I'll
2. Ash and the Ha - zel shall mourn - ing say, My bon - ny Cuc - koo don't go a - way, Don't

1. rove with you un - til the next spring, And then my Cuc - koo shall sweet - ly sing. Cuc -
2. go a - way, but tar - ry here, And make the sea - son last all the year. Don't

1. koo, Cuc - koo, un - til the next spring, And then my Cuc - koo shall sweet - ly sing.
2. go a - way, but tar - ry here, And make the sea - son last all the year.

Bunting tells us that he obtained this pretty melody in Ballinascreen in 1793; the words are a close translation of the original Irish. Another version of the tune is to be found in the same author's *Ancient Irish Music*, 1796, under the title of "The Little and Great Mountain." "My Bonny Cuckoo" was first published in Bunting's third work of 1840, and in Fitzgerald's *Old Songs of Old Ireland*, 1843. Thomas Davis refers to it in his poem, "A Christmas Scene; or, Love in the Country."

Be quiet, and sing me "The Bonny Cuckoo,"
For it bids us the summer and winter love through,
And then I'll read out an old ballad that shows
How Tyranny perished, and Liberty rose.
          (Ballads and Songs, Dublin, 1846.)

142

My Celia! smiling gladness.

LITTLE CELIA CONNELLAN.

Translated from the Irish by JOHN D'ALTON.

Allegretto.

VOICE.

PIANO. { *con espress.*   *cres.*   *poco rit.*   p

1. My
2. In
3. How

1. Ce - lia! smil - ing glad - - ness, My on - - ly love!— my
2. wine, in wine, to drown care, In wine I'll plunge, a
3. blithe the breez - es gam - - bol Thro' yon - der val - ley

1. pear - ly dear!— My days must end in sad - - ness, If
2. mad - d'ning tide, If heav'n re - fuse my one . . pray'r, To
3. wild and free; Oh! were my love to ram - - ble From

cres.

cres.

As "The Peeler and the Goat" this air was published in Hudson's *Native Music of Ireland* (Citizen Magazine, Nov., 1842),
I have omitted the accidentals which I cannot but think are spurious. The old verses associated with the tune are a skit upon
the police force which Peel introduced into the country, and which was so universally detested for its tyrannical and

1. long you leave me lone - ly here. Or should you still so
2. be my snow - y fair be - side. Far soft - er to your
3. dawn to sun - set there with me; Where none should see our

1. doom .. me Thro' sigh - ing glens un - blest to rove; De -
2. lov - - - er You seem than down or silks so gay; Oh!
3. bliss - - es, But heath birds or the coo - ing dove: Nor

1. -spair shall soon con - sume me, And leave my heart in ru - ins, love!
2. words can ne'er dis - cov - er My lone - li - ness when you're a - way!
3. mor - tal count my kiss - es With Ce - lia Con - nel - lan, my lit - tle love!

inquisitorial character. The song which I have adapted to the melody, is from Hardiman's *Irish Minstrelsy*, vol. i., 1831. There
is an air in Bunting's third collection, entitled "Celia Connallon," which is possibly the original air to the Irish song; but
Bunting's setting is not vocal and the compass is too large.

L

My countrymen, awake! arise!

DENIS FLORENCE M'CARTHY.

Spiritoso.

VOICE.

PIANO.

mf   *rall.*   *f a tempo.*   *mf*

1. My
2. As
3. Too
4. There's

1. coun - try - men, a - wake! a - rise! Our work be - gins a new; . . . Your
2. long as E - rin hears the chink Of base ig - no - ble chains,—. . As
3. long we've borne the ser - vile yoke,— Too long the sla - vish chain,— . . Too
4. not a man of all our land Our coun - try now can spare; . . . The

1. min - gled voi - ces rend the skies, Your hearts are firm and true, . . . You've
2. long as one de - test - ed link Of for - eign rule re - mains,—. . As
3. long in fee - ble ac - cents spoke, And ev - er spoke in vain;— . . Our
4. strong man with his sin - ewy hand, The weak man with his pray'r! . . No

M'Carthy's stirring song, which he entitles "A New Year's Song," was printed with the melody in Duffy's *Spirit of the Nation*, 1846. The air is modern, and was probably written to M'Carthy's song.

1. brave - ly marched, and no - bly met, Our lit - tle green isle
2. long as of our right - ful debt One small - est frac - tion's
3. wealth has filled the spoil - er's net, And gorg'd the Sax - on
4. whin - ing tone of mere re - gret, Young Ir - ish bards, for

cres.

1. through ; . . But, oh ! my friends, there's some - thing yet For
2. due, ... So long, my friends, there's some - thing yet For
3. crew ; . . . But oh ! my friends, we'll teach them yet What
4. you ; . . . But let your songs teach Ire - land yet What

f

1. Ir - ish - men to do ! . . . .
2. Ir - ish - men to do ! . . . .
3. Ir - ish - men can do ! . . . .
4. Ir - ish - men should do ! . . . .

ff

L 2

My gentle harp.

THOMAS MOORE.

Andante.

VOICE.

1. My   gen - tle
2. And   yet   since
3. But   come,— if

PIANO.

mf con espress.

dim.

con Ped.

mf

1. harp!   once   more   I   wak - en   The   sweet-ness   of . . .   thy   slumb' - ring
2. last   thy   chord   re - sound - ed   An   hour of   praise . .   and   tri - umph
3. yet   thy   frame   can   bor - row   One   breath of   joy, . . .   oh!   breathe   for

mf

sempre Ped.

mf

1. strain;   In   tears   our   last   fare - well   was   tak - en,   And   now in
2. came,   And   many   an   ar - dent bo - som   bound - ed   With   hopes that
3. me,   And   show   the   world   in   chains and   sor - row,   How   sweet thy

mf

Like so many Celtic airs "The Coina" is common to both Ireland and Scotland. The Scottish form is called *Cha trid mis a rioudh*; or, "I shall not willingly go," and was published in Alexander Campbell's *Albyn's Anthology*, vol. i., 1816, set to Scott's poem "Nora's Vow." Sir Walter's song is based upon the original Gaelic verses, a few of which are printed in Campbell's work. Moore's song with the air, "The Conn, or Dirge" was printed in the seventh number of the *Melodies*, 1818.

1. tears. . . we meet a - gain. No light of joy . . . hath o'er thee
2. now . . . are turn'd to shame. Yet ev - en then, . . while peace was
3. mu - - sic still can be. How gai - ly ev'n, . . . 'mid gloom sur-

1. brok - en, But like those harps whose heav'n - ly skill Of slav - 'ry
2. sing - ing Her hal - cyon song o'er land and sea, Tho' joy and
3. -round - ing, Thou yet canst wake at plea - sure's thrill, Like Mem -non's

1. dark as thine hath spok - en, Thou hangst up - on . . . . the wil - lows still.
2. hope to oth - ers bring - ing, She on - ly brought . . new tears to thee.
3. brok - en im - age sound - ing Mid de - so - la - - tion tune - ful still.

My home's on the mountain.

FAIRY HAUNTS.

JOSEPH FITZGERALD.

1. home's on the moun-tain, my dance by the foun-tain, The mu-sic I dote on is
2. love to rove on-ly at mid-night when lone-ly, And play with the moon in the

1. sung by the rill, The gam-bols I squan-der are by the well yon-der, Where
2. old Ab-bey wall, The old-en days seem-ing, me-thinks, the harp's dream-ing, Its

This air, called "Jackson's Morning Brush" has been long a favourite in both Ireland and Scotland. It was evidently composed by Jackson, a musician of last century, who seems to have resided in Ballingarry, barony of Upper Connello, Co. Limerick, and who was celebrated for his skill on the violin and Irish bagpipes, and for the composition of many lively airs.

1. leans the grey oak at the foot of the hill. Of the flow'rs of the wil-low I
2. long - fad - ed dir - ges in bow'r and in hall. Where youth's grave lies wrin-kled, with

1. weave my light pil - low, My slum-bers are wing - èd, and fleet - ing, and blest, And
2. snow gar - land sprin-kled, I love to still lin - ger till twi - light ap - pears, Wher-

1. sun-light a-dorn - ing the bow'rs of young morning, I wing my way back to the hills I love best.
2. ev - er woe weep-eth, or fair vir-tue sleep-eth, They be-long not to night, they're my own dew - y tears.

The "Morning Brush" was printed in Edmund Lee's publication of *circa* 1775, entitled *Jackson's Celebrated Irish Tunes*; it was also used by Arnold in his opera, *The Agreeable Surprise*, 1781; Thompson included it in his *Country Dances for* 1779, and Aird in his *Selection*, vol. i., 1782. I have taken the song "Fairy Haunts," from Fitzgerald's *Old Songs of Old Ireland*, London, 1843.

My love, still I think that I see her.

GEORGE REYNOLDS.

VOICE.

Poco allegretto.   *p Andantino.*

1. My love, still I think that I
2. Her hair gloss-y black— her
3. She milk'd the dun cow that ne'er
4. She sat at the door one
5. Oh, cold was the night-wind that

PIANO.

Poco allegretto.   *Andantino.*

p   *poco rit.*   *p*

1. see her once more, But a - las! she has left me her loss to de - plore, My
2. eyes were dark blue, Her col - our still chang - ing, her smiles ev - er new, So
3. of - fer'd to stir; Tho' wick - ed to all, it was gen - tle to her, So
4. cold af - ter - noon To hear the wind blow, and to gaze on the moon, So
5. sigh'd round her bow'r, It chill'd my poor Kath-leen, she droop'd from that hour, And I

rit.

1. own lit - tle Kath-leen, my poor lit - tle Kath-leen, My Kath - leen O' - More! . . . .
2. pret - ty was Kath-leen, my sweet lit - tle Kath-leen, My Kath - leen O' - More! . . . .
3. kind was my Kath-leen, my poor lit - tle Kath-leen, My Kath - leen O' - More! . . . .
4. pen - sive was Kath-leen, my poor lit - tle Kath-leen, My Kath - leen O' - More! . . . .
5. lost my poor Kath-leen, my poor lit - tle Kath-leen, My Kath - leen O' - More! . . . .

rit.

This pretty little song is the composition of George Nugent Reynolds, the author of a musical interlude called *Bantry Bay,* performed in London in 1797, the music to which was written by William Reeve; Reynolds died in 1802. The composer of the air, "Kathleen O'More," has drawn upon some well known Irish melodies for his inspiration, notable among these being the "Black Joke."

My love she was born in the north countrie.

Air: "Fair maidens' beauty will soon fade away." Regarding this song, Dr. Joyce remarks, "I learned both the air and the words of the song from my father. It was well known in my early days among the people of the south; and there are more verses in the song; but those I give are all that I can remember." (Anc. Irish Music, 1873, p. 66.)

My love's the fairest creature.

Lady Morgan.

Andante espressivo.

VOICE.

PIANO.

p

poco rit.

p

con Ped.

1. My love's the fair - est
2. Her sigh is like the

1. crea - - ture, And round her flut - ters ma - ny a charm, Her
2. sweet gale That dies up - on the vio - let's breast, Her

cres.

1. star - ry eyes, blue - - beam - - ing, Can e'en the cold - est
2. hair is like the dark mist On which the even - ing

cres.

As "My Love's the fairest creature, or Shelah na Conolan," this air and song were published in *Twelve Original Hibernian Melodies with English Words, imitated and translated from the Works of the Ancient Irish Bards. By Miss Owenson. London, 1805.* This is the collection of Irish Melodies alluded to in the advertisement attached to the first edition of the first number of Moore's Irish

1. bo - som warm. Her lip is, like a cher - - - - - - ry,
2. sun - beams rest; Her smile is like the false light, Which

1. Ripe - ly su - ing to be cull'd, Her cheek is like a
2. lures the tra - vel - ler by its beam; Her voice is like a

1. May . . . rose, In dew - y fresh - ness new - ly pull'd.
2. soft . . . strain Which steals its soul from pas - sion's dream.

Melodies, 1807. Under the same title, "My love's the fairest creature," the air was printed in Aird's Collection, vol. vi., c. 1802-3, and in Mulholland's Irish and Scots Tunes, Edinburgh; this work is undated, but is advertised for sale in a newspaper of April, 1804. Miss Owenson was the daughter of Robert Owenson, the Irish actor and singer, and was born about 1778; she married Sir T. Morgan, M.D., in 1812, and died in London on April 13th, 1859.

154

Nay, tell me not, dear.

Thomas Moore.

1. Nay, tell me not, dear, that the gob-let drowns One charm of feel-ing, one fond re - gret; Be - lieve me, a few of thy an - gry frowns Are all I've sunk in its bright wave yet, Ne'er hath a beam Been

2. They tell us that Love, in his fai - ry bow'r Had two blush - ro - ses of birth di - vine; He sprin-kles the one with a rain - bow - show'r But bathed the o - ther with mant - ling wine. Soon did the buds That

As " Dennis, don't be threatening " the air is in Bunting's Collections of 1796 and 1809, the *Irish Repository*, 1808, Mulholland's *Ancient Irish Airs*, 1810, and, with Moore's song in the fourth number of the *Melodies*, 1811. It is the progenitor of the air known as " The Dandy O " (see p. 251). As " O, rouse yourself, it's cold you've got," Dr Petrie has printed a setting of " Dennis, don't be threatening," which he obtained in 1854 from the singing of a blind ballad-singer in Limerick. Another version was used by Shield in the " Poor Soldier," 1783, set to verses beginning, " Out of my sight, or I'll box your ears."

1. lost in the stream That e - ver was shed from thy form or soul; The balm of thy sighs, The
2. drank of the floods Dis - till'd by the rain-bow de - cline and fade; While those which the tide Of

1. spell of thine eyes, Still float on the sur - face, and hal - low my bowl; Then
2. ru - by had dyed All blush'd in - to beau - ty, like thee, sweet maid; Then

1. fan - cy not, dear-est, that wine can steal One bliss - ful dream of the heart from me; Like
2. fan - cy not, dear-est, that wine can steal One bliss - ful dream of the heart from me; Like

1. founts, that a - wak - en the pil - grim's zeal, The bowl but brightens my love for thee!
2. founts, that a - wak - en the pil - grim's zeal, The bowl but brightens my love for thee!

No, not more welcome.

THOMAS MOORE.

Andante con espressione.

VOICE.

PIANO.

p

rit.

p

con Ped.

1. No, not more wel - come the fai - ry
2. Sweet voice of com - fort! 'twas like the

1. num - bers Of mu - sic fall on the sleep - er's ear, When half a -
2. steal - ing Of sum - mer wind thro' some wreath - èd shell, Each se - cret

cres.

1. -wak - ing from fear - ful slum - bers, He thinks the full quire of heav'n is
2. wind - ing, each in - most feel - ing Of all my soul e - choed to its

cres.

This air, known as " Lnagelaw," was supplied to Moore by Dr. George Petrie about 1808 (Petrie Collection, p. viii). The air bearing the same title, published by Hoffmann in the collection of tunes taken from the Petrie MSS., 1877, bears no resemblance to the above melody. Moore's song was published in the sixth number of the *Melodies*, 1815.

1. near,   Then came that voice, when, all for - sak - en,   This
2. spell!   'Twas whis - per'd balm,— 'twas sun - shine spok - en,   I'd

1. heart long had sleep - ing lain,   Nor thought its cold pulse would ev - er
2. live years of grief and pain,   To have my long sleep of sor - row

1. wak - en To such be - nign bless - ed sounds a - gain.
2. brok - en By such be - nign bless - ed sounds a - gain.

O Bay of Dublin.

HELEN SELINA DUFFERIN.

1. O Bay of Dub - lin! my heart you're
2. Sweet Wicklow moun - tains, the sun - light
3. How oft - en when at work I'm

1. troub - lin', Your beau - ty haunts me like a fe - ver'd dream, Like fro - zen
2. sleep - ing On your green banks is a pic - ture rare: You crowd a -
3. sit - ting And mus - ing sad - ly on the days of yore, I think I

1. foun-tains that the sun sets bub - blin' My heart's blood warms when I but hear your
2. - round me like young girls peep - ing, And puzz - ling me to say which is most
3. see . . . my Ka - tey knit - ting, And the chil - dren play - ing round the cab - in -

This Limerick air, which I have adapted to Lady Dufferin's well-known song, is from Hoffmann's Collection, 1877; I am indebted to Messrs Pigot & Co. for permission to reprint it in the present work. Lady Helen Selina Dufferin was the author of some beautiful Irish poems; she was born in 1807, and died in London in 1867.

1. name.   And nev - er till . . . this life pulse ceas - es,   My ear - liest
2. fair;   As tho' you'd see . . . your own sweet fa - ces   Re - flect - ed
3. door;   I think I see . . . the neighbours' fa - ces   All ga - ther'd

a tempo.   p

sempre con Ped.

cres.

1. thought . . . you'll cease to   be;   O no one   here   knows how fair that
2. in   that smooth and sil - ver   sea;   My fer - vid   bless - ing on those lone - ly
3. round, their long - lost friend to   see;   Tho' no one   knows . . .   how fair that

cres.

mf   dim. rit.

1. place   is,   And   no   one   cares how dear it   is   to   me.
2. pla - - ces,   Tho' no   one   cares how dear they are   to   me.
3. place   is,   Heav'n knows how   dear my poor home was   to   me.

mf   dim. rit.

M

Oh haste and leave this sacred isle.

ST. SENANUS AND THE LADY.

Thomas Moore.

1. "Oh! haste, and
2. "Oh! fa - ther,
3. The la - dy's

1. leave this sa - cred isle, Un - ho - ly bark, ere morn - ing
2. send not hence my bark, 'Thro' win - try winds and o'er bil - lows
3. pray'r Sen - an - us spurn'd; The wind blew fresh, and the bark re -

Air: *Drohhneann donn* or. "The Brown Thorn," and preserved in Bunting's *General Collection of the Ancient Irish Music*, 1796. On p. xvii. of *The Ancient Music of Ireland*, 1855, Dr. Petrie criticises Bunting's version of the air somewhat severely. Moore's song appeared in the second number of the *Melodies*, 1807.

1. smile; For on thy deck, tho' dark it be, A fe - male
2. dark; I come with hum . - ble heart to share Thy morn and
3. -turn'd; But le - gends hint, that had the maid Till morn -ing's

1. form I see; And I have sworn this saint - ed
2. ev'n - - - - - - - - ing pray'r, Nor mine the feet, O ho - ly
3. light de - lay'd, And giv'n the saint one ros - y

1. sod Shall ne'er by wo - - man's feet be trod."
2. saint, The bright - ness of . . . thy sod to taint."
3. smile, She ne'er had left . . his lone - ly isle.

M 2

O, love is the soul of a neat Irishman.

A SPRIG OF SHILLELAH.

HENRY B. CODE.

1. love is the soul of a neat I - rish - man, He loves all that's love - ly, loves
2. e'er had the luck to see Don - ny - brook fair? An I - rish - man all in his
3. coun - try, say I, that gave Pa - trick his birth! Bless the land of the oak and its

1. all that he can, With his sprig of shil - le - lah and sham-rock so green. His
2. glo - ry is there, With his sprig of shil - le - lah and sham-rock so green. His
3. neigh-bour - ing earth: Where grow the shil - le - lah and sham-rock so green. May the

This air was evidently a great favourite in England about the beginning of last century : indeed, were it not for the tradition that it originally came from Ireland, I should be inclined to consider it English : it seems to lack that sprightly feeling, so peculiar to Irish jig-tunes. It was introduced as "The Black Joke" in *Pills*, or *The Beggar's Wedding*, 1729, *The Lottery*, 1732, *Achilles*, 1733, etc., and as "The Coal Black Joak," in Watt's *Musical Miscellany*, vol. vi., 1731. It is to be observed, however, that the setting of that period is somewhat different from the tune now generally known as "The Sprig of Shillelah." The Ballad

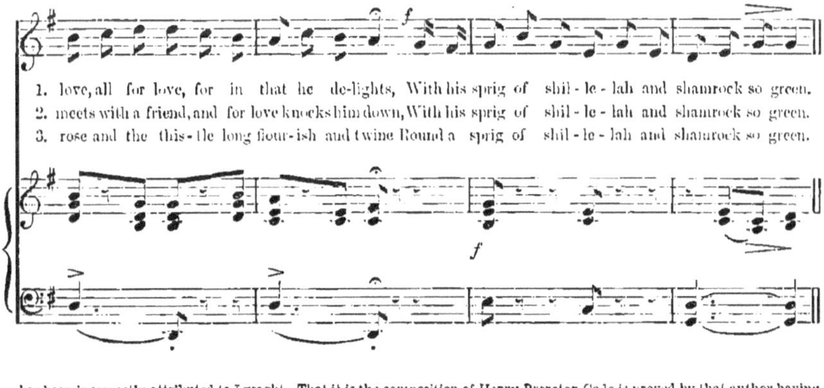

Lyrics (verse lines beneath staves):

1. heart is good hu-mour'd,'tis hon - est and sound, No mal - ice or ha - tred is
2. clothes spruce and span new, with - out e'er a speck, A new Bar - ce - lo - na tied
3. sons of the Thames, and the Tweed, and the Shan-non, Drub foes who dare plant on our

1. there to be found, He courts and he mar - ries, he drinks and he fights, For
2. round his neat neck; He en - ters a tent and spends half - a - crown, He
3. con - fines a can - non, U - ni - ted and hap - py, at loy - al - ty's shrine, May the

1. love, all for love, for in that he de-lights, With his sprig of shil - le - lah and shamrock so green.
2. meets with a friend, and for love knocks him down, With his sprig of shil - le - lah and shamrock so green.
3. rose and the this-tle long flour-ish and twine Round a sprig of shil - le - lah and shamrock so green.

has been incorrectly attributed to Lysaght. That it is the composition of Henry Brereton Code is proved by that author having introduced it in his drama *The Russian Sacrifice or Burning of Moscow*, 1813, with the following note. "This song, ['The Sprig of Shillelah'] written by the author of the play some years ago, having been so long before the public, it was held expedient that he should forego his intention of introducing it, however applicable in the representation, and substitute the following original song." Then follows the song, "If you'd search the world round, all from Howth to Killarney," tune: Langolee."

O, wearily, wearily lags the day.

VOICE.

Andante.

1. Oh, wea - ri - ly, wea - ri - ly...
2. I am wind - ing my thread on this

PIANO.

p con molto espressione e ritard. . . . . . .

poco rit.

1. lags . . . the day, When the one . . . we love is far . . . a -
2. wil - - low wand, But ev - er it breaks in my trem - - bling

poco rit.

1. - way; The sun has set, and the day - light is gone, And
2. hand; A - way to - mor - row the task will be o'er, To -

This pretty air and song are from Horncastle's *Music of Ireland*, pt. i., 1844; the verses are evidently the translation of some old Irish peasant song.

1. I . . . am here, and here a - lone. The sun has
2. - night, . . a - las! I can wind no more. A - way to -

1. set, and the day - light is gone, And I am here, And
2. - mor-row the task will be o'er, To - night, a - las, I can

pp Lento.

1. here a - lone.
2. wind no more.   Oh,   ul- la - gone, ...   Oh,   ul -la - gone.

pp

con Ped.

Och hone! oh, what will I do?

MOLLY CAREW.

Con spirito.   *f rit.*   *mf a tempo.*   SAMUEL LOVER.

VOICE.

PIANO.   *f*   *rit.*   *a tempo. mf*

1. Och hone! Oh, what will I do? Sure my love is all crost, Like a
2. Och hone! But why should I speak of your fore-head and eyes, When your
3. Och hone! Don't pro-voke me to do it; There's girls by the score, That

1. bud in the frost! And there's no use at all in my go-ing to bed, For 'tis dhrames and not sleep that comes
2. nose it de-fies Pad-dy Blake, the schoolmaster, to put it in rhyme. Tho' there's one, Burke, he says, who would
3. love me and more; And you'd look very queer if some morning you'd meet My wed-ding all march-ing in

1. in-to my head. And 'tis all a-bout you, My sweet Molly Carew, And in-deed 'tis a sin and a
2. call it snub-nose. And then for your cheek, Throth 'twould take him a week, Its beauties to tell, as he'd
3. pride down the street; Troth, you'd o-pen your eyes, And you'd die with surprise, To think 'twasn't you was come

1. shame, You're com-plet-er than Na-ture in ev-e-ry feature, The snow can't compare with your
2. ra-ther; Then your lips, oh, Ma-chree, in their beau-ti-ful glow, They a pat-thern might be for the
3. to it; And faith, Kat-ty Naile, and her cow, I go bail, Would jump if I say, "Kat-ty

Hardiman and Lover attribute this air to Carolan, but do not state their authority. Its name, "Planxty Reilly" certainly
resembles the titles of many of our bard's compositions, most of which were named after his patrons and friends. But
"Planxty Reilly" does not occur in Thumoth's octavo publications, nor in the volume of Carolan's compositions published by

1. fore - head so fair, And I ra - ther would see just one blink of your eye, Than the
2. cher - ries to grow. "Twas an ap - ple that tempt - ed our mo - ther, we know, For
3. Naile, name the day." And tho' you're fair and fresh as a morn - ing in May, While

1. pur - ti - est star that shines out of the sky, And, by this and by that, for the
2. ap - ples were scarce, I sup - pose, long a - go, And, by the time o' day, For my
3. she's short and dark like a cold win - ter's day; Yet if you don't re - pent Be - fore

1. mat - ther of that You're more dis - tant, by far, than that same, *Och hone!* *wie - ra - sthru, och*
2. conscience I'll say, Such cher - ries might tempt a man's fa - ther, *Och hone!* *wie - ra - sthru, och*
3. Eas - ter when Lent Is o - ver, I'll mar - ry for spite, *Och hone!* *wie - ra - sthru, och*

colla voce.

1. *hone!* I'm a - lone, I'm a - lone, in this world with - out you.
2. *hone!* I'm a - lone, I'm a - lone, in this world with - out you.
3. *hone!* When I die my ghost will haunt you ev' - ry night!

f

John Lee in 1780. It is printed in Bunting's Collection of 1809, and in Mulholland's *Irish Airs*, 1810, but in neither of these collections is Carolan's name connected with the air. Regarding his song "Molly Carew," Lover writes: "The intensely Irish character of the air stimulated me to endeavour that the words should partake of that quality, and the rapid replication of the musical phrases made me strive after as rapid a ringing of rhyme, of which our early bards were so fond." (*Lyrics of Ireland*, 1858, p. 94.) I ought to observe that "Planxty Reilly" apparently underwent considerable alteration in Lover's hands; but I think he was justified in doing so, because of the unvocal nature of the air as printed by Bunting and Mulholland.

Of all the fish that roam the sea.

HERRING THE KING.

VOICE.

Allegretto.

mf

1. Of
2. I
3. Oh!
4. Then

PIANO.

mf

con Ped.

1. all	the	fish	that	roam	the	sea,	The	Her - ring a - lone our
2. think	with	me	you'll	all	a - gree,	We	to	our King should
3. who	would not	a	fish - er	be,	And	lead	a	life so
4. once	more heark - en	un - to	me,	The	Her - ring	a - lone	our

1. King	shall	be!	So	fill	your	cups,	ye	fish - ers strong, And
2. thank - ful	be.	He	clothes	us,	feeds	us,	pays	the rent, And
3. wild	and	free?	Grim	care	we	leave	up - on	the shore To
4. King	shall	be!	So	fill	your	cups,	ye	fish - ers strong, And

The air and words are from Horncastle's *Music of Ireland*, pt. i., 1844. As "The Brink of the White Rocks" the tune was published four years earlier in Bunting's third collection ; Bunting states that he obtained it from a blind man in Westport in 1802. An ancient air called *Thugamar féin a samhra lín* ; or, "We have brought the Summer with us," is printed in Bunting's

mf CHORUS.

1. drink   his   health   full   deep   and   long.
2. cheers   us   in   the   time   of   Lent.
3. wait   un - til   our   voyage   is   o'er.
4. drink   his   health   full   deep   and   long.

Sing *hu - ga - mar   fein   an

mf

dim.

sam - - ra   lin,   The   storm   is   o'er,   'tis   calm   a - gain;   And

dim.

we have brought the   sum - mer in,   In   hold - ing   chase   with   Her-ring   our King.

f

* Irish for " We have brought the summer in."

Collection of 1796. An earlier and probably more genuine setting of it is to be found in Burk Thumoth's *Twelve Scotch and Twelve Irish Airs*, London, c. 1745, entitled *Hugar mu Feta*, and another as *Hugar mon foco souraline*, in Mulholland's *Irish Tunes*, 1804. The air adopted here has all the appearance of antiquity. Dr. Petrie gives four settings of it in the *Ancient Music of Ireland*; the fourth one he considers the oldest and the parent version. In this I cannot agree with Dr. Petrie; a close comparison of "The Brink of the White Rocks" with the ancient air *Coin dubh delish*, must prove that the resemblance existing between the two melodies is not merely accidental. The air *In braoch na carraige baine*; or, "The Brink of the White Rocks," printed with Davis's song "The lament for the Milesians" in the *Spirit of the Nation*, 1846, is an entirely different air (see p. 190).

Oh! amber-hair'd Nora.

Translated from the Irish by EDWARD WALSH.

1. Oh! am - ber - hair'd No - ra, That thy fair head could rest On the arm that would shel - ter Or cir - cle thy breast: Thou hast stol'n all my brain, love, And then left me lone — Tho' I'd cross o'er the main, love, To call thee my own.

2. My fair one is dwell - ing By Moy's love - ly vale, Her rich locks of am - ber Have left my cheek pale; May the king of the Sab - bath Yet grant me to see My herds in the green lanes Of fair Baile - ath - Buidhe!

From Dr. Joyce's Collection, 1873. The air was noted in the County of Limerick, in 1853; Dr. Joyce considers it to be a minor setting of "Do you remember that night" (see p. 28). The song "Oh, Amber-hair'd Nora" seems to have been associated with an air known under a similar title and which we have printed on p. 140 of this work.

Oh! Arranmore.

Thomas Moore.

1. Oh! Ar - ran-more, lov'd
2. How blithe up - on thy
3. That E - den where th'im-

1. Ar -ran-more, How oft I dream of thee, And of those days when, by thy shore, I
2. breez-y cliffs At sun - ny morn I've stood, With heart as bound -ing as the skiffs That
3. -mor-tal brave Dwell in a land se-rene,— Whose bow'rs be -yond the shin - ing wave At

1. wan-der'd young and free. Full man-y a path I've tried since then Thro' plea-sure's flow - 'ry
2. danc'd a - long thy flood; Or, when the west-ern wave grew bright With day-light's part - ing
3. sun - set oft are seen. Ah, dream too full of sadd'n-ing truth! Those man - sions o'er the

1. maze, But ne'er could find the bliss a - gain I felt in those sweet days.
2. wing, Have sought that E - den in its light Which dream-ing po - ets sing.
3. main Are like the hopes I built in youth,—As sun - ny and as vain!

For note to this song see Appendix.

Oh! blame not the bard.

Thomas Moore.

Andante.

Voice.

mf

Piano.

p con espress.

poco rit. . . .

1. Oh! blame not the
2. But a - las for his
3. But tho' glo - ry be

1. bard if he fly to the bow'rs, Where plea - sure lies care - less - ly
2. coun - try! her pride has gone by, And that spi - rit is bro - ken, which
3. gone, and the' hope fade a - way, Thy name, lov - èd E - rin, shall

1. smil - ing at fame; He was born for much more, and, in hap - pi - er
2. nev - er would bend; O'er the ru - in her chil - dren in se - cret must
3. live in his songs; Not ev'n in the hour when his heart is most

Air. "Kitty Tyrrell." This favourite air appears in the following works prior to its having been adopted by Tom Moore in the third number of the *Melodies*, 1810. Bunting's Collection, 1796, *Town Magazine*, vol. i., 1797, O'Farrell's *National Irish Music*, 1797-1800, Miss Owenson's *Hibernian Melodies*, 1805, Mulholland's *Irish and Scots Tunes*, 1804, Holden's Collection, vol. i., 1806, Murphy's *Irish Airs and Jiggs*, 1809, Mulholland's *Irish Airs*, 1810, and many other works.

1. hours, His soul might have burn'd with a ho-li-er flame. The
2. sigh, For 'tis trea - son to love her, and death to de - fend. Un -
3. gay, Will he lose the re - mem-brance of thee and thy wrongs. The

1. string, that now lan - guish - es loose . . o'er the lyre, Might have bent a proud
2. -priz'd are her sons, till they've learn'd . to be - tray; Un - dis - tin - guish'd they
3. stran - ger shall hear thy la - ment . . on his plains, The . . sigh of thy

1. bow to the war - - ri - or's dart; And the lip, which now breathes but the
2. live, if they shame . . . not their sires; And the torch that would light . . them thro'
3. harp shall be sent . . . . o'er the deep, Till thy mas-ters them - selves, . as they

1. song of de - sire, Might have pour'd the full tide of the pa - tri - ot's heart.
2. dig - ni - ty's way, Must be caught from the pile where their coun - try ex - pires.
3. ri - vet thy chains, Shall pause at the song of their cap-tives and weep!

Oh! breathe not his name.

Thomas Moore.

Andantino.

PIANO.

p con espress.

poco rit.

p

p

1. Oh, breathe not his name, let it sleep in the shade Where
2. But the night - dew that falls, tho' in si - lence it weeps, Shall

1. cold and un - hon-our'd his re - lics are laid! Sad, si - lent, and dark be the
2. bright - en with ver - dure the grave where he sleeps, And the tear that we shed, tho' in

rit.

1. tears that we shed, As the night - dew that falls on the grass o'er his head.
2. se - cret it rolls, Shall long keep his mem - 'ry green in our souls.

rit.

Bunting includes this air in his first Collection, 1796, as *Cailin Donn; or,* "The Brown Maid." Holden's air, *Cailin Donn,* in vol. ii. of his *Old Established Irish Tunes,* is quite different; in his later work entitled *Periodical Irish Melodies,* he gives the above air as "The Brown Maid." Moore's song was written for the first number of the *Melodies,* 1807.

Oh, dark, sweetest girl.

PEGGY BROWNE.

Translated from the Irish by THOMAS FURLONG.

Andantino.

VOICE.

PIANO.

mf   *ppi*   *ppi*   *p*

1. Oh, dark, sweet-est
2. I dreamt that at
3. Dear, dear is the

1. girl, are my days doom'd to be, . . While my heart bleeds in si - lence and
2. eve - ning my foot - steps were 'bound To yon deep spread-ing wood where the
3. bark to its own cher - ish'd tree, . But dear - er, far dear - er is my

1. sor - row for thee; In the green spring of life to the grave I go
2. shades fall a - round; I sought, 'midst new scenes, all my sor - rows to
3. lov'd one to me; In my dreams I draw near her, un - check'd by a

1. down, Oh! shield me, and save me, my lov'd Peg - gy Browne.
2. drown, But the cure of my sor - row rests with thee, Peg - gy Browne.
3. frown, But my arms spread in vain to em - brace Peg - gy Browne.

Diarmid ua Duib ; or, " Dermot O'Dowd," was published in Bunting's Collections of 1796 and 1809. The song " Peggy Browne " is attributed to Carolan by Hardiman, from whose *Irish Minstrelsy* I have taken Furlong's translation. The heroine of the song was the daughter of George Browne of Brownstown, in the county of Mayo.

Oh, deep in my soul is my Paistheen Fion.

There are many forms of this air; I have chosen the one given above not only because I consider it the finest I have as yet seen, but because it appears to me to best suit the passionate sentiment of the song; it is from Horncastle's *Music of Ireland*, pt. ii., 1844. The translation of the Irish song is by John D'Alton, and was published in Hardiman's *Irish Minstrelsy*, vol. i., 1831. *Paistheen Fion*, pronounced *Fin*, means either fair youth or maiden, who, in this case, is supposed by many to be the son of James II. Versions of the air are to be found in *The Vocal Magazine*, vol. i., 1797, Holden's Collection, vol. i., 1806, Mulhollan's Collection, 1804, etc.; but Horncastle's setting differs considerably from these.

f poco accel.

1. fair, And her neck with the March swan's can more than com - pare.
2. bright, Can but drink her a bless - ing from morn - ing to night.
3.-lone Will I che - rish— till life and its mem - o - ries are gone.

Then

Your - neen, fly with me, fly with me, fly with me, With thy nut - brown ..

f poco accel. . . . .

. . . . poco rit.   *mf a tempo.*

ring - lets so art - less - ly curl'd. Here is the one that will

. . . . poco rit.   *mf a tempo.*

cres.   *f*   *poco rit.*

live and die with thee, Thy guard and thy guide thro' the wilds of the world.

cres.   *f*   *poco rit.*

n 2

Oh, did you ne'er hear of the Blarney.

Moderato.

SAMUEL LOVER.

PIANO.

1. Oh, did you ne'er hear of the Blar - ney, That's found near the banks of Kil -
2. For the Blar-ney's so great a de - sai - ver That a girl thinks you're there—tho' you
3. Oh, say, would you find this same Blar - ney, There's a cas - tle not far from Kil -
4. Like a mag - net its in - flu-ence such is, That at - trac-tion it gives all it

1. - lar - - - ney? Be - lieve it from me No girl's heart is free, Once she
2. have . . . . her, And nev - er finds out All the thricks you're a - bout Till she's
3. - lar - - - ney, On the top of the wall—But take care you don't fall,—There's a
4. touch - - es, If you kiss it, they say That from that bless - ed day, You may

poco rit. *f*

1. hears the sweet sound of the Blar - - ney, Once she hears the sweet sound of the Blar - ney.
2. quite gone her-self with your Blar - - ney, Till she's quite gone her-self with your Blar - ney.
3. stone that con-tains all this Blar - - ney, There's a stone that con-tains all this Blar - ney.
4. kiss whom you plaze, with your Blar - - ney, You may kiss whom you plaze, with your Blar - ney.

poco rit. *f colla voce.*

Samuel Lover wrote this song to the tune, "The Beardless Boy," better known as "Kate Kearney." As Lady Morgan's ballad is too closely associated with that air to admit of its being separated, I have adopted Lover's verses to an Irish air used by J. Daniel in connection with Lover's "Widow Malone," and published at Dundee as a sheet song, about 1841. A comparison of this tune with the well-known one, "Open the door to me, O," to which Moore wrote the song, "She is far from the land," will show that the resemblance they bear to one another is so strong as to admit of the probability of their having had one common origin. The "Blarney Stone" is also the subject of a little song by Father Prout.

Oh! my sweet little rose.

ROISIN DUBH.

Translated from the Irish by Thomas Furlong.

Andante espressione.

VOICE.

PIANO.

p

con Ped.

1. Oh! my sweet lit - tle
2. There's no flow - er that e'er
3. The moun-tains, high and

1. rose, cease to pine for the past, For the friends that come east - ward shall
2. bloom'd can my rose ex - cel, There's no tongue that e'er mov'd half my
3. mis - ty, thro' the moors must go, The riv - ers run back - ward, and the

cres.

1. see thee at last; They bring bless - ings, they bring fa - vours which the past nev - er
2. love can tell; Had I strength, had I skill the wide world to sub -
3. lakes o - ver-flow; And the wild waves of old o - cean wear a crim - son

cres.

p   *vit.*   *Last time.*

1. knew, To pour forth in glad - ness on my Rois - in Dubh.
2. - due, Oh! the queen of that wide world should be Rois - in Dubh.
3. hue, Ere the world sees the ru - in of my Rois - in Dubh.

p   *vit.*   *sf p*

For note to this song see Appendix.

Oh! did you not hear of Kate Kearney?

Lady Morgan.

1. Oh, did you not hear of Kate
2. Oh, should you e'er meet this Kate

1. Kear -ney? She lives on the banks of Kil - lar - ney; From the
2. Kear -ney, Who lives on the banks of Kil - lar - ney, Be -

1. glance of her eye, Shun dan - ger and fly, For fa - tal's the glance of Kate
2. -ware of her smile, For man - y a wile Lies hid in the smile of Kate

Although this melody is generally designated "Kate Kearney," a glance at the ninth air in Bunting's Collection of 1796, will show that it is merely an adaptation from the old air, "The Beardless Boy." Lady Morgan's sweet little song must have met with great success. It appears to have been a great favourite with the celebrated English ballad-singer, Charles Incledon.

1. Kear - ney.   For that eye is so mod - est - ly
2. Kear - ney.   Tho' she looks so be - witch - ing - ly

con espress.

1. beam - ing,   You'd ne'er think of mis - chief she's dream - ing,   Yet,
2. sim - ple,   Yet there's mis - chief in ev - er - y dim - ple,   And

1. oh! I can tell How fa - tal the spell That lurks in the eye of Kate Kear - ney.
2. who dares in - hale Her sigh's spic - y gale, Must die by the breath of Kate Kear - ney.

(1764-1826); it is printed with the air in Crosby's *Irish Musical Repository*, 1808, and in many subsequent song-books. John Murphy names it "Kate Martin" in his *Irish Airs*, 1809. Lady Morgan's song was seized upon by the ballad-mongers of Dublin and Limerick at an early date, and issued in rough chap-book form.

Oh, for the swords of former time!

THOMAS MOORE.

Allegro con energia.

VOICE.

PIANO.

1. Oh, for the swords of for - mer time! Oh, for the men who bore them! When
2. Oh, for the kings who flour - ish'd then! Oh, for the pomp that crown'd them! When

1. arm'd for right they stood sub - lime, And ty - rants crouch'd be - fore them! When
2. hearts and hands of free - born men Were all the ram - parts round them! When

As "Unknown," this air with Moore's stirring song was printed in the seventh number of the *Melodies*, 1818. I have not been able to ascertain the original name of the tune, but in 1783 it was used by William Shield in that repository of Irish Melodies, the opera entitled *The Poor Soldier*. The following is the first verse of the song to it in that work, the libretto of which was written by John O'Keefe, the clever Irish dramatist:—

(Kathleen) Dermot's welcome as the May, cheerful, handsome and good-natur'd,
Foolish Darby, get away, awkward, clumsy, and ill-featur'd;
Dermot prattles pretty chat, Darby gapes like any oven,
Dermot's neat from shoe to hat, Darby's but a dirty sloven.
Lout, looby, silly looby, come no more to me a-courting,
Was my dearest Dermot here,—all is love and gay sporting.

1. pure yet, ere courts be-gan With hon-ours to en-slave him, The
2. safe built on bo-soms true, The throne was but the cen - tre Round

1. best hon - ours worn by man Were those which vir - tue gave him.
2. which Love a cir - cle drew, That Trea-son durst not en - ter.

1. Oh, for the swords of for - mer time! Oh, for the men who bore them! When
2. Oh, for the kings who flour-ish'd then! Oh, for the pomp that crown'd them! When

1. arm'd for right they stood sub - lime, And ty - rants crouch'd be - fore them!
2. hearts and hands of free - born men Were all the ram - parts round them!

Oh! had we some bright little isle.

THOMAS MOORE.

Moderato con grazia.

PIANO.

1. Oh! had we some bright lit - tle
2. There with souls ev - er ar - dent and

1. isle of our own, In a blue sum - mer o - cean, far off and a -
2. pure as the clime, We should love as they lov'd in the first gold - en

1. -lone, Where a leaf nev - er dies in the still bloom - ing bow'rs, And the
2. time; The glow of the sun - shine, the balm of the air, Would

dim.

As "Chiling O'guiry," the air is in a little octavo work, entitled *Twelve Scotch and Twelve Irish Airs with Variations by Mr. Burk Thumoth,* undated but *circa* 1745. Hoffmann's Collection of Dr. Petrie's traditional airs contains a tune called "Sheela, my love," but it bears no resemblance to the above ancient melody. The following extract from one of Moore's letters to Power, his music publisher (Jan. 1813), shows that he either intended to, or did re-write his song: "I hope you have not engraved 'Oh, had I a bright little Isle' as I must put a totally new set of words to it." Moore's song was published in the fifth number of the *Melodies,* Dec., 1813.

1. bee ban - quets on thro' a whole year of flow'rs, Where the sun loves to
2. steal to our hearts, and make all sum - mer there. With af - fec - tion as

1. pause With so fond a de - lay, That the night on - ly draws A thin
2. free From de - cline as the bow'rs, And with hope like the bee, Liv -ing

1. veil o'er the day; Where sim - ply to feel that we breathe, that we
2. al - ways on flow'rs, Our life should re - sem - ble a long day of

1. live, Is worth the best joy that life else -where can give.
2. light, And our death come on ho - ly and calm as the night.

186

Oh! Irishmen! Never forget.

OUR OWN LITTLE ISLE.

FERMOY.

Spiritoso.

VOICE.

PIANO.

1. Oh! Ir - ish-men! Nev-er for - get!—'Tis a *for - eign - er's farm*— your
2. Rise! heart - i - ly! shoul-der to shoul - der— We'll show them strength with good
3. Think, think what your fore - fa - thers fought for; When to O' - Neil, or O'-
4. Strength! yes, to make Ir - ish - men free a - gain; On - ly *u - nite*, and we'll

1. own lit - tle isle :— . . Oh! Ir - ish-men! When will you get Some
2. hu - mour go *leor,* . . . Rise! Rise! Show each for - eign be - hold - er We've
3. -Don - ell A - bu, ... *Sas-sen-achs* ev' - ry -where sunk in the slaugh - ter, O!
4. con - quer the foe, ... Nev - er on earth shall a for - eign - er see a - gain

* Go leor = plentifully.   † Sassenachs = Saxons.

This stirring song, with its air, is from the celebrated *Spirit of the Nation*, Dublin, 1846. The author of the verses, signed "Fermoy," was John Edward Pigot, an Irish barrister: Mr. Pigot died in 1871 at the age of fifty-one. He is said to have left a large collection of Irish airs in MS. behind him. The air is called "The Carnbha Jig" in the *Spirit of the Nation*.

1. life in your hearts for your poor lit-tle isle? Oh! yes! we've a
2. not lost our love to thee, E - rin a - store! Oh! yes! 'tis a
3. Vengeance for in - sult, dear E - rin, to you! Oh! yes! 'tis a
4. E - rin a pro-vince, tho' late - ly so low! Oh! yes! we've a

1. dear lit-tle spot of it! Oh! yes!— a sweet lit-tle isle! Yes! yes!— if
2. dear lit-tle spot of it! Oh! yes!— a sweet lit-tle isle! Yes! yes!— the
3. dear lit-tle spot of it! Oh! yes!— a sweet lit-tle isle! Yes! yes!— if
4. dear lit-tle spot of it! Oh! yes!— a sweet lit-tle isle! Yes! yes!— the

rit. . . . . . .

1. Ir - ish-men thought of it, 'Twould be a dear lit-tle, sweet lit-tle isle!
2. Ir - ish *have* thought of it, E - rin for ev - er!—*our own* lit-tle isle!
3. Ir - ish-men thought of it, E - rin once more is *our own* lit-tle isle!
4. Ir - ish *have* thought of it, E - rin for ev - er—*our own* lit-tle isle!

sf

Oh! Love is a hunter boy.

Thomas Moore.

Allegretto viro.

Voice.

Piano.

mf

1. Oh! Love is a hun - ter boy Who ...
2. But 'tis his joy most sweet, At ....

1. makes young hearts his prey; ... And in ... his nets of joy En - -
2. ear - ly dawn to trace ... The print of Beau - ty's feet, And ...

Bunting obtained this air in Dublin in 1839; he gives its name as *As fada annsa me*, "Long am I here" or "The Gentle Maiden," and considers that it is the original of the English melody, "My lodging is on the cold ground." He places it in his list of ancient tunes and observes that "the characteristic national tone of the sub-mediant in the fourth bar, continued at intervals through the melody," proves it to be pure Irish. Bunting's singular theories regarding Irish melody have been so often refuted, that it would be waste of labour to re-open the discussion. The following extract from the *Ancient Music of Ireland*, p. 48, shows Dr. Petrie's views regarding the tone of the sub-mediant or major sixth in the scale, which in Bunting's opinion "distinguishes

1. - snares them night and day. . . . In vain con-ceal'd they lie, Love. . .
2. give the trem - bler chase. . . And if, thro' vir - gin snow, She . . .

1. tracks them ev - 'ry - where; . . . In vain a - loft they
2. tracks her foot - steps fair, . . . How sweet for love to

1. fly, — Love . . . shoots them fly - ing there. .
2. know None . . . went be - fore him there! .

all Irish melody."—"That such a tone is indeed a characteristic one, both of Irish and Scottish melodies, I by no means deny; but I cannot concur with Mr. Bunting that it is an essential, or even the most characteristic feature of a true Irish melody." Bunting's theory that the air "My lodging is on the cold ground" was taken from "The Gentle Maiden" is strangely at variance with Mr. Chappell's remarks on p. 529 of *Popular Music of the Olden Time*; alluding to "My lodging is on the cold ground" that author remarks: "I believe there is no ground whatever for calling it Irish. The late Edward Bunting . . . . distinctly assured me that he did not believe it to be Irish—that no one of the harpers played the tune,—and that it had no Irish character."

Oh! proud were the chieftains of green Innis-Fail.

Thomas Davis.

VOICE.

Andante. mf

1. Oh! proud were the chief-tains of
2. 'Gainst Eng-land long bat - tling, at
3. How fair were the mai - dens of
4. Their fa - mous, their ho - ly, their

PIANO.

p con espress.   rit.   dim.   mf

con Ped.   sempre con Ped.

cres.   mf

1. green In - nis - Fail, *As throo - a gon i - ra na var - - ra! The
2. length they went down; As throo - a gon i - ra na var - - ra! But they
3. fair In - nis - Fail! As throo - a gon i - ra na var - - ra! As
4. dear In - nis - Fail! As throo - a gon i - ra na var - - ra! Shall it

cres.   sf

cres.

1. stars of our sky, and the salt of our soil, As throo - a gon i - ra na
2. left their deep tracks on the road of re - nown, As throo - a gon i - ra na
3. fresh and as free as the sea - breeze from soil; As throo - a gon i - ra na
4. still be a prey for the stran - ger to spoil? As throo - a gon i - ra na

mf   cres.

* A's truagh gan oidhre 'na bh-farradh ; or, What a pity that there is no heir of their company.'

Air: *An bruach na carraige;* or, "The Brink of the White Rocks." In the *Ancient Music of Ireland,* 1855, Dr. Petrie writes: "The air has been already twice printed; first, as set by myself—indifferently enough, I must confess—in the collection of Irish Tunes published in 1806, by my young friend, the late Francis Holden, Mus. Doc.; and secondly in Mr. O'Daly's recent

1. var - ra! Their hearts were as soft as a child in the lap, Yet
2. var - ra! We are heirs of their fame, if we're not of their race— And
3. var - ra! Oh! are not our maid-ens as fair and as pure? Can our
4. var - ra! Sure, brave men would la-bour by night and by day To

1. they were "the men in the gap"— . . And now that the cold clay their
2. dead-ly and deep our dis - grace, . . If we live o'er their se-pul-chres,
3. mu - sic no lon-ger al - lure? . . . And can we but sob, as such
4. ban-ish that stran-ger a - way; . . . Or, dy-ing for Ire-land, the

rit.

1. limbs doth en-wrap— As throo - a gon i - ra na var - - ra!
2. ab - ject and base;— As throo - a gon i - ra na var - - ra!
3. wrongs we en-dure? As throo - a gon i - ra na var - - ra!
4. fu - ture would say As throo - a gon i - ra na var - - ra!

publication, "The Poets and Poetry of Munster." Dr. Petrie errs here: in O'Farrell's *National Irish Music for the Union Piper,* c. 1797–1800, p. 36, the air is printed as "Carraga Bawn," i.e., "The White Rock," and again, in *The Spirit of the Nation,* 1846, p. 236, not only do we find the same melody, but the identical version as that printed in Dr. Petrie's work. In the fourth volume of his *Pocket Companion,* c. 1810, O'Farrell prints another setting as "Carolan's Cup." The air must not be confounded with one known by the same name, and given on p. 168 of this work. Indeed, Dr. Petrie considers the true name of the air to be *Ar thaobh na Carraige Baine,* which means " On the brink of the White Rocks." Davis's stirring song is printed in the *Spirit of the Nation,* and in the collection of his poems printed in 1846—just one year after the poet's death.

Oh! the boys of Kilkenny.

VOICE.

PIANO.

1. Oh! the boys of Kil - ken - ny are
2. Thro' the town of Kil - ken - ny there
3. Her eyes are as black as Kil -
4. Oh! Kil - ken - ny's a town that

1. stout rov - ing blades, And if ev - er they meet with the nice lit - tle maids, They
2. runs a clear strame; In the town of Kil - ken - ny there lives a sweet dame, Her
3. Ken - ny's fam'd coal, And 'tis they thro' my bo - som have burn'd a big hole; Her
4. shines where it stands, And the more I think on it, the more my heart warms, And

1. kiss them and coax them, they spend their mon - ey free, Oh! of all towns in Ire - land, Kil -
2. cheeks are like ros - es, her lips much the same, Like a dish of ripe strawber - ries
3. mind, like its wa - ters, is deep, clear, and pure; But her heart is more hard than its
4. if in Kil - ken - ny I'd think my - self home, For it's there I'd get sweethearts, but

1. ken - ny for me, Oh! of all towns in Ire - land, Kil - ken - ny for me!
2. smoth - er'd in crame, Like a dish of ripe straw - ber - ries smoth - er'd in crame.
3. mar - ble, I'm sure, But her heart is more hard than its mar - ble, I'm sure.
4. here I get none, For it's there I'd get sweet-hearts, but here I get none.

For the history of this air known as "The Head of Old Dennis," I must refer the reader to p. 205. The authorship of the song is not known. Early in the century it was printed with the air as a sheet song entitled: *The Boys of Kilkenny. A Favourite Irish Song. Inscribed to Col. Doyle by Mr. Kelly.* Michael Kelly, the Irish composer, was born in Dublin in 1762. He wrote and compiled the music to various musical dramas, now long forgotten; his *Reminiscences*, 1826, are still read with enjoyment; he died at Margate in 1826. It is possible that Kelly wrote the ballad "The Boys of Kilkenny," but beyond the title quoted above, I have been unable to obtain direct proof of his being the author.

On the green hills of Ulster.

RORY O'MORE.

Dr. Drennan.

Maestoso. *mf*

VOICE.

PIANO.

1. On the green hills of Ul-ster the white cross waves high, And the bea-con of war throws its flames to the sky, Now the taunt and the threat let the cow-ard en-dure, Our hope is in God and in
2. Do you ask why the bea-con and ban-ner of war On the moun-tains of Ul-ster are seen from a-far? 'Tis the sig-nal our rights to re-gain and se-cure, Through God and our La-dy and
3. For the mer-ci-less Scots, with their creed and their swords, With war in their bo-soms, and peace in their words, Have sworn the bright light of our faith to ob-scure, But our hope is in God and in
4. Oh! lives there the trai-tor who'd shrink from the strife, Who, to add to the length of a for-feit-ed life, His coun-try, his kin-dred, his faith would ab-jure? No! we'll strike for old E-rin and

CHORUS.

1. Ro - ry O' - More, Our hope is in God and in Ro - ry O'-More.
2. Ro - ry O' - More, Through God and our La - dy and Ro - ry O'-More.
3. Ro - ry O' - More, But our hope is in God and in Ro - ry O'-More.
4. Ro - ry O' - More, No! we'll strike for old E - rin and Ro - ry O'-More.

From *Ancient Music of Ireland*, 1873. The following is Dr. Joyce's note to the air: "I noted this tune in 1853, from the singing of John Dinan, of Glenansir, in the county of Limerick. I also took down the Irish song, every verse of which ended with the name of the air as chorus, 'We'll take again a cruiskeen, a cruiskeen lawn.'" I have adapted Drennan's words to the air; they were printed in vol. iii. of *Irish National Poetry*, 1846. Rory, or Roger O'More was one of the most influential actors of the rising of 1641. He was of ancient extraction and descended from the chief branch of the O'Mores of Co. Leix, and was related by marriage to many of the best English families. The phrase "God and our Lady be our assistance, and Rory O'More," was common in Ireland last century.

Oh! the days are gone when beauty bright.

LOVE'S YOUNG DREAM.

THOMAS MOORE.

Poco allegro.

mf

VOICE.

PIANO.

1. Oh! the
2. Tho' the
3. No,—that

ten.

1. days   are gone   when beau - ty bright   My heart's   chain   wove,   When my
2. bard   to   pur - er   fame   may soar,   When wild   youth's   past ;   Tho'   he
3. hal - low'd form   is   ne'er   for - got   Which first   love   traced ;   Still   it

mf

colla voce.

1. dream   of life,   from morn   till night,   Was   love,   still   love!   New
2. win   the wise,   who frown'd   be - fore,   To   smile   at   last ;   He'll
3. ling - 'ring haunts   the green - est spot   On   mem - 'ry's   waste,   'Twas

This air as *An Thseann Bheann Bhocht*, or, "The Old Woman," is from Bunting's *Ancient Music of Ireland*, 1809. An apparently older setting of the tune was recovered by R. A. Smith for *The Irish Minstrel*, 1825, as "Oriek's fair daughter." Moore's song appeared in the third number of the *Melodies*, issued January, 1810. *An t-sean bean bochd :* or, *Shan van vocht*, as it is usually called, literally means "The Poor Old Woman," and is one of the names for Ireland. The original song seems to have been written in 179, when the French fleet arrived in Bantry Bay.

poco cres.   *ten.*

1. hopes may bloom, and days may come Of mild - er, calm - er beam, But there's
2. nev - er meet a joy so sweet In all his noon of fame, As when
3. o - dour fled as soon as shed, 'Twas morn - ing's wing - èd dream; 'Twas a

poco cres.   *colla voce.* . . . .

1. no - thing half so sweet in life As love's young
2. first he sung to wo - man's ear His soul - felt
3. light that ne'er can shine a - gain On life's dull

f ten.

1. dream! No, there's no - thing half so sweet in life As
2. flame, And, at ev - 'ry close, she blush'd to hear The
3. stream, Oh! 'twas light that ne'er can shine a - gain On

f colla voce.

rit.

1. love's young dream! . . .
2. one lov'd name. . . .
3. life's dull stream. . . .

Oh! the marriage.

THOMAS DAVIS.

Allegro.

VOICE.

PIANO.

mf sf

1. Oh! the mar-riage, the mar-riage With love and *mo bou -chal* for me, The
2. hair is a show - er of soft gold, His eye is as clear as the day, His
3. kins-men are hon - est and kind, The neigh-bours think much of his skill, And
4. meet in the mar - ket and fair, We meet in the morn -ing and night, He

1. la - dies that ride in a car -riage Might en - vy my mar-riage to me; For
2. conscience and vote were un - sold, When oth - ers were car - ried a - way, His
3. Eog-han's the lad to my mind, Tho' he owns nei - ther cas - tle or mill. But
4. sits on the half of my chair, And my peo - ple are wild with de - light. I

1. Eog-han† is straight as a tow - er, And ten - der and lov - ing and true, He
2. word was as good as an oath, And free - ly 'twas giv - en to me, Oh,
3. he has a till - och of land, A horse and a stock-ing of coin, A
4. long thro' the win - ter to skim, Tho' Eog - han longs more I can see, When

---

1.
2. His
3. His
4. We

* Mo bhuachail (mo buchal) = my boy. † Eoghan = Owen

Thomas Davis's song, with the air, "The Swaggering Jig," was printed in James Duffy's work entitled *The Spirit of the Nation*, Dublin, 1846, and in the following year in Henderson's little publication issued at Belfast, as *The Flowers of Irish Melody*.

1. told me more love 'in an hour Than the squires of the coun-ty could do.
2. sure 'twill be hap-py for both, The day of our mar-riage to see.
3. foot for the dance, and a hand In the cause of his coun-try to join.
4. I will be mar-ried to him, And he will be mar-ried to me.

Then,

Oh! the mar-riage, the mar-riage, With love and *mo bou-chal* for me, The

la-dies that ride in a car-riage Might en-vy my mar-riage to me!

Oh! 'tis sweet to think.

Thomas Moore.

1. sweet to think that wher-e'er we rove, We are sure to find some-thing bliss-ful and dear, And that,
2. shame, when flow-ers a - round us rise, To make light of the rest if the rose is not there, And the

1. when we're far from the lips we love, We have but to make love to the lips we are near! The
2. world's so rich in re-splen-dent eyes, 'Twere a pi - ty to lim - it one's love to a pair. Love's

1. heart, like a ten - dril, ac - cus-tom'd to cling, Let it grow where it will, can - not
2. wing and the pea-cock's are near - ly a - like, They are both of them bright, but they're

"Oh! 'tis sweet to think" was written for the third number of the *Melodies*, 1810: Moore designa'ed the air, "Thady, you gander," but I have been unable to discover upon what authority. As "She is the Girl that can do it," Holden included the air in his *Old Established Irish Tunes*, vol. i., 1806; it must be admitted, however, that Moore's setting is superior to the one given by Holden. The original name of the air is *Donall na Greine*, or, "Daniel of the Sun;" both O'Farrell (*Pocket Companion*, Bk. i., c. 1805) and O'Daly (*Poets of Munster*, 1849) give it this title, and in the latter work an old Irish song is printed which has been long associated with the tune; the following is a translation of the first verse:

Wild Donall na Greine!—his frolics would please ye,
Yet Wallace, confound him, came trickishly round him!
He'd sit, without winking, in alehouses drinking
For days without number, nor care about slumber!

1. flou - rish a - lone, But will lean to the near - est and love - li - est thing It can
2. change - a - ble too; And wher - ev - er a new beam of beau - ty can strike, It will

1. twine with it - self, and make close - ly its own.
2. tinc - ture love's plume with a dif - fer - ent hue.

Then oh, what plea - sure, wher -

- e'er we rove To be doom'd to find some - thing still that is dear; And to

know, when far from the lips we love, We have but to make love to the lips we are near!

Oh, weary's on money.

THE DEAR IRISH BOY.

1. O! wea-ry's on money, and wea-ry's on wealth, And sure we don't want them while we have our health; 'Twas they tempt-ed Con - - nor ov-er the

2. My Cou-nor was hand-some, good-hu-mour'd, and tall, At hurl-ing and danc-ing, the best of them all; But when he came court-ing be-neath our old

3. The morn-ing he left us I ne'er will for-get, Not an eye in our vil-lage but with cry-ing was wet. "Don't cry an-y more, Ma-vour-neen," said

4. Sad as I felt then, hope mix'd with my care, A-las! I have no-thing left now but de-spair. His ship it went down in the midst of the

As "My Dear Irish Boy" this version of the above noble air is printed in F. N. Crouch's *Songs of Erin; being a Collection of Original Irish Melodies. The Poetry by Desmond Ryan*. London, 1841; and, with the ballad, in *The Native Music of Ireland* ("Citizen Magazine," March, 1842) as "The Wild Irish Boy; or, My Connor." In Lynch's *Melodies of Ireland, c. 1845*, it is named "The Dear Irish Boy." Holden's setting of the air as "Oh, my Connor, his cheeks are like the rose" in his *Irish Tunes*, vol. ii., 1806, is not so good although it is possibly an earlier form. I have extracted the accidentals from the tune as given by Crouch and others; they appear to me to be a modern interpolation.

1. sea,   And   I   lost   my   lov - er,   my   cush - la   ma - chree.
2. tree,   His   voice   was   like   mu - sic,   my   cush - la   ma - chree.
3. be,   "For   I   will   re - turn   to   my   cush - la   ma - chree.
4. sea   And its   wild   waves   roll   o - ver   my   cush - la   ma - chree.

cres.   *dim.*

Smil - ing,— be - guil - ing— cheer - ing— en - dear - ing— Oh! dear - ly   I

lov'd   him,   and   he . . .   lov'd   me;   By   each   o - ther   de - light - ed,   and

fond - ly   u - ni - ted,   My   heart's   in   the   grave   with   my   cush - la   ma-chree!

One bumper at parting.

THOMAS MOORE.

This air entitled "Moll Roe" was sung in Henry Brooke's ballad-opera, *Jack the Giant Queller*, which was performed in Dublin in 1748. Commenting on this work, Bladen (*New Theatrical Dict.*, 1792) remarks that "there being in it two or three satirical songs against bad Governors, Lord Mayors, and Aldermen, it was prohibited after the first night's performance." The air sung by Darby in Shield's *Poor Soldier*, 1783, to verses beginning, "Tho' late I was plump round and jolly," is a setting of "Moll Roe"; but it differs considerably from Moore's version; it is included in Mulhollan's *Irish and Scots Tunes*, 1804, as "Ditherum Doodle,"—a name obviously taken from O'Keefe's song in the *Poor Soldier*; another setting was published by O'Farrell in the fourth book of his *Pocket Companion* c. 1810. Moore's song was written for the fifth number of the *Melodies*, issued in December, 1813; he designated the air "Moll Roe in the morning."

ten.

1. sweet-ness that plea - sure has in it Is al - ways so slow to come forth, That
2. time, like a pit - i - less mas - ter, Cries, "On-ward," and spurs the gay hours, Ah,
3. saw how he fin - ish'd, by dart - ing His beam o'er a deep bil - low's brim, So,

sf

1. sel - dom, a - las, till the min - ute It dies, do we know half its worth; But
2. nev - er doth time tra - vel fast - er Than when his way lies a - mong flow'rs, But
3. fill up, let's shine at our part - ing In full li - quid glo - ry like him, And

ten.

1. oh! may our life's hap - py mea - sure Be all of such mo - ments made up; They're
2. come! may our life's hap - py mea - sure Be all of such mo - ments made up; They're
3. oh! may our life's hap - py mea - sure Of mo - ments like this be made up; 'Twas

ten.

1. born on the bo - som of plea - sure, They die midst the tears of the cup.
2. born on the bo - som of plea - sure, They die midst the tears of the cup.
3. born in the bo - som of plea - sure, It dies midst the tears of the cup.

One clear summer morning, near blue Avonree.

Translated from the Irish by EDWARD WALSH.

Moderato.

VOICE.

PIANO.

1. One clear sum - mer
2. Her slight waist was
3. At the birth of the
4. A sting from her

1. morn - ing, near blue A - von - ree A state - ly brown maid - en flash'd
2. grace - ful, her foot light and smooth Glanc'd air - lift - ed o - ver the
3. maid - en, a hum-ming bee flew With a rich hon - ey - show - er to her
4. red lip sped, swift as a dart, Its way to my bo - som— how

1. full on my way; More white was her brow than the foam - or the
2. wild grass - y slope— "Fair light of the val - ley," I said to her
3. ber - ry - red lip— I snatch'd from the fair one, the sweet fra - grant
4. wo - ful to say; 'Tis strange that I live with the dart in my

1. sea, More ho - ly her voice than the fai - ry choir's lay!
2. sooth, "My heart's health is gone if you yield me no hope!"
3. dew: 'Twas rap - ture en - tranc-ing— but what did I sip?
4. heart, While thou-sands have died of her love since that day!

poco rit.

poco rit.

For note to this song see Appendix.

One morning in July.

MARY OF LIMERICK TOWN.

Moderato.

PIANO.

mf

poco rit.

mf

mf

1. One morn-ing in Ju - ly a - lone as I stray'd By the banks of the . .
2. As she tripp'd o'er the mea-dows so green and so gay, She far out - shone
3. "For - bear, sir," she said, "for your suit is in vain, For the lad that I . .
4. Then find - ing the maid - en so loy - al and true, I said, " Sweet-heart
5. Then she flew in my arms— with joy and sur - prise, And on me she
6. Soon af - ter, with great joy, to - geth - er we went, And mar - ried we

1. Shan -non, I met a fair maid, Her cheeks were like ros - es, her
2. Flo - ra, the god - dess of May. I told her I'd free - ly re -
3. love is cross'd ov - er the main. In Lon - don he mar - ried a
4. Ma - ry, I've re - turn'd un - to you. These sev - en long years, love, I've
5. gaz'd with her bright spark-ling eyes, By the banks of the Shan - non to -
6. were, with her par -ents' con - sent, We have great stores of rich - es our

1. hair a dark brown; She is beau - ti - ful Ma - ry of sweet Lim'-rick town.
2. sign a king's crown To be lov'd by fair Ma - ry of sweet Lim'-rick town.
3. maid of re - nown, Therefore I will live sin - gle in sweet Lim'-rick town."
4. rav'd up and down, But my heart was still with you in sweet Lim'-rick town."
5. -geth - er we sat down, On a bank of prim - ros - es by sweet Lim'-rick town.
6. plea - sures to crown, And now live in splen - dour in sweet Lim'-rick town.

This is the second version of "Nora of the Amber Hair" given in the Petrie Collection, and to which I have alluded on p. 140 of this work. The ballad is one of those Anglo-Irish productions of the early part of the century ; it was issued in rough chap-book form by Goggins of Limerick, many years ago. I may mention, however, that I have been obliged to slightly alter some of the original verses.

One eve as I happen'd to stray.

FOR IRELAND I'D NOT TELL HER NAME.

Translated from the Irish by EDWARD WALSH.

Moderato.

VOICE.

PIANO.

sf p *sf p* *rit.* *p*

con Ped.

1. One eve as I
2. A mai - den young,

1. hap - pen'd to stray . . On the lands that are bor - der - ing mine, A
2. ten - der, re - fined, . . On the lands that are bor - der - ing mine, Hath

1. mai - den came full in my way, . . Who left me in an - guish to
2. vir - tues and gra - ces of mind, . . And fea - tures sur - pass - ing - ly

I am indebted to Dr. P. W. Joyce for permission to use this version of the air "For Ireland I'd not tell her name," which was first printed in *Irish Music and Song, Dublin,* 1888. In this work Dr. Joyce observes that it is well-known in the Munster counties and in the southern counties of Leinster. It is often called by the English name "Nancy, the pride of the East [or West]" from a song with that refrain. Another setting of the air is preserved in the Petrie Collection, p. 99, but it is not so good as the one noted by Dr. Joyce.

1. pine. The slave of the charms and the mien, . . And the
2. fine. Blent amber and yel-low com-pose . . The

1. sil-ver-ton'd voice of the dame, . . . To meet her I
2. ring-let-ed hair of the dame, . . . Her cheek hath the

1. sped o'er the green; . . Yet for Ire-land I'd not tell her name!
2. bloom of the rose; . . . Yet for Ire-land I'd not tell her name!

P

208

One morn when mists did hover,

THE GRACEFUL MAIDEN.

Translated from the Irish by EDWARD WALSH.

Andantino.

VOICE.

PIANO.

p espressione.   *rit.*

1. One morn when mists did
2. When thro' the val - leys
3. "And now with white sails

1. hov - er The green - woods' fol - iage o - ver, 'Twas
2. roam -ing I see my bright love com -ing, Like
3. flow - ing, To Flan - ders I'll be go - ing; I'll

1. then I did dis - cov - er How pain - - ful love may
2. gar - den rose all bloom-ing, Or flow'r of the ap - ple -
3. seek the vine -yards grow - ing, In dis - - tant Gaul or

This popular ballad tune is from Dr. Petrie's Collection, 1855; it was noted down about 1810 from the singing of a Dublin ballad-singer. I have taken four verses from Walsh's translation, printed in *Irish Popular Songs, Dublin*, 1847.

1. be,   A   maid,   'mid   shades   con - ceal - ing,   Pour'd
2. -tree,   Bright   Ve - - nus   she's   ex - cel - ling,   Fresh
3. Spain.   Proud   maid,   no   more   I'll   woo   thee,   No

1. forth . . her voice of feel - ing,   And   love   came   o'er me   steal-ing,   She's a
2. from . . her o - cean dwell - ing,   Her   soft,   round   bo -som   swell-ing,   Her
3. more . . with love pur - sue   thee,   An - oth - er   mate may   sue thee,   And

1. dear   maid   to   me.
2. foot - falls   light   and   free.
3. plough   for   thee   the   plain!"

One night in my youth.

Moderato.

VOICE.

PIANO.

mf con energia.

1. One night in my youth as I
2. My chant - er I plied with my

1. rov'd with my mer - ry pipe, List'n - ing the e - choes that rang to the tune, I
2. heart beat - ing gai - ly, I pip'd up the strain, while so sweet - ly she sung, The

1. met Kit - ty More with her two lips so cher - ry ripe; "Phe - lim," says she, "give us
2. soft melt - ing mel - o - dy fill'd all the val - ley, The green woods a - round us in

This tune has been long known in the Highlands of Scotland as *Bhannarach dhon a cruidh* ; or, "The Brown dairy-maid." Versions of it were printed in Johnson's *Scots Musical Museum*, vol. ii., 1788, p. 105, in Captain Fraser's *Airs and Melodies peculiar to the Highlands*, 1815, p. 29, and in *Albyn's Anthology*, vol. i., 1816, p. 8 : in the last-mentioned work the long original Gaelic song is

1. El - len A - roon." "Dear Kit - ty," says I, "thou'rt so charm - ing - ly free; Now,
2. har - mo - ny rung. Me-thought that she ver - i - ly charm'd up the moon! Now,

1. if thou wilt deign thy sweet voice to the mea - sure, 'Twill make all the e - choes run
2. still, as I wan - der in vil - lage or ci - ty, When good peo - ple call for some

1. gld - ly with plea - sure, For none in fair E - rin can sing it like thee!"
2. fa - vour - ite dit - ty, I give them sweet Kit - ty, and El - len A - roon.

given with an English translation. The Irish version was first printed as "The Lass that wears green," in Smith's *Irish Minstrel*, 1825. It was to the "Brown dairy-maid" that Burns wrote his song. "The Banks of Devon"; in Cromek's *Reliques of Robert Burns*, 1808, the Scotch poet remarks: "I first heard the air from a lady in Inverness and got the notes taken down for this work"—alluding, of course, to Johnson's *Museum*. The air is in O'Farrell's Collection, Bk. iv., but with the title of Burns's song.

One Sunday after Mass.

This air was obtained by Dr. Petrie about the beginning of the century from the singing of a relative. In inserting it with the first verse of the song in his Collection, p. 112, Dr. Petrie was evidently unacquainted with its origin. As "An Irish Song—Set by Mr. Leveridge," the original melody along with the entire song, was published in Thomas D'Urfey's *Pills to Purge Melancholy*, vol. iv., 1719, p. 276. A perusal of the original air from that work will satisfy the reader how much a tune can

p SOLO.

1. -lone, and all a - lone.   He ask'd her for a póg,*   But she
2. -lone, and all a - lone."   "Now Der - mot, dear, be good,   You
3. hone, and och hone.   And now he sees her wish,   Not

p

1. call'd him a rogue,   And she beat him with her brogue,†   Och
2. know you real - ly should,   You must not be so rude,   Och
3. think - ing it a - miss,   Her cher -ry lips does kiss,   Och

f

L.H. marcato.

CHORUS.   poco rit.

1. hone, and och hone!   Och hone, and och hone!
2. hone, and och hone!   Och hone, and och hone!
3. hone, and och hone!   Och hone, and och hone!

poco rit.

* Kiss.   † Shoe.

change in a century (through passing about from singer to singer (see Appendix No. XX.). The verses given above are a close imitation of D'Urfey's song in the *Pills*. It may be observed that the word "set," so much used in old English song books, does not always mean "composed," but quite as often *arranged* or *adapted*. I am inclined to think, however, that this melody is an original composition by Leveridge.

Our mountain brooks were rushing.

ANNIE DEAR.

THOMAS DAVIS.

Andantino.   *p*

VOICE.

PIANO.

p   *pp rit.*   *p*

1. Our moun-tain brooks were rush - ing, An-nie dear, The
2. Ah! but our hopes were splen-did, An-nie dear, How
3. For once when home re - turn - ing, An-nie dear, I
4. But why a - rose a mor - row, An-nie dear, Up-

1. au - tumn eve was flush - ing, An - nie dear, But bright - er was your blush-ing When
2. sad - ly they have end - ed, An - nie dear, The ring be-twixt us brok - en, When
3. found our cot - tage burn - ing, An - nie dear, A - round it were the yeo - men, Of
4. - on that night of sor - row, An - nie dear, Far bet - ter, by thee ly - ing, Their

1. first, your mur-murs hush-ing, I told my love out - gush - ing, An - nie dear.
2. vows of love were spok - en, Of your heart was a to - ken, An - nie dear.
3. ev' - ry ill an o - men, The coun-try's bit - ter foe - men, An - nie dear.
4. bay - o - nets de - fy - ing, Than live in ex - ile sigh - ing, An - nie dear.

This air, "Maids in May," with Thomas Davis's verses, is from James Duffy's *Spirit of the Nation*, 1846. It was republished in the following year by Henderson of Belfast in his little work entitled *The Flowers of Irish Melody*. The song portrays an incident of 1798, at which period the yeomanry, owing to their many acts of violence, had gained the deep-set hatred of the people.

Peacefully, my baby, sleep.

LULLABY.

ALICE ROSE DENNY.

VOICE.

Andante molto tranquillo.

PIANO.

p L.H.
con espress.

con Ped.   *sempre con Ped.*

1. Peace - ful -ly, my ba - by sleep, Stars in heav'n be-
2. Now the moon be - gins to rise, Sail - ing thro' the

1. -gin to peep. O'er thy bed of yel - low gold, An-gels bright their wings un-fold.
2. peace -ful skies; 'Mong the leaves her sil - ver rays Shim-mer in the ghost - ly haze.

1. Sho -heen sho, .. loo la loo, Birds of eve their ves - pers sing, Sho-heen sho, . . .
2. Sho -heen sho, .. loo la loo, Ho - ly Mo -ther, Ma - ry mild! Sho-heen sho, . . .

1. loo la loo, With their hymns the vale doth ring. Sho - heen sho!
2. loo la loo, Thro' the night pro - tect my child! Sho - heen sho!

poco rit.

I have taken this air from J. P. Lynch's *Melodies of Ireland, c,* 1845, where it is entitled "A Cradle Song, never before published." I am indebted to Miss Denny for supplying me with suitable verses to the melody.

Remember the glories of Brien the brave.

Thomas Moore.

Tempo di marcia, poco maestoso.

1. Re - mem - ber the glo - ries of
2. Mo - no - nia! when na - ture em-
3. For - get not our wound - ed com-

1. Bri - en the brave, Tho' the days of the he - ro are o'er; Tho'
2. - bel - lish'd the tint Of thy fields and thy moun - tains so fair, Did she
3. - pan - ions who stood In the day of dis - tress by our side; While the

1. lost to Mo - no - nia, and cold in the grave, He re - turns to Kin - cor - a no
2. ev - er in - tend that a ty - rant should print The foot - steps of sla - ver - y
3. moss of the val - ley grew red with their blood, They stirr'd not, but con - quer'd and

This air. "Molly Macalpin," is preserved in Bunting's *Ancient Irish Music*, 1796. In his work of 1840, he states it to be the composition of William O'Connallon, born about 1645; it is quite evident, however, that many of Bunting's statements must be taken "with a grain of salt." In John Mulholland's *Ancient Irish Airs*, Belfast, 1810, the air is designated "Molly Halfpenny." Moore's noble song was written for the first number of the *Melodies*, 1807.

1. more! That star of the field, which so of-ten has pour'd Its
2. there? No, Free-dom, whose smile we shall nev-er re-sign, Go
3. died! The sun, that now bless-es our arms with his light, Saw them

1. beam on the bat-tle, is set; But e-nough of its glo-ry re-
2. tell our in-va-ders, the Danes, That 'tis sweet-er to bleed for an
3. fall up-on Os-so-ry's plain:— Oh! let him not blush, when he

1. -mains on each sword To light us to vic-to-ry yet!
2. age at thy shrine Than to sleep but a mo-ment in chains!
3. leaves us to-night, To find that they fell there in vain!

Rich and rare were the gems she wore.

THOMAS MOORE.

Andantino.

VOICE.

PIANO.

1.
2.
3. Sir

p *rit.*

1. Rich and rare were the gems she wore, And a bright gold
2. La - - dy! dost thou not fear to stray So lone and
3. knight, I feel not the least a - larm, No son of

p

1. ring on her wand she bore; But oh! her beau - ty was
2. love - ly thro' this bleak way? Are E - - rin's sons so
3. E - rin will of - fer me harm:— For tho' they love wo - men and

We are indebted to Edward Bunting for the preservation of this fine air ; it is printed in his *General Collection of the Ancient Irish Music,* 1796, as "The Summer is coming." Moore's verses are in the first number of the *Melodies,* 1807. The following quotation from Bunting's work will show how much importance that author attached to the existence of the air in Ireland. "The ancient air *Ta an samradh tuacht,* or the *Summer is coming,* is used upon the opening of summer in different parts of the kingdom. Strange as it may appear, this proves to be the same song in essence, both as to poetry and music, which Dr. Burney has published and written so voluminous a critique on, as the first piece of music ever set in score in Great Britain. The extreme improbability of its being *borrowed* by the ancient Irish, from a country that has no national music of its own (the

1. far . . be - yond   Her   spark - ling   gems   or   snow - white
2. good or so   cold   As   not   to   be   tempt - ed   by   wo - man   or
3. gold - en   store,   Sir   knight, they love   hon - our   and   vir - tue

1. wand.   But   oh!   her   beau - ty was   far . . . be - yond   Her
2. gold?   Are   E - - rin's   sons   so   good   or   so   cold   As
3. more.   For   tho'   they love   wo - men and   gold - - en   store,   Sir

1. spark - - ling   gems   and   snow - - white wand.
2. not   to   be   tempt - ed   by   wo - man   or   gold?
3. knight, they   love   hon - our   and   vir - - tue   more.

Welsh excepted) is sufficiently evident. The devoted attachment to their own music, and the praises it received from other countries ; their ignorance of the English language, and their rooted aversion to their invaders, were effectual bars to any such plagiarism or adoption." (Collection of 1796, p. iv.). It is hardly necessary to say that the old score referred to is the celebrated early English MS. copy of "Summer is icumen in." which Mr. Chappell considers to have been written in the year 1220. An inspection of this ancient composition proves that beyond the first four notes, but little affinity can be said to exist between it and the Irish air. The similarity of titles evidently caused Bunting to form his opinion ; in designating England a country with no national music of its own, Bunting only showed how limited his knowledge was of the subject.

Remember thee.

Thomas Moore.

Andante.

VOICE.

PIANO.

1. Re - mem - ber thee!
2. Wert thou all that I
3. No, thy chains as they

1. yes, while there's life in this heart It shall nev - er for - get thee, all
2. wish thee, great, glo - rious, and free— First flow - er of the earth, and first
3. ran - kle, thy blood as it runs, But make thee more pain - ful - ly

1. lorn as thou art, More dear in thy sor - row, thy gloom and thy
2. gem of the sea, I might hail thee with proud - er, with hap - pi - er
3. dear to thy sons,— Whose hearts, like the young of the des - ert - bird's

mf

poco rit.

Last time.

1. show'rs, Than the rest of the world in their sun - ni - est hours.
2. brow, But, oh! could I love thee more deep - ly than now?
3. nest, Drink love in each life - drop that flows from thy breast.

mf   *poco rit.*   *p rit.*

For note to this song see Appendix.

She is far from the land.

THOMAS MOORE.

Andante.

VOICE.

1. She is   far   from the land where her
2. She   sings the wild songs of her
3. He had lived for his love, for his
4. Oh! make her a grave where the

PIANO.

rit.

1. young   he - ro   sleeps,   And   lov - ers   are   round her   sigh - - ing;   But
2. dear   na -tive   plains,   Ev' -ry note which he   lov'd   a - wak - - ing;   Ah!
3. coun - try he   died,   They were all that to   life had en - twin'd . .   him;   Nor
4. sun - beams   rest,   When they pro -mise   a   glo - ri - ous   mor - - - row;   They'll

poco rit.

1. cold - ly she turns from their   gaze,   and weeps, For her   heart in   his   grave is   ly - ing.
2. lit - tle they think who de - light in   her strains, How the   heart of   the   minstrel is   break - ing.
3. soon shall the tears   of his   coun-try   be dried,   Nor   long will his   love stay be - hind   him.
4. shine o'er her sleep, like a   smile from the West, From her   own lov - ed   is-land of   sor - row.

poco rit.

Air: "Open the Door." Alluding to this air Professor Stanford remarks in his edition of Moore's *Melodies* "restored": "An air from Bunting's first Collection, of which Moore scarcely left a note unaltered, omitting the flat seventh and vulgarizing the close." The following will prove that this grave assertion against the poet is entirely unfounded. Moore's "She is far from the land" was published in the fourth number of the *Melodies*, 1811, and the version of "Open the Door" used by him is found in the following works. As "Open the door to me, oh, oh. Irish air," in Corri's *Scots Songs, including a few English and Irish*, vol. ii., 1783. As ditto in the *Musical Miscellany, Perth*, 1786; *Calliope, U'd*; George Thomson's *Scottish Airs*, Set. i., 1793; *The British Musical Miscellany, Edinburgh, 1805*, etc. The version in Bunting's and Miss Owenson's Collections is possibly purer than the more popular one, but it will be seen that Tom Moore merely published the usually accepted version of the melody, and did not alter a note of it. (See also note on p. 178).

Silence is in our festal halls.

Thomas Moore.

Andante molto sostenuto.

VOICE.

PIANO.

mf *ritard.* *p*

con Ped.

1. Si - lence is in our
2. Yes, E - rin, thine a -

1. fes - tal halls, Oh! son of song, thy course is o'er,
2. - lone . . . the fame, Or, if thy bard have shar'd the crown,

sf p

cres.

1. In vain on thee, sad E - rin calls, Her min - strel's voice res - ponds no
2. From thee the bor - rowed glo - ry came, And at thy feet is now laid

cres.

Moore's song was written for the supplement to the tenth and concluding number of the *Melodies*, 1834: it was a tribute from the poet to the memory of Sir John Stevenson, who died in Dublin in Sept., 1833, at the age of seventy-one. I have given two of the four verses of the song. The air, as "The Green Woods of Truigha," was printed in Bunting's *Ancient Music of Ireland*,

1. more: All si - lent as th' E - o - lian shell . . . Doth sleep at close, at
2. down. E - nough if Free- dom still in - spire . . . His lat - est song, and

1. close of some bright day, When the sweet breeze that wak'd its swell, At
2. still there be, As even - ing clos - es round his lyre, One

1. sun - ny morn, hath died a - way.
2. ray up - on its chords from thee.

1808, to "a literal translation of the original Irish" by Mary Balfour, beginning "In ringlets curl'd thy tresses flow." As shown on p. 244. "The Green Woods of Truighn," is one of the older versions of "The Morven" to which Moore wrote his immortal song "The Minstrel Boy." The melodies called "The Green Woods of Treugh" in the collections of John Murphy, John Mulholland, and R. A. Smith, are all different, and have nothing in common with the above beautiful air. (See p. 4.)

Silent, O Moyle! be the roar of thy water.

THE SONG OF FIONNUALA.

THOMAS MOORE.

Andante maestoso.

VOICE.

PIANO.

mf

sf p ritard.

con Ped.

1. Si - lent, O Moyle! be the   roar   of thy wa - ter,   Break   not, ye breez -es!   your
2. Sad - ly, O Moyle! to thy   win - ter wave weep-ing,   Fate   bids me lan -guish long

1. chain   of   re-pose,   While,   mur - mur-ing mourn -ful - ly,   Lir's   lone -ly daugh-ter
2. a - ges   a -way;   Yet   still   in her dark - ness doth   E - rin lie sleep -ing,

This melody was supplied by Dr. Petrie to Holden's Collection, vol. i., 1806, where it appears as "Arah my dear Ev'leen." Moore, who is indebted to Holden's work for so many of his airs, wrote the above song to "Arrah my dear Eveleen" for the second number of the *Melodies*, 1807. It will be seen by glancing at Holden's tune, which I give in the Appendix No. XXI, that the following remark by Professor Stanford in his "restored" edition of Moore's *Melodies*, is quite incorrect. "'Silent O Moyle.'

1. Tells to the night - star her tales of woes, When shall the swan, her
2. Still doth the pure light its dawn - ing de - lay! When will that day - star,

1. death - note sing - ing, Sleep with wings in dark - ness furl'd?
2. mild - ly spring - ing, Warm our isle with peace and love?

1. When will heav'n, its sweet bell ringing, Call my spi-rit from this stormy world?
2. When will heav'n, its sweet bell ringing, Call my spi-rit to the fields a - bove?

Moore destroyed the character of the tune and obliterated the scale by sharpening the seventh (G sharp for G natural). The song refers to Fionnuala, the daughter of Lir, who by some supernatural power was transformed into a swan and condemned to wander for many hundred years over certain lakes and rivers in Ireland till the coming of Christianity, when the first sound of the Mass-bell was to be the signal of her release (original note by Moore).

Q 2

Sleep on, for I know 'tis of me you are dreaming.

FLORENCE BEAMISH.

Andante tranquillo.

VOICE.

PIANO.

1. Sleep on, for I know 'tis of
2. Yes, sleep on, Ma-vour-neen, my

con Ped. *sempre con Ped.*

1. me you are dream-ing, Sleep on, till the sun comes to give you a call; Tho' the
2. joy, and my trea-sure, Not of-ten does sleep get a com-rade so fair; And no

1. pride of my heart is to see your eye beam-ing, Yet still to be dreamt of is
2. won-der it is that his eye takes a plea-sure To watch by your pil-low while

This is another *Suantraidhe* or Lullaby, a species of composition for which Ireland is unrivalled; it was obtained by that enthusiastic collector of folk-airs, R. A. Smith, and published in his work, *The Irish Minstrel, c.* 1825. This volume, which was issued by Purdie of Edinburgh, is in the form and style of the same publisher's *Scottish Minstrel,* 1822; it was suppressed, however, by Power, Moore's publisher, who raised an action against Purdie for infringement of copyright. "Sleep on" was published in Hayes' *Ballads of Ireland,* vol. ii., 1855.

1. bet - ter than all.   For   then, 'tis to yours that my heart's al - ways speak-ing, And
2. you slum - ber there!   Then   sleep, soft-ly sleep, till the   day - dawn is   break-ing, And

1. then   'tis the   spell that   en - chains it   gives way,   And re - veals all   the   love   that I
2. peeps   in to   give you   a   smile and   a   call;   For tho' great as   my   joy   is, to

1. ne - ver,when waking, Could get round my tongue in the daylight to say.
2. see you when waking, Yet   still to   be dreamt of   is sweeter than all!

Sweet babe, a golden cradle holds thee.

THE FAIRIES' LULLABY.

Andante tranquillo.

VOICE.

PIANO.

p

p

Ped.

sempre con Ped.

1. Sweet babe, a gold - en cra - dle holds thee,
2. Rest thee, babe, for soon thy slum - bers,

1. Shu-heen sho, lu - lo lo— Soft the snow-white fleece en-folds thee, Shu-heen sho,
2. Shu-heen sho, lu - lo lo— Fly at the ma - gic *Koelshee's numbers, Shu-heen sho,

1. lu - lo lo. In air - y bow'rs I'll watch thy sleeping, Shu-heen sho, lu - lo lo, Where
2. lu - lo lo. In air - y bow'rs I'll watch thy sleeping, Shu-heen sho, lu - lo lo, Where

rit. *pp*

1. branch - y trees to the breeze are sweeping, Shu-heen sho, lu - lo lo, shu - heen sho.
2. branch - y trees to the breeze are sweeping, Shu-heen sho, lu - lo lo, shu - heen sho.

p

rit. *ppp*

* Koelshee = Fairy music.

In giving another version of this air in the *Ancient Music of Ireland*, 1855, Dr. Petrie evidently overlooked the fact that Hornecastle had already printed the above setting in his *Music of Ireland*, pt. iii., 1844. A comparison of the two settings will prove, I think, that Hornecastle's is the purer and more vocal of the two. The verses were translated from the Irish by Edward Walsh. "A child is supposed to be led into the fairy fort of Lisroe where she sees her little brother, who had died about a week before, laid in a rich cradle, and a young woman singing as she rocks him to sleep." (Note to song in McCarthy's *Irish Ballads*, 1846.)

Sweet babe, a golden cradle holds thee.

LULLABY.

Edward Walsh and P. W. Joyce.

This is another beautiful lullaby, or nurse-tune, obtained by Dr. George Petrie in the county of Londonderry, and preserved in that author's magnificent collection of traditional Irish melodies. The song is a modification, by Dr. Joyce, of Walsh's translation from the original Irish, given on the preceding page.

Speed thy flight.

Poco andantino.

VOICE.

1. Speed thy flight,
2. And at fair

PIANO.

1. riv - er bright, Full of joy, full of light; Glee - ful - ly take thy path,
2. Eas - ter - tide I shall claim her my bride; O'er the moor, thro' the grove,

1. And at the mos - sy rath Tell my love wait - ing there, Wait - ing for the
2. Riv - er, speed to my love; Kiss her cheek ten - der - ly, Whis - per low of

1. Spring fair— Tell her that the time is nigh, Win - ter and sor - row die.
2. joys to be— Tell her that the time is nigh, Win - ter and sor - row die.

This is one of those traditional tunes picked up by F. W. Horncastle, and published by him in the work entitled *The Music of Ireland*, bk. 1. London, 1844; it is there designated "The Quern Time."

The earth is fair around us.

ELLEN MARY DOWNING.

Molto andante.

VOICE.

PIANO.

p con espress.

poco rit.

a tempo.

1. The earth is
2. Your eyes,— your
3. Are you glad to
4. And I felt your

1. fair a - round us, The sun is bright a - bove, But more
2. eyes so ten - der Look fond - ly in - to mine, And they
3. be so near me? For your smile is ve - ry bright, And a
4. light hand trem - bling Tho' so fear - less is my own; Are you

rit.

1. glo - rious is our hap - pi - ness, More glow-ing is our love.
2. clasp me like a bless - - ing, Those dar - ling hands of thine.
3. smile is some - times com - - ing, As of new - ly found de - light.
4. glad to be so near . . . me? Would you grieve if I were gone?

rit.

Air: "When she answered me her voice was low," preserved in the Petrie Collection, 1855. It was obtained about 1815 from the county of Cavan. Ellen Mary Downing was born at Cork in 1828; she contributed poems to the *Nation, United Irishman, Cork Magazine*, etc. She entered a convent and died in 1869.

232

The day went down.

THE LAST LAY OF THE DYING BARD.

DESMOND RYAN.

VOICE.

1. The
2. He
3. "Where
4. The

PIANO.

1. day went down, and the sun's last ray Had pass'd where the dy - ing harp - er lay, His
2. strikes the chords from the sil - ver strings, A low and tune - less pre - lude rings; Ah!
3. are ye now, ye prin - ces all! Who led the dance in the fes - tive hall? I -
4. min - strel rose and brush'd a - way The dews of woe on his lids that lay, He

1. snow-white locks in the breeze did play As it swept thro' the aisles of Kin - co - ra. "A -
2. vain the time-worn min - strel sings A la - ment for the days of Kin - co - ra. His
3. - er - ne's burn - ing tears will fall As she dreams o'er the days of Kin - co - ra. On
4. stood on the height o'er the waves whose spray Once lash'd the proud halls of Kin - co - ra. One

Air: "The Princess Royal." In an interesting article on this celebrated air, now almost universally known as "The Arethusa," Mr. Frank Kidson points out the following facts: Shield never claimed the air as his composition; Preston's edition of the *Lock & Key*, in which the "Arethusa" appears, has on the title, "composed and selected" by Mr. Shield; contemporary issues of the song in sheet-form bear "arranged" and "adapted." The tune was printed about 1730 in Walsh's *Compleat Country-Dancing-Master* as "The Princess Royal, the new way," and in vol. i. of Wright's *Country Dances*. Mr. Kidson then observes that the air must have fallen into disfavour, and it is not until 1787 that it re-appeared in McGlashan's *Scots Measures*; and it was probably from seeing it in this work that gave Shield the suggestion to insert it in his opera. (See *The Musical Times*, Oct., 1901.) The fact of the air having been first printed in London is not in itself proof that it was not originally Irish. The early English music publishers seized greedily upon any fine Scotch or Irish airs they could find, and their country-dance collections especially teem with such. Daniel Wright evidently took an interest in Irish music; the title-page of his *Aria di Camera*, c. 1730, shows that he employed a "Mr. Derm' O'connar of Limerick" to supply him with Irish airs. The "Princess Royal" does not occur in the *Aria di Camera*; but in another collection which contains many similar airs, and evidently published by Wright not later than 1735, we find the "Princess Royal" printed along with "Limerick's Lament" and other Irish tunes. The book I allude to is an oblong quarto

p

1. - wake, my harp!" he faint - ly cried, From his eyes then flash'd a gleam of pride As he
2. bro - ken mur - murs melt in the air, Tho' his voice was gone, yet his soul was there, And he
3. Shan-non's banks the wild winds mourn For glo - ries, a - las! that no more re-turn; Thro' the
4. strain of joy he wild - ly sung, In the o - cean stream his harp he flung, Then

sf   *p*

cres.

1. look'd back on days of the re - gal might When the chief-tain bold and the war - rior knight And
2. wept for the tow'rs and the walls laid low, For the halls where no more the gob - lets flow, Where
3. moul - dering aisles dark shades ap - pear, The spi - rits of for-mer guests are here; Grim
4. sink - ing down by the rush - ing tide, His lips grow pale and his eyes' dark pride Waxed

cres.

poco rit.

1. beau-ty in jew-els and rings shone bright, As they glanc'd thro' the halls of Kin - co - ra.
2. joy ran high, and soft cheeks did glow To his strains in the days of Kin - co - ra.
3. he-roes have stol'n from their tomb - less bier To sigh o'er the days of Kin - co - ra."
4. glass-y and dim thro' the gloom, and died With a smile the last bard of Kin - co - ra.

poco rit.

preserved in the Wighton Collection, Dundee Public Library; although the title-page is missing there is unmistakable evidence to show that the work is one of Wright's publications. The first to claim the tune as being the composition of Carolan seems to have been O'Farrell in bk. iv. of his *Companion for the Irish or Union Pipes, c.* 1810; he merely heads it "Air by Carolan. Irish." Bunting also obtained a version from O'Neill the harper in 1809, and remarks in his Collection of 1840, that it was composed by Carolan for the daughter of Macdermott Roe, the representative of the old Princes of Coolavin; here, at any rate, is a traditional explanation of the title. "The Princess Royal." In a list of tunes composed by Carolan, James Hardiman includes an air entitled "Abigail Judge," or, as Bunting has it, "Madam Judge." Now, if Carolan wrote this melody, and I see no reason to doubt his having done so, then it is not at all improbable that he was also the composer of the "Princess Royal." There is a great similarity in the style of the two airs; without being particularly Irish in character, they have that spirited ring in them which the old English melodies in the minor mode lack so much. In case this air should be unknown to the reader, I have inserted it in the Appendix No. XXXI. for his perusal. Various printed versions of "Abigail Judge" exist, but the one I have chosen is from George Thomson's *Irish Airs,* bk. ii. 1816; it appears to me to be the finest setting. Although we refuse to give up our claim to the "Princess Royal" being of Irish origin, we must admit that the accusation brought by Lover and other writers against Shield for having "shabbily purloined" and issued it as his own composition is entirely unfounded. Ryan's fine song was first printed in F. N. Crouch's *Songs of Erin,* 1841. Since writing the above I find that a poor and incorrect setting of the air is included in Messrs. Parry and Rowland's *Cambrian Minstrelsie* with the following remark: "Though the title of this air is English, there can be no question about its Welsh origin." Assertions of this description scarcely deserve notice: they are easily made, and are certainly not worth refuting.

The dew each trembling leaf enwreath'd.

MARY BALFOUR.

Andante.

VOICE.

1. The
2. But

PIANO.

p

rit.

1. dew   each   trem - bling   leaf   en - wreath'd, The   red - breast   sweet - ly
2. now   o'er   drear - y   scenes   I . . range, Where   once   such   beau - ties

p

1. sung,   The   balm - y   air   with   fra - grance breath'd   From
2. shone,   Yet   bloom - ing   na - ture   knows   no   change,   A -

I have taken this pretty melody known as "Nancy of the Branching Tresses," from Bunting's Second Collection, 1809, where it is printed with Miss Balfour's verses. An entirely different air is given in Holden's *Old Established Irish Tunes*, vol. ii., 1806, as "Nancy of the pleasing tresses."

1. bow'rs with ros - es hung. The set - ting sun still
2. -las! 'tis all . . . my own. The rose . . still holds its

1. faint - ly gleam'd, And swift and sweet the mo - ments flew With
2. love - ly form, The dew still spar - kles on the tree, But

1. her, whose smile too art - less seem'd To hide a heart un - true.
2. oh, the smile that gave the charm No long - er beams for me.

The fairies are dancing.

VOICE.

PIANO.

Vivace.

p

tr

rit.

p

1. The fair - ies are danc -ing by brake and by bow'r, By
2. Their queen is in youth and in beau - ty there, In
3. She'll meet thee at dark like a la - - dy fair, A

1. brake and by bow'r, By brake and by bow'r, The fair - ies are danc - ing by
2. beau - ty there, In beau - ty there, Their queen is in youth and in
3. la - dy fair, A la - dy fair, She'll meet thee at dark like a

Several settings of this sprightly jig tune exist under different titles. In O'Farrell's *National Music for the Union Piper, c.* 1797-1800, it is called "Round the World for Sport," and as such was reprinted in Holden's *Irish Tunes,* 1806. Hudson obtained a setting from the "Farmer and O'Reilly MS." which he printed in the *Citizen Magazine,* April, 1841, as "Diversion everywhere." Another setting was noted by Dr. Petrie, and, as "Better let them alone," published in Hoffmann's *Ancient Music of Ireland from the Petrie Collection,* 1877. The verses are from *Irish National Poetry,* bk. iii., Dublin, 1846.

1. brake and by bow'r, For this in their land is the mer - ri - est hour. Their
2. beau - ty there, The daugh-ters of earth are not half so fair. Her
3. la - dy fair, But go not, for dan - ger a - waits thee there! She'll

1. steps are so soft, and their robes are so bright, Their robes are so bright, Their
2. glance is so quick, and her eyes are so bright, Her eyes are so bright, Her
3. take thee to ram - ble by grove and by glen, By grove and by glen, By

1. robes are so bright, Their steps are so soft, and their robes are so bright, As they
2. eyes are so bright, Her glance is so quick, and her eyes are so bright, But they
3. grove and by glen; She'll take thee to ram - ble by grove and by glen, And the

1. trip it at ease in the clear moonlight.
2. glit -ter with wild and un - earth - ly light.
3. friends of thy youth will ne'er know thee a -gain!

The first day of Spring in the year Ninety-three.

HUNTING SONG.

Allegro spirituoso.

VOICE.

PIANO.

f

ten.

mf

mf

1. The first day of spring in the year Nine - ty - three, The
2. When Rey - nard was start - ed be fac - ed Tul - la - more, And
3. But Rey - nard, sly Rey - nard, lay hid there that night, And they
4. When Rey - nard was tak - en, his wish - es to ful - fil, He
5. "To you, Mis -ter Ca - sey, I give my whole es - tate, And to

1. first re - cre - a - tion was in this countrie; The King's coun -ty gen -tle-men o'er
2. Ark - low and Wick - low a - long the sea-shore, We kept his brush in view ev' - ry
3. swore they would watch him un - til the day-light; So ear - ly next morn - ing the
4. call'd for ink and pa - per, and pen to write his will; And what he made men-tion of, they
5. you, young O'-Brien, my mo-ney and my plate; I give to you, Sir Fran - cis, my

Air: "Reynard the Fox," from Dr. P. W. Joyce's Collection. "The song of 'Reynard the Fox' has long been a favourite ; and to the present day continues to be printed as a street ballad. The old people of the Midland counties still retain some traditions of this great hunt, which, according to my version of the song, took place in 1793. I learned the air and words from my father ;

1. hills, dales and rocks, They rode out so jo - vial - ly in
2. yard of the way, And he straight took his course thro' the
3. woods did re - sound With the e - cho of horns and the
4. found it no blank, For he gave them a cheque on the
5. whip, spurs, and cap, For you crossed walls and ditch - es, and ne'er

f

1. search of a fox.
2. street of Ros-crea.
3. sweet cry of hounds. } Tal - ly - ho! hark a-way! Tal - ly - ho! hark a-way! Tal - ly -
4. na - tion - al bank!
5. look'd for a gap!"

ho! hark a-way, my boys, a - way, hark a-way!

but the version now commonly printed on sheets is a little different, for both date and names are altered to suit a later time. All the versions that I have seen or heard agree in the line 'Arklow and Wicklow along the sea-shore,' which appears absurd, as these two places lie far out of the line of the chase. It is probably a corruption." (*Ancient Irish Music*, 1873, p. 50.)

R

The gold rain of eve was descending.

THE CAILIN DEAS.

Dr. George Sigerson.

Allegretto con grazia.

Voice.

Piano.

poco rit.

1. The
2. Dark
3. "At
4. Her

1. gold rain of eve was de-scend-ing, Bright pur-ple rob'd mountain and tree, As
2. clouds where a gold tinge re-pos - es, But pic-ture her brown wa - vy hair; And her
3. last, o'er that long night, dear E - rin, Dawns the Sun of thy Free-dom!" sang she; "But thy
4. tears on a sad - den brimm'd ov - er, Her voice trem-bled low and less clear; To

Air: *Cailin deas cruidhidh na mho*, or "The pretty girl milking the cow." We are indebted to Bunting for the preservation of this sweet little air; it occurs in his first Collection, 1796. Holden has a slightly different version of it in his *Old Established Irish Tunes*, vol. i., 1806, and *Periodical Irish Melodies*; in the latter collection, the air is set to the well known song "The beam on the stranded wave playing." Written by J. S., Esq." O'Farrell prints "The pretty girl milking her cow" in his *National Irish Music for the Irish Pipes*, 1795-1800, as "Doneing for Sport." Dr. George Sigerson is one of the leading Irish poets of the present time; under the pseudonym of *Erionnach* he edited the second series of *The Poets and Poetry of Munster*, Dublin, 1860.

1. I thro' Glen-mor-neen was wend-ing, A wan-d'rer from o'er the blue sea. 'Twas the
2. teeth look'd as if in a ros-e's Red bo-som a snow-flake gleam'd there. As her
3. moun-tain-eers still are de-spair-ing— Ah, he who 'mid bond-men was free. Ah, my
4. list-en, I stepp'd from my cov-er, But the bough-rus-tle broke on her ear: She

1. lap of a west-look-ing moun-tain, Its wood-y slope bright with the glow, Where
2. tones down the green dell went ring-ing, The list'n-ing thrush mimicked them low, And the
3. Diar-mid, the pa-tri-ot heart-ed Who would fill them with hope for the blow. Far,
4. start-ed—she red-den'd—"A stoir-in! My Diar-mid! O can it be so?" And I

1. sang by a mur-mur-ing foun-tain An coll-yeen das croo-tia na mo.*
2. brook-let harped soft to the sing-ing Of coll-yeen das croo-tia na mo.
3. E-rin! from thee is he part-ed, Far from coll-yeen das croo-tia na mo."
4. clasp'd to my glad heart, sweet Moir-in, . Mo coll-yeen das croo-tia na mo!

* An Cailin deas g-cruidadh na mbo = The pretty girl milking the cows.

R 2

The harp that once thro' Tara's halls.

THOMAS MOORE.

Andantino.

VOICE.

PIANO.

mf

con l'ed.

mf　　　　　　　　　　　　　　　　　　　　　　*cres.*

1. The harp that once thro' Ta - ra's halls The soul of mu - sic shed, Now
2. No more to chiefs and la - dies bright The harp of Ta - ra swells, The

mf

f

1. hangs as mute on Ta - ra's walls As if that soul were fled. So
2. chord a - lone that breaks at night Its tale of ru - in tells. Thus

f

The earliest printed form of the air is to be found in William McGibbon's Collection of *Scots Tunes*, bk. ii., p. 2, Edinburgh, 1746, under the title of "Will you go to Flanders?" (See Appendix, No. XXII.); it is worthy of notice that bars three and fifteen of the Scotch version are more similar in character to "Molly, my Treasure," the setting obtained by Bunting from Fannin the Harper, in 1792, and printed in his work of 1840, than the ordinary accepted version which was introduced by Sheridan in the *Duenna*, 1775, set to the well-known stanzas beginning, "Had I a heart for falsehood framed." As "My Heart's Delight," a dance setting of the air was printed in Charles and Samuel Thompson's *Country Dances for* 1775, and from this year until the

1. sleeps the pride of for - mer days, So glo - ry's thrill is o'er, And
2. Free - dom now so sel - dom wakes, The on - ly throb she gives Is

cres.

1. hearts that once beat high for praise Now feel that pulse no more.
2. when some heart in - dig - nant breaks To show that still she lives.

rall.

appearance of the first number of the *Melodies,* 1807, "Gramachree" is to be met with in many printed collections of songs and tunes, sometimes set to Ogle's "As down on Banna's banks I stray'd," and sometimes to that strange ballad, "The Maid in Bedlam." Two verses of the old song are preserved in David Herd's *Ancient and Modern Scottish Songs,* vol. ii., 1776; it will be seen that the lady's name contained in the Irish title occurs:—

Will ye go to Flanders, my Mally O?
Will ye go to Flanders, my Mally O?
There we'll get wine and brandy, and suck and sugar candy;
Will ye go to Flanders, my Mally O?

The minstrel boy.

Thomas Moore.

Andante maestoso.

Voice.

Piano.

mf

con Ped.

1. The
2. The

1. min - strel boy to the war is gone, In the ranks of death . . you'll
2. min - strel fell!— but the foe - man's chain Could not bring his proud soul

dim.

sempre con Ped.

dim.

1. find . . . him; His fa - ther's sword he has gird - ed on, And his
2. un - - - der; The harp he loved ne'er spoke a - gain, For he

dim.

dim.

Regarding this air, called "The Moreen" (*Moirin*, diminutive of *Mor* or *Moria*, a girl's name), Professor Stanford makes the following remark in his edition of Moore's *Melodies* "restored." "It is a reel tune altered by Moore into a march." Yet curiously enough, the original, or, at least, *one* of the original versions of "The Moreen" is to be found in Professor Stanford's book, namely, the beautiful air "The green woods of Truigha," to which Tom Moore wrote the song "Silence is in our festal halls." A reference

1. wild harp slung . . be - hind . . . him. "Land of song," said the
2. tore its chords . . a - sun - - - der; And said, "No chains shall

1. war - rior bard, "Tho' all the world be - trays . . . thee, One
2. sul - ly thee, Thou soul of love and bra - ve - ry! Thy

colla voce. *poco rit.* *a tempo.*

1. sword, at least, thy rights shall guard, One faith-ful harp . . shall praise thee!"
2. songs were made for the pure and free, They shall nev - er sound . in sla - ve - ry!"

dim.

to p. 222, will show the reader to what I allude. Bunting, in whom Professor Stanford places so much faith, states that "The green woods of Truigha" "is of great antiquity, as is proved by its structure, and by the fact of its being known by so many different names in different parts of the country. Thus it is known in Ulster as 'The green woods of Truigha,' in Leinster as 'Edmund of the Hill,' in Connaught as 'Colonel O'Gara,' and in Munster as 'More No Beg,' with a variety of other aliases.' (*Ancient Music of Ireland*, 1840, p. 16.)

The night was still.

Andante.

CALLANAN.

1. The night was still, the air was balm, Soft
2. With mod-est air she droop'd her head, Her

1. dews a-round were weep - ing; No whis-per rose o'er o-cean's calm, Its waves in light were
2. cheek of beau-ty veil - ing; Her bo-som heav'd—no word she said; I mark'd her strife of

1. sleep - ing, With Ma - ry on the beach I stray'd, The stars beam'd joys a - bove me, I
2. feel - ing; "Oh, speak my doom, dear maid," I cried, "By yon bright heav'n a - bove thee!" She

poco rit.

1. press'd her hand, and said, "Sweet maid, Oh! tell me, do you love me?"
2. gent - ly rais'd her eyes and sigh'd, "Too well you know I love thee!"

poco rit.

This air, as "The Lame Yellow Beggar," was printed in Bunting's third Collection, 1840; it was obtained by that author in 1792 from Black the harper. In the Index of his work, Bunting gives the author and date of the composition as "O'Cahen, 1610;" on the music sheet, "By O'Caghan in 1659." Whether we are intended to believe that this bard composed the air in his tenth year or not, is uncertain. One point, however, is quite certain, and that is, the air existed centuries before O'Cahen tuned his lyre. A reference to p. 265, will show the reader that the "Lame Yellow Beggar" is nothing more than a version of the ancient Celtic melody known now as "The Old Head of Dennis," "Robin donn goraeh," etc. A florid setting of the tune occurs in that somewhat rare book, Irish Airs and Jiggs, by John Murphy, Performer on the Union Pipes, at Eglinton Castle, 1809, as "Th' Lame Beggar—an Old Irish Air."

The pigeons coo—the spring's approaching now.

CORMAC OGE.

Translated from the Irish by EDWARD WALSH.

VOICE.

PIANO.

1. pi - geons coo— the spring's approaching now, The bloom is burst - ing
2. are the fruits the haz' - ly woods dis-play,— A slen - der vir - gin
3. lit - tle birds pour mu-sic's sweet-est notes, The calves for milk dis -

1. on the leaf - y bough; The cress - es green o'er streams are clust'ring low, And
2. vir-tuous, fair and gay, With steads and sheep, of kine a man-y score, By
3. tend their bleat-ing throats, A - bove the weirs the sil - ver sal - mon leap, While

1. hon - ey - lives with sweets a - bund - ant flow.
2. trout - stored Lee whose banks we'll see no more.
3. Cor - mac Oge and I all lone - ly weep.

Noted by Dr. Petrie when a boy from the Dublin ballad singers, during which time it was associated with an Anglo-Irish ballad, called "Pretty Sally." The air is also known in the Isle of Man, as "Isbel Falsey," or, "False Isobel"; a setting of it was published in C. St. George's *Mona Melodies, A Collection of Ancient and Original Airs of the Isle of Man,* 1820 (see Appendix, No. XXIII). Walsh's translation is from *Irish Popular Songs,* 1847. Of the River Lee, Spenser says in the *Fairy Queen :—*
The spreading Lee, that, like an island fair
Encloseth Cork with his devided flood.

248

The silent bird is hid in the boughs.

Rosa Mulholland (Mrs. Gilbert).

1. The si - lent
2. A lit - tle

1. bird . . is hid in the boughs, The scythe is hid . . . . . in the
2. door . . is hid in the boughs, A face is hid - - - - ing with -

1. corn, The la - zy ox - - - en wink and drowse, The grate - ful
2. in; When birds are si - lent and ox - en drowse, Why should a

Air: "The Bastard." This is another of those melodies which were forwarded to me last January from Dublin, by an anonymous correspondent. Although I have not been able to trace it to any printed source, as in the case of the air set to "Shane Glas," I have no doubt that it is of considerable antiquity. I have adapted it to Miss Rosa Mulholland's beautiful song, which it seems to suit extremely well. "The Bastard" is an example of a class of tunes which, on account of their construction, Dr. Petrie has termed "narrative;" they are peculiar to Ireland and the Highlands and Western Isles of Scotland.

mf

1. sheep . . . . . are shorn, Red - der and red - - - - der burns the
2. maid - - - - - - en spin? Slow - er and slow - - - - er turns the

mf

1. rose, The li - - - ly was ne'er so pale, Still - er and
2. wheel, The face turns . . . . red and pale, Bright - er and

1. still - er the ri - ver flows, A - long the path . . . . to the vale.
2. bright -er the looks that steal A - long the path . . . . to the vale.

rit.

rit.

The winter it is past.

From the Petrie Collection, 1855, as "The Winter it is past, or, The Curragh of Kildare;" words and air noted about the commencement of the century. Dr. Petrie remarks, "I have found that this song has been more than once published in Scotland as a Scottish one, connected with a melody undoubtedly of Scottish origin, but, as I think, of no great antiquity, and most probably a composition of Oswald's, in whose *Caledonian Pocket Companion* it first appeared." I think Dr. Petrie errs here; the air was certainly not composed by Oswald, and I have been unable to find the slightest reason to suppose that it was "obviously composed" for the song. In fact, although differing considerably from the Irish "Curragh of Kildare," there appears to be sufficient ground to conclude that in the distant past the Scotch and Irish forms of the air had one origin. I give Oswald's setting in the Appendix, No. XXV., and particularly draw the reader's attention to the *flow* of the melody which is much the same as in Petrie's version. As this work is one which deals with the printed history of the *airs*, and not of the *ballads*, I shall refrain from criticising the claims for the ballad set forth by rival writers; the following quotation from Dean Christie's magnificent collection of *Traditional Ballad Airs procured in the counties of Aberdeen, Banff and Moray*, 2 vols., 1876 and 1881 seems to show that whether the composition of a Scotchman or an Irishman, the hero of the song, at any rate, was a native of Erin. I may mention that the Scotch version was printed as early as 1787, in Johnson's *Scot's Musical Museum*, vol. ii., p. 208. "Commenting on his [Dr. Petrie's] version of the Ballad, he rightly traces it to about 1750; but, not having found the first six lines of the second stanza here given, he was unable to discover that the hero of the ballad was Johnson, a highwayman, who was hung in the middle of last century for the many robberies he committed on the Curragh of Kildare" (Christie's Collection, vol. i., p. 114). It is highly probable that the air is much older than the ballad, or at any rate, than that portion of the ballad relating to an incident which took place at as late a period as 1750.

1. black - bird sings on ev'-ry tree: . . . The hearts of these are glad, But
2. joy to the lin - net and the bee; . . . Their lit - tle hearts are blest, But
3. al - ways proves con - stant and true; . . . But his is like the moon That

1. mine is ve - ry sad Since my true love is ab - - sent from
2. mine is not at rest, While my true love is ab - - sent from
3. wan - ders up and down, And ev' - - ry month it is

1. me.
2. me.
3. new.

2. The
3. My

f

The wren, the wren.

THE WREN-BOYS' SONG.

Allegro spiritoso.

VOICE.

PIANO.

f   *dim.*

mf

1. The wren, the wren, the king of all birds, Saint
2. My box would speak if it had but a tongue, And
3. And if you draw it of the best, I

mf

1. Ste - phen's Day was caught in a furze, Al -though he is lit - tle, his
2. two or three shil - lings would do it no wrong, So show us some pi - ty in
3. hope in hea - ven your soul it may rest, But if you draw it

This song and air are from F. W. Horncastle's *Music of Ireland,* pt. iii., London, 1844. The following is the note attached to the song in that work :—"On the anniversary of St. Stephen's Day groups of young villagers carry about a holly bush adorned with ribbons and with several wrens depending from it. This is conveyed from house to house with much ceremony, the wren-boys chanting several verses, the burthen of which may be collected from the lines of the song. Contributions are, of course, levied and the evening spent in merriment."

1. fam - i - ly's great; I pray you, good land - la - dy, give us a treat. Sing
2. or - der that we May drink you good health for your kind cha - ri - ty. Sing
3. of the small, It won't a - gree with the wren-boys at all! Sing

1. hey! sing ho! Sing hol - ly, sing hol - ly! A drop just to drink, it would
2. hey! sing ho! Sing hol - ly, sing hol - ly! A drop just to drink, it would
3. hey! sing ho! Sing hol - ly, sing hol - ly! A drop just to drink, it would

f CHORUS.

1. cure me - lan - cho - ly. Sing hey! sing ho! Sing hol - ly, sing
2. cure me - lan - cho - ly. Sing hey! sing ho! Sing hol - ly, sing
3. cure me - lan - cho - ly. Sing hey! sing ho! Sing hol - ly, sing

1. hol - ly! A drop just to drink, it would cure me - lan - cho - ly.
2. hol - ly! A drop just to drink, it would cure me - lan - cho - ly.
3. hol - ly! A drop just to drink, it would cure me - lan - cho - ly.

The young May moon.

THOMAS MOORE.

1. The young May moon is beam - ing, love, The glow - worm's lamp is
2. Now all the world is sleep - ing, love, But the sage his star - watch

1. gleam - ing, love, How sweet to rove Thro' Mor - na's grove, While the
2. keep - ing, love, And I, whose star, More glo - rious far, Is the

Moore's song was published in the fifth number of the *Melodies*, 1813. The air, which he designates "The Dandy, O," was introduced by Shield as an "Irish Tune" in his comic opera, *Robin Hood*, 1784, with verses beginning "My name's Honest Harry O." George Thomson also printed it in his Collection, vol. iv., 1805, in conjunction with a song by Boswell; it is there entitled "Pat and Kate." A good dance version is to be seen in Pringle's *Reels and Jigs*, *Edinburgh*, 1801, as "The Irish Wedding." The name, "The Dandy O," is a misnomer, and was evidently taken from the second verse of the song in *Robin Hood*, one of the

1. drow - sy world is dream-ing, love! Then a - wake! the heav'ns look bright, my dear! 'Tis
2. eye from that case-ment peep - ing, love! Then a - wake!—till rise of sun, my dear, The

poco rit.

1. ne - ver too late for de - light, my dear! And the best of all ways To
2. sa - - ge's glass we'll shun, my dear! Or, in watch - ing the flight Of

poco rit.

1. length-en our days, Is to steal a few hours from the night, my dear!
2. bod - ies of light, He might hap - pen to take thee for one, my dear.

lines of which is "And I'm her-a-dandy O." The tune printed in Brysson's *Curious Selection of Fifty Irish Airs*, 1791, and in O'Farrell's *Pocket Companion*, vol. iv., as "The Dandy O," is entirely different, being, in fact, the air to which Moore wrote the song "Eveleen's Bower," and which he marked "unknown" in the second number of the *Melodies*. But a close examination of the so-called "Dandy O" will show the reader that, after all, it is merely a pretty version of the old tune "Dennis don't be threatening" (see p. 154).

s

The time I've lost in wooing.

THOMAS MOORE.

1. The time I've lost in woo - ing, In watch-ing and pur - su - ing The light that lies In wo-man's eyes, Has been my heart's un - do - ing. Tho' wis-dom oft has sought me, I scorn'd the lore she brought me; My on - ly looks Were wo-man's looks, And fol - ly's all they've taught me.

2. Her smile when beau -ty grant - ed, I hung with gaze en - chant - ed, Like him, the sprite, Whom maids by night Oft meet in glen that's haunt - ed. Like him, too, beau-ty won me, But while her eyes were on me, If once their ray Was turn'd a - way, Oh! winds could not out - run me!

3. And are those fol - lies go - ing? And is my proud heart grow - ing Too cold or wise For bril -liant eyes A - gain to set it glow - ing? No,' vain, a - las! th'en -dea - vour From bonds so sweet to sev - er;—Poor wisdom's chance A - gainst a glance Is now as weak as ev - er.

As "Pease upon a Trencher" this air is to be seen in Aird's Selection of *Scotch, English and Irish Airs*, vol. i. 1782; in the following year Shield introduced it in his opera *The Poor Soldier*, and again in 1798 in *The Mountains of Wicklow*. On p. 32 of the *Ancient Music of Ireland* Dr. Petrie prints an air obtained in 1836 from Bannagher, Co. Londonderry, and which he conceives to be the original of "Pease upon a Trencher." Dr. Petrie's usually clear judgment seems to be somewhat at fault in this instance : a portion of the air, which I give in the Appendix No. XXIV., will show the reader that "O Jenny, you have borne away the palm," has little in common with "Pease upon a Trencher." In fact, I can see no reason to suppose that Dr. Petrie's air is even anterior to that fine old tune.

There are flowers in the valley.

YOUNG KATE OF KILCUMMER.

Moderato.

VOICE.

PIANO.

1. There are flow'rs in the
2. Oh! I'll wan - der from

1. val - ley And fruit on the hill, Sweet scent - ed and smil - ing, Ro -
2. day-break Till night's gloom-y fall, Full sure . . such an - oth - er I'd

1. - sort where you will. But the sweet - est and the brightest, In spring - time or
2. ne'er meet at all. As the rose to the bee, As the sun - shine to

1. sum - mer, Is the girl of my heart, The young Kate of Kil-cum-mer.
2. sum - mer, So wel - come to me Is young Kate of Kil-cum-mer.

This air is in the Petrie Collection as "My Love has gone—my heart is sore": it was supplied by Mr. P. J. O'Reilly, of Westport, county of Mayo. As no words were sent with it to Dr. Petrie, I have adapted it to "Young Kate of Kilcummer," a song which appeared in "The Rapparee," a tale printed in a Cork periodical publication called Bolster's *Quarterly Magazine*, August, 1828. In this work the ballad is stated to be "a favourite Irish song, which we have endeavoured to translate, preserving as much as possible the simplicity of the original." In *Popular Songs of Ireland*, 1839, Thomas Croker observes that he does not recognise anything to induce him to credit this statement; he believes it to be an original composition. Kilcummer is in the county of Cork, not far from the town of Doneraile.

s 2

There are sounds of mirth.

THOMAS MOORE.

Allegretto.

VOICE.

PIANO.

1. There are
2. And
3. Thus

1. sounds of mirth in the night air ring-ing, And lamps from ev'-ry
2. see the lamps still live-li-er glit-ter: The si - ren lips more
3. sung the sage, while, sly - ly steal-ing, The nymphs their fet-ters a-

1. case-ment shown, While voi ces blithe with - in are sing-ing, That
2. fond-ly sound; No, seek, ye nymphs, some vic - tim fit-ter To
3.-round him cast, And, their laugh-ing eyes the while con-ceal-ing, Led

Air: "The Priest in his Boots." The tune known as "Murphy Delaney," but which also occurs in Rutherford's 200 *Country Dances*, 1756, as "The Miser," was evidently associated with an old song entitled "The Parson in his boots," and under this name we find Bremner printing it in his *Reels and Country Dances*, book ii., 1757. I am inclined to think that the above air is merely a transformation of "Murphy Delaney." As "The Priest in his Boots," a variation of it is in C. and S. Thompson's

1. seem to say, "Come," in ev' - - ry strain. Ah! once how light, in
2. sink in your ro - sy bon - - dage bound. Shall a bard, whom not the
3. Free - dom's bard their slave at last. For the Po - et's heart, still

1. Life's young sea - son, My heart had bound-ed at that sweet lay; Nor
2. world in arms Could bend to ty - ran - ny's rude con - trol, Thus
3. prone to lov - ing, Was like that rock of the Dru - id race, Which the

1. paused to ask of grey-beard Rea-son If I should the si - ren call o - bey.
2. quail at sight of wo - man's charms, And yield to a smile his free - born soul?
3. gent - lest touch at once set mov-ing, But all earth's pow'r couldn't cast from its base.

Compleat Collection of 120 Favourite Hornpipes, issued some time between the years 1765 and 1777. (See Appendix, No. XXVa.)
This dance setting shows the tune in its evolutionary stage, between "Murphy Delaney" and the air used by Moore. Moore's song, "There are sounds of mirth," was printed in the tenth and concluding number of the *Melodies*, issued May, 1834, and prior to that, versions of the air were published in Aird's *Selection*, vol. i., 1782, Gow's *Repository*, vol. ii., 1802, Holden's *Irish Tunes*, vol. i., 1806, Mulhollan's *Irish and Scots Tunes*, 1804, Murphy's *Irish Airs*, 1809, etc.

There blooms a bonnie flower.

THE HEATHER GLEN.

Dr. George Sigerson.

1. There blooms a bon-nie flow-er,
2. There sings a bon-nie lin-net,
3. O might I pull the flow-er That's

1. Up the heath-er glen; Tho' bright in sun, in show-er 'Tis just as bright a-gain. I
2. Up the heath-er glen; The voice has ma-gic in it Too sweet for mor-tal men! It
3. bloom-ing in that glen, Nae sor-rows that could low-er Would make me sad a-gain! And

1. nev-er can pass by it, I nev-er dar' go nigh it, My heart it won't be qui-et
2. brings joy down be-fore us Wi' win-some, mel-low cho-rus, But flies far, too far, o'er us,
3. might I catch that lin-net, My heart,—my hope are in it! O heav'n it-self, I'd win it,

Dr. Joyce has kindly supplied me with the above air, the name of which is *An Smachtoan Crón*, or, "The brown little mallet," meaning a piece of tobacco shaped like the head of a mallet. *Smachtoan Crón* was applied to a stout description of tobacco smuggled into Ireland about the middle of last century and in which an extensive traffic was carried on in Munster.

1. Up the heath - er glen.
2. Up the heath - er glen. Sing O! the blooming heath-er, O! the heath - er glen, Where
3. Up the heath - er glen.

fair - est fair - ies gath-er To lure in mor - tal men; I nev - er can pass by it, I

nev - er dar' go nigh it, My heart it won't be qui - et, Up the heath - er glen.

A poor setting of the tune is given in the second edition of O'Daly's *Poets and Poetry of Munster*, 1850, as "The brown little mallet." The air is merely a version of "Hoche, my Jocky" in Holden's Collection, vol. ii., 1806, to which Moore wrote his song "Drink to her who long hath waked the poet's sigh" for the third number of the *Melodies*, 1810. I am indebted to Dr. Sigerson for kindly allowing me to print his beautiful song.

There came to the beach.

THE EXILE OF ERIN.

Thomas Campbell.

Andante molto espressivo.

Voice.

1. There came to the beach a poor
2. Sad is my fate! (said the
3. E - rin, my coun - try! tho'
4. Yet all its sad re - col-

Piano.

poco rit.

p

con Ped.

1. ex - ile of E - rin, The dew on his thin robes was hea - vy and chill; For his
2. heart-brok-en stran - ger,) The wild deer and wolf to a co - vert can flee; But
3. sad and for - sak - en, In dreams I re - vi - sit thy sea - beat-en shore; But a
4. - lec - tion sup - press - ing,— One dy - ing wish my lone bo - som can draw;

1. coun - try he sigh'd, when at twi - light re - pair - ing, To wan-der a - lone by the
2. I have no re - fuge from fam - ine and dan - ger, A home and a coun - try re-
3. -las! in a far for - eign land I a - wak - en, And sigh for the friends who can
4. E - rin! an ex - ile be - queaths thee his bless - ing:— Land of my fore - fa-thers,

Air: Savourneen Deelish. Versions are in the following works: "Farewell, ye groves" in Shield's opera, *The Poor Soldier*, 1783; "Erin go Bragh" in O'Farrell's *National Irish Music*, c. 1797–1800; "Savournah Delish" ("Oh! the moment was sad") in Arnold's opera, *The Surrender of Calais*, 1791, and in Attam's *Musical Repository*, 1799; "Savournah Deelish" in Gow's Collection,

1. wind - beat - en hill; But the day - star at-tract - ed his eye's sad de - vo - tion, For it
2. -main not to me: Nev - er a - gain in the green sun - ny bowers Where my
3. meet me no more. Oh, cru - el fate! wilt thou nev - er re - place me In a
4. E - rin go bragh! Bu - ried and cold, when my heart stills her mo - tion,

1. rose .. o'er his own na - tive isle of the o - cean, Where once, in the fire of his
2. fore - fa -thers liv'd, shall I spend the sweet hours, Or cov - er my harp with the
3. man - sion of peace when no per - ils can chase me? Nev - er a - gain shall my
4. Green be thy fields, sweet-est isle of the o - cean! And thy harp - strik-ing bards sing a -

1. youth - ful e - mo - tion, He sang the bold an - them of E - rin go bragh!
2. wild - wov -en bow - ers, And strike to the num - bers of E - rin go bragh!
3. bro - thers em - brace me? They died to de - fend me, or live to de - plore!
4. -loud with de - vo - tion, - E - rin ma vour - neen, E - rin go bragh!

vol. iv., 1806, Holden's Collection, 1806, Murphy's Collection, 1809, etc. Campbell's song, which was written in Hamburg in 1801, is set to "Savourneen Deelish" in Elouis' Collection, vol. i, 1805, and also to a curious version of the air, in Bunting's second Collection, 1809; in the last named volume the air is designated Bladh na seada, or, "Thou blooming treasure." Moore wrote his song "'Tis gone and for ever," to "Savourneen Deelish"; it was published in the sixth number of the Melodies, 1815.

There is a gentle gleam.

Samuel Lover.

1. There
2. There
3. There are

1. is a gen-tle gleam, when the dawn is nigh, That sheds a ten-der light in the
2. is a blush-ing bud on the spring-tide bough That tells of com-ing fruit, tho' 'tis
3. mem-'ries of the past which we all love well, The pre-sent rings its chime like a

1. east - ern sky: When we see that light, we know That the
2. fruit - less now; So the blush I love to trace O'er the
3. sil - ver bell, But the fu - ture all un-known Has a

1. noon - tide soon will glow, Oh! such the light I know that's in my true love's eye.
2. beau - ty of that face Tells that love will come a - pace as I breathe my vow.
3. mu - sic of its own For the pro - mise of its tone can all ex - cel.

This air with Lover's song was published in the series of songs entitled "Irish Evenings," issued by Duff and Hodgson about 1846.

There is not in the wide world.

THE MEETING OF THE WATERS.

Thomas Moore.

Andante.

VOICE.

PIANO.

p con espress. *poco rit.* *p*

Ped. con Ped.

1. There is not in the wide world a
2. It was not that na -ture had
3. 'Twas that friends, the be - lov'd of my
4. Sweet Vale of A - vo - ca! how

1. val - ley so sweet, As that vale in whose bo - som the bright wa - ters meet; Oh! the
2. shed o'er the scene Her pur - est of crys - tal and bright-est of green: 'Twas
3. bo - som, were there, Who made ev' - ry dear scene of en - chant-ment more dear, And who
4. calm could I rest In thy bo - som of shade, with the friends I love best,   Where the

1. last rays of feel - ing and life must de - part, Ere the bloom of that val - ley shall
2. not her soft ma - gic of stream-let or hill; Oh! no, it was something more
3. felt how the best charms of na - ture im -prove, When we see them re - flect - ed from
4. storm that we feel in this cold world should cease, And our hearts, like thy wa - ters, be

ten. *rit.*

1. fade from my heart, Ere the bloom of that val - ley shall fade from my heart.
2. ex - quis - ite still, Oh! no, it was some-thing more ex - quis - ite still.
3. looks that we love, When we see them re - flect - ed from looks that we love.
4. min-gled in peace, And our hearts like thy wa - ters, be min-gled in peace.

rit.

For note to this song see Appendix.

There's a beech=tree grove by the river=side.

NELLY, MY LOVE, AND ME.

P. W. Joyce, LL.D., M.R.I.A.

Moderato.

Voice.

1. There's a
2. There's a
3. Be -
4. And I

Piano.

p

1. beech - tree grove by the riv - er - side, Sweet scent - ed with new - mown
2. sweet lit - tle cot - tage hard by the grove As white as the driv - en
3. -side the cot - tage my gar - den blooms, With a hedge of sweet briar all
4. love my Nel - ly with all my heart Much bet - ter than I can

p

1. hay,. . . And two young peo - ple that I know well Come and
2. snow;. . . And round the win - dows and up the wall Sweet
3. round;. . . You nev - er could think of a sin - gle flow - er That
4. tell;. . . And I know by her eyes when she looks at me That she

Both air and words are from Dr. Joyce's *Ancient Irish Music*, 1873. Regarding the tune the author remarks: "For this air I am indebted to Mr. Charles Morris, of Enniskillen Model School, who heard it sung, and noted it down, in the neighbourhood of that town. I was so impressed with its graceful and playful beauty, that I could not resist the temptation of writing a song for it."

1. meet there ev' - ry day; . . . . They're the hap - pi - est cou - ple that
2. pea and ros - es grow; . . . . 'Tis neat and co - sy with-
3. in it can - not be found. . . . . And the flow'rs are laugh - ing like
4. loves me quite as well. . . . . There's no one at all like my

1. ev - er were born, As you may plain - ly see; And if
2. -in and with - out, As you may plain - ly see; And that
3. me for joy, As you may plain - ly see; For I
4. dar - ling Nel - ly, As you may plain - ly see; We're to be

1. ev - er you wish to know their names, 'Tis Nel - ly, my love, and me. . . .
2. pret - ty cot - tage my fa - ther built For Nel - ly, my love, and me. . . .
3. plant - ed them all with my own two hands, For Nel - ly, my love, and me. . . .
4. mar - ried to - mor - row morn - - ing, Nel - ly, my love, and me. . . .

There's a colleen fair as May.

Verses translated from the Irish by Dr. PETRIE.

VOICE.

Andante.

1. There's a col - leen fair as May, For a
2. O thou blooming milk-white dove, To

PIANO.

p

con Ped.

1. year and for a day, I have sought by ev'-ry way Her heart to gain. There's no
2. whom I've giv'n true love, Do not ev - er thus re-prove My con-stan - cy. There are

1. art of tongue or eye Fond youths with maidens try, But I've tried with ceaseless sigh, Yet tried in
2. maidens would be mine, With wealth in land and kine, If my heart would but in-cline To turn from

Air: "The Pearl of the White Breast." "For this beautiful melody and its accompanying words I have great pleasure in acknowledging myself indebted to the kindness of my valued friend, Mr. Eugene Curry. . . . The melody is given exactly as noted from Mr. Curry's singing of it, and as he learnt it from the singing of his father in his native home, upon the ocean beaten cliffs of the southern extremity of the lands of the *Dal Cais*" (Petrie Collection, p. 9). Bunting's tune bearing the same title in

1. vain.   If to France or far-off Spain   She'd cross the wa-t'ry main,   To
2. thee.   But a kiss with wel-come bland,   And touch of thy fair hand,   Are

1. see her face a-gain—The seas I'd brave.   And if 'tis heav'n's de-cree   That
2. all that I de-mand—Would'st thou not spurn.   For if not mine, dear girl,   Oh,

poco rit.

1. mine she may not be,   May the Son of Ma-ry me—In mer-cy save.
2. Snow-y-breast-ed Pearl! May I nev-er from the Fair—With life re-turn.

poco rit.

Irish, and translated by him as "The Snowy-breasted Pearl" in his *Ancient Irish Music*, 1796, has nothing in common with the above air; regarding it Petrie remarks: "It is of a rhythm, time and general construction so different, that it could never have been united with the words of the old song; it is very probably misnamed, as many of the airs in Bunting's Collections often are." The song is a translation by Petrie of the Irish verses associated with the air, which were also supplied by Mr. Curry.

This rock that overhangs the foam.

JOSEPH FITZGERALD.

As "The Foggy Dew" this air is printed in Bunting's third Collection, 1840. I have taken the verses from Horncastle's *Music of Ireland*, 1844, where they are set to Bunting's air. In his interesting collection of *Traditional Tunes* (Oxford, 1891) Mr. Frank Kidson gives a tune entitled "The Foggy Dew" taken from a MS. book of tunes for the violin noted down by a Yorkshire

1. flow. Oh! tear - less I dwell on this wild steep, O'er -
2. more. My fa - thers sleep, their sor - rows past, While
3. chains. Like the ro - sy wreath which sun - set links, At

1. look - ing that vast sea, And think the tears of
2. I a - lone re - main, Like the last cold link that
3. ev' - ning o'er the sea, Thus when my part - ing

1. all who weep Can bring no tears for me.
2. breaks at last Of Sor - row's i - ron chain.
3. spi - rit sinks, Then hope may smile for me.

performer about 1825; but Mr. Kidson's air is in the major mode and unlike the one given above. I have seen an old broadside in the British Museum Library entitled "The Foggy Dew," printed by T. Birt, Seven Dials, London, beginning "When I was a batchelor, early and young." It is interesting to note that this ballad suits the rhythm of Bunting's air.

T

Tho' dark are our sorrows.

THOMAS MOORE.

1. dark are our sor - rows, to - day we'll for - get them, And smile thro' our tears, like a
2. tempt on the min - ion who calls you dis - loy - al! Tho' fierce to your foe, to your
3. loves the Green Isle and his love is re - cord - ed In hearts which have suf - fer'd too

1. sun - beam in show'rs; There nev - er were hearts, if our rul - ers would let them, More
2. friends you are true; The tri - bute most high to a heart that is roy - al Is
3. much to for - get; And hope shall be crown'd and at - tach - ment re - ward - ed, And

1. form'd to be grate - ful and blest than ours! But, just when the chain Has
2. love from a heart that loves li - ber - ty too. While cow - ards, who blight Your
3. E - rin's gay ju - bi - lee shine out yet. The gem may be broke By

Dr. Petrie alludes to this air, "St. Patrick's Day," as being in Playford's *Dancing Master*. If this is so, it must be in one of the editions of that work which I have not seen. "St. Patrick's Day" seems to have been a favourite in England during last century and we find it in many works. It is sufficient to say that in 1748 Rutherford printed it in his 200 *Country Dances*, vol. i., and that it was introduced into Bickerstaffe's opera called *Love in a Village*, 1762. Moore's song was written for the fourth number of the *Melodies*, 1811.

1. ceased to pain, And hope has en-wreath'd it round with flow'rs, There
2. fame, your right, Would shrink from the blaze of the bat - tle ar - ray, The
3. ma - ny a stroke, But no - thing can cloud its na - tive ray, Each

cres.   *mf*

1. comes a new link, Our spi - rits to sink!— Oh! the joy that we taste, like the
2. stan-dard of green In front would be seen!— Oh! my life on your faith! were you
3. frag-ment will cast A light to the last!— And thus E - rin, my coun - try, tho'

cres.   *mf*

f

1. light of the poles, Is a flash a-mid dark-ness, too bril - liant to stay; But
2. sum-mon'd this min - ute, You'd cast ev' - ry bit - ter re - membrance a - way, And
3. bro - ken thou art, There's a lus - tre with - in thee that ne'er will de - cay, A

1. tho' 'twere the last lit - tle spark in our souls, We must light it up now, on our Prin-ce's Day.
2. show what the arm of old E - rin has in it When roused by the foe, on her Prin-ce's Day.
3. spi - rit which beams thro' each suf - fer-ing part, And now smiles at all pain on the Prin-ce's Day.

f

T 2

Tho' the last glimpse of Erin.

THOMAS MOORE.

Andante con espressione.

VOICE.

1. Tho' the last glimpse of
2. To the gloom of some
3. And I'll gaze on thy

1. E - rin with sor - row I see, Yet wher - ev - - - er thou
2. de - sert, or cold rock - y shore, Where the eye . . . of the
3. gold hair as grace - ful it wreathes, And hang . . . o'er thy

PIANO.

Air: "The Coolun." The following is Professor Stanford's note to the above melody in his edition of Moore's *Melodies* restored: "This beautiful air has been mercilessly altered and spoilt by Moore. I have restored Bunting's version." I am glad to be able to prove that Professor Stanford's statement is incorrect. Moore printed his song with the air in the first number of the *Melodies*, 1807. "The Coolun" appeared in the following works prior to that date, and a reference to any of them will show the reader that Tom Moore's version is not only correct and unaltered, but that in substituting Bunting's air, which, by the way, was not published until 1840, and in appending the note which I have quoted, Professor Stanford is unjust to the memory of the poet. Walker's *Irish Bards*, 1786, air x.; Urban's *Scots Songs*, vol. ii., 1804; Aird's Collection, vol. v., 1797; Adam's *Musical Repository*, 1799; McGoun's *Repository*, c. 1803; Mulhollan's *Irish Tunes*, 1804; Owenson's *Hibernian Melodies*, 1805; Holden's Collection, vol. i., 1806, etc. An examination of these works will show that although slight variations of the grace-notes occur, the air itself practically remains the same. Shield also made use of "The Coolun" in the opera, *The Mountains of Wicklow*, 1798. Dr. Petrie noted down a melody which he called "The Old Coolun," (see Hoffmann's Collection, p. 88), but it has nothing in common with Bunting's hybrid tune. Mr. C. F. Cronin of Limerick has kindly forwarded me the following interesting communication:—The origin, authorship, and original name of this world-famed melody are unknown. Neither the Act of 29 Edward I., A.D. 1295, quoted by Lynch ("The Dublin Penny Journal" for April 13, 1833, nor that of 28 Henry VIII., A.D. 1589, quoted by Walker ("Historical Memoirs of the Irish Bards," 1786, p. 131,) on the fanciful authority of Beauford, had any connection whatever with its origin. The "Culan," mentioned in Lynch's memoir, is certainly not its original name; nor is there the slightest foundation in fact for that writer's beautiful story of the bard, the virgin and her lover,—a story manifestly borrowed from Walker and *fabricated* by his friend Beauford. Not less unwarranted and misleading is the latter's audacious interpolation of the word "Coolun" after that of "Glibbes." It is not mentioned, nor even implied, in the Act of Henry VIII., which was directed against the wearing of the "Glibbes" only—then, and for long afterwards, the popular hair-fashion among the natives. This tune (according to O'Curry) was only called "The Coolin" about a hundred years ago *for the first time*, and then only in reference to Irish words (see Dr. Douglas Hyde's "Love Songs of Connacht," 1893, pp. 70, 71) written to it by Father Oliver O'Hanley, a Gaelic poet of that period (*circa* 1700-1750), in praise of a beauty of the county of Limerick of the name of Nelly O'Grady. The title, "The Coolin," is a corruption of the Gaelic original, *i.e.*, "An Chuilfhionn" (*pronounced* "Cooleen" or "Coolin"), meaning "the maiden of fair flowing locks."

poco cres.

1. art   shall   seem   E - rin   to   me;   In   ex - ile   thy
2. stran - ger   can   haunt   us   no   more,   I   will   fly   with   my
3. soft   harp,   as   wild - ly   it   breathes;   Nor   dread   that   the

poco cres.

p

1. bo - som   shall   still   be   my   home,   And   thine
2. Cou - lin,   and   think   the   rough   wind   Less
3. cold - - heart - ed   Sax - on   will   tear   One

p

poco rit.

1. eyes . . . make my cli - mate wher - ev - er we roam.
2. rude . . . than the foes we leave frown - ing be - hind.
3. chord . . . from that harp, or one lock . . . from that hair

poco rit.

Tho' dark fate hath 'reft me.

FAREWELL.

J. J. Callanan.

VOICE.

Andantino.

p

1. Tho' dark fate hath
2. How sad were the
3. But why should I

PIANO.

p

p

con Ped.

1. 'reft me Of all that was sweet, And wide - ly we sev - er, Too
2. glan - ces At part - ing we threw, No word was there spok - en, But the
3. dwell thus On scenes that but pain, Or think on thee, Ma - ry, When

1. wide - ly to meet, Oh! yet, while one life -pulse Re - mains in this
2. sti - fled a - - dieu: My lips o'er thy cold cheek All rap - ture - less
3. think - ing is vain? Thy name to this bo - som Now sounds like a

1. heart, 'Twill re - mem - ber thee, Ma - ry, Wher - ev - er thou art. . .
2. passed, 'Twas the first time I press'd it, It must be the last. . .
3. knell; My fond one, my dear one, For ev - er, Fare - well!. . .

f

This air, entitled "Kitty O'Hara," is from the *Ancient Music of Ireland*, 1840; Bunting obtained it at Castlebar in 1802.

Thou bidst me sing.

Thomas Moore.

1. bidst me sing the lay I sung to thee, In o - ther days, ere joy had left this
2. rose thou wear'st to - night is still the same We saw this morn - ing on its stem so
3. first that mu - sic touch'd thy heart and mine, How many a joy and pain o'er both have

1. brow; But think, tho' still unchanged the notes may be, How
2. gay; But, ah! that dew of dawn, that breath which came, Like
3. past,— The joy, a light too pre - cious long to shine, The

1. dif - rent feels the heart that breathes there now.
2. life o'er all its leaves, hath pass'd a - way.
3. pain, a cloud whose sha - dows al - ways last.

This melody was obtained by Bunting in 1799 from a gentleman in Belfast, and as "I am a poor rambling boy," he published it in the *Ancient Music of Ireland*, 1840.

Though full as 'twill hold of gold.

THE RED-HAIR'D MAN'S WIFE.

KATHARINE TYNAN.

1. Though full as 'twill hold of gold the har - vest has smil'd, I'll ne'er have re - lief from grief . . . . for that
2. That fond va - len - tine of mine a let - - ter I sent, That I'd soon sail with store ga - - lore . . . . to
3. Oh, child and sweet - heart, their art had you but with - stood Till I had come home o'er foam . . for our

Bunting prints this air as "Red Man's Wife" in his third Collection; it was obtained from Dr. Petrie in 1839. There are several airs known as *Bean an fhir ruaidh*, or "The red-hair'd man's wife," Bunting's "O Molly dear" being one of them. Holden gives an air in minor as "The Red Man's Wife," and a florid version of the air adopted here is included in O'Daly's *Poets and Poetry of Munster*, 1849. In the last mentioned work one stanza of the old song is given, of which the following is a translation:—

> I spent nine months in prison fettered and bound,
> My body chained round and bolted secure with locks.
> I gave a dart like the swan on the lake
> In hopes to sit down beside the red-hair'd man's wife.

I may mention that Mrs. Hinkson's beautiful song was first adapted to the air by Mr. A. P. Graves, in whose *Irish Song Book* it is printed.

1. fond grey - eyed child, Whom kin - dred most cru - el, poor
2. wed her ere Lent. Her friends stole the note . . . I
3. great joy and good, I had not now to go, . . . un - der

1. jew - el, in - to love - less wed-ded life, With an - guish be it
2. wrote, and far worse than with knife, Have slain my bright
3. woe . . . o'er the salt sea's strife, A wan - d'rer to

1. told, have sold to be the Red - hair'd Man's wife. . . .
2. pearl for a churl: . . . . she's the Red - hair'd Man's wife. . . .
3. France from the glance . . . . of the Red - hair'd Man's wife. . .

Thy welcome, O'Leary.

1. wel - come, O' - Lea - ry, be joy - ous and high As the dwell - ing of fair - y can
2. har - per and po - et we'll place high thy seat, O' - Lea - ry, we owe it to

1. e - cho re - ply, The Ba - ra - boo's wild - ness is meet for the fray, The
2. pi - per so sweet; The clar - seach is meet - er for bow - er and hall, But thy

From Horncastle's *Music of Ireland*, 1844. The air is named "Contented am I," and to it Davis wrote his song "The Battle-eve of the Brigade," published in the *Spirit of the Nation*, 1846. But a slight examination proves it to be merely one of the many versions of the air known in Ireland as "Drunk at night and dry in the morning" (O'Farrell's *National Irish Music*), and in Scotland as "Whistle and I'll come to ye, my lad." The Scottish claim for the tune is based upon the authority of Robert Burns,

1. cro - tal's soft mild - ness for fes - ti - val gay. The clar-seach and cro - tal and
2. chant - er sounds sweet - er, far sweet - er than all, And fai - ries are braid - ing, such

1. loud Ba - ra - boo Shall sound not a note till we've mu - sic from you, The
2. fav' - rite art thou, Fresh lau - rels un - fad - ing to cir - cle thy brow, The

1. clar-seach and cro - tal and loud Ba - ra - boo Shall sound not a note till we've mu - sic from you.
2. fai - ries are braid - ing, such fav'- rite art thou, Fresh lau - rels un - fad - ing to cir - cle thy brow.

who asserted that it was composed by John Bruce, a Dumfries fiddler of the first half of last century. Burns stated that Bruce always claimed the air, and that the old musical folk of Dumfries believed him to be the author of it. It is difficult to decide whether to believe or disbelieve this tradition. The tune was used in *The Poor Soldier*, 1783, and in this work it is generally supposed to have first appeared in print. But this is a mistake : it was adapted to a ballad and issued in sheet form fully ten years prior to Shield's opera, with the following title, *The Irish Lover's Morning Walk*. *The Music an original Irish Tune.*

'Tis believed that this harp.

THE ORIGIN OF THE HARP.

Thomas Moore.

Moderato.

VOICE.

mp

1. 'Tis be -
2. But she
3. Still her
4. Hence it

PIANO.

mf

poco rit.

1. -liev'd that this harp which I wake now for thee, Was a sy - ren of
2. lov'd him in vain, for he left her to weep, And in tears all the
3. bo - som rose fair— still her cheeks smil'd the same—While her sea beau-ties
4. came that this soft harp so long hath been known To min - gle love's

mp

1. old who sang un - der the sea; And who of - ten at eve thro' the
2. night her gold tress - es to steep; Till heav'n look'd with pi - ty on
3. grace - ful - ly form'd the light frame; And her hair as lot loose o'er her
4. lan - guage with sor - row's sad tone; Till *thou* didst di - vide them and

1. bright wa - ters rov'd To meet on the green shore a youth whom she lov'd.
2. true love so warm, And chang'd to this soft harp the sea - maid - en's form.
3. white arm it fell, Was chang'd to bright chords ut - t'ring me - lo - dy's spell.
4. teach the fond lay To speak love when I'm near thee, and grief when a - way!

p

rit.

p

rit.

Air "Gage Fane," from Holden's Collection, vol. ii., 1806; Moore's song was written for the third number of the *Melodies*, 1810. The tune "The Wild Geese," which Bunting obtained from Quin the harper in 1803 and published in his third Collection, 1840, is merely a variated version of "Gage Fane." The oldest form of the air which I have been able to find in print is in minor, and in that somewhat rare work entitled *A Favourite Collection of Scots Tunes. By the Late Mr. Chs. McLean.* This volume is undated, but through the kindness of Mr. John Glen, who showed me an advertisement of the book in a contemporary Edinburgh paper, I am enabled to fix the date of its issue as being June, 1772. McLean calls the air "Old Ireland, Rejoice."

'Tis pretty to be in Ballinderry.

As "Ballinderry and Chorus" this pretty little melody, with the verses, was first printed in Edward Bunting's Collection, 1840; it was obtained from Dr. Crawford, Lisburn, in 1808. Bunting attaches much importance to this air, "which, although now sung to English words in the counties of Down and Antrim, bears unequivocal marks of high antiquity, and at the same time possesses the extraordinary peculiarity of a very nearly regular bass, called the *Cronan*, running concurrently with the melody through the entire composition." (*Anc. Mus. of Ireland*, 1840, p. 8.)

'Tis pretty to see the girl of Dunbwy.

THE GIRL OF DUNBWY.

THOMAS DAVIS.

1. 'Tis pret - ty to see the girl of Dun - bwy,
2. But pale as her cheek is, there's fruit on her lip, Her
3. I saw her but once, and I look'd in her eye, She
4. I nev - er can think on Ban - try's bright hills, Her

1. Step - ping the moun - tain state - li - ly; Tho' rag - ged her gown, and
2. teeth flash as white as the cres-cent moon's tip, Her form and her step like the
3. knew that I wor-shipped in pass - ing her by; The saint of the way - side, she
4. im - age starts up, and my long - ing eye fills; I whis - per her soft - ly, "A -

1. na - ked her feet, No la - dy in Ire - land to match her is meet.
2. reed-deer's go past, As light - some, as love - ly, as haugh - ty, as fast.
3. grant - ed my pray'r, Tho' we spoke not a word, for her mo - ther was there.
4. gain, love, we'll meet: And I'll live in your bo - som and lie at your feet."

As *Cossolohe Oir* this air was printed in Bunting's two collections of Irish melodies of 1796 and 1809. In the first book Bunting incorrectly translated the Irish name as "The Blossom of the Raspberry"; in the second this error is rectified and the English title given as "The Captivating Youth." A more florid version of the air is to be seen in Mulholland's *Ancient Irish Airs, Belfast*, 1810. Davis's song was published in the *Spirit of the Nation*, 1845.

'Tis the last rose of summer.

Andante espressivo.

THOMAS MOORE.

PIANO.

p

rit.

con Ped.

p

sempre con Ped.

1. 'Tis the last rose of sum-mer, Left bloom - ing a - lone; All her love - ly com -
2. I'll not leave thee, thou lone one, To pine . . on the stem; Since the love - ly are
3. So soon may I fol - low When friend - ships de - cay ; And from Love's shin-ing

1. - pan - ions Are fad - ed and gone; No flow'r of her kin - dred, No
2. sleep - ing, Go, . sleep thou with them. Thus kind - ly I scat - ter Thy
3. cir - cle The gems drop a - way! When true hearts lie with - er'd, And

p

rit.

1. rose- bud is nigh . . To re - flect back her blush-es, To give sigh for sigh.
2. leaves o'er the bed, . . Where thy mates . . of the gar-den Lie scent - less and dead.
3. fond ones are flown, . Oh! who would in - hab - it This bleak world a - lone?

p

rit.

* This note is E♭ in Moore's version of the air ; as it is so obviously wrong and sounds so commonplace, I have retained the D♭.

The following are the various versions of this celebrated air. "The Young Man's Dream," in Bunting's *Ancient Irish Music*, 1796, p. 10 ; "The Groves of Blarney," in Holden's *Old Established Irish Tunes*, vol. i., 1806, p. 14 ; "Castle Hyde," in Fitzsimon's *Irish Minstrelsy*, 1814, p. 41, and R. A. Smith's *Irish Minstrel*, 1825, p. 10. *Bodhran an Eassan*, or, "The Cottage adjoining the Fall," in Captain Fraser's *Airs Peculiar to the Highlands of Scotland*, 1815, p. 80 ; "Groves of Blarney" and "Anonymous Air" in George Thomson's *Original Irish Airs*, vol. ii., 1816, pp. 50 and 90 ; "The Last Rose of Summer" in Moore's *Melodies*, no. v., Dec., 1813, p. 15. Of these versions "The Young Man's Dream" (see Appendix, No. XXVI.) is considered by Petrie and others to be the oldest ; Fraser's air, which greatly resembles it, was obtained by the captain's father in the Scottish Highlands. It is highly improbable that the present beautiful variation of the old Irish tune was wholly composed by either Moore or Stevenson, although we find the poet stating in a letter of January, 1831, to James Power, that he had made some alterations in it. George Thomson's settings may be cited as examples of the evolutionary state of the air between Holden's "Groves of Blarney" and "The Last Rose of Summer" ; it must not be forgotten, however, that Thomson's airs were published subsequent to the appearance of the fifth number of the *Melodies*, and it is impossible to decide whether they were influenced in any way by Moore's setting or not.

To dhrink wid the Divil, though may be hilarious.

Spiritoso.

VOICE.

PIANO.

1. To dhrink wid the Div - il, tho'
2. The Ould Bhoy had stat - ed how
3. "And if there is thruth in the
4. Och, had the Fiend chos - en to
5. But as they the top of the

1. may be hi - lar - i - ous, Must be re - gard - ed as some - what pre - car - i - ous,
2. well he was trayt - ed, 'Twas quite a mis - take to sup - pose he was hat - ed, And
3. pop - u - lar say - in' That prints prove love, then there's no use de - lay - in' To
4. make a se - lec - tion Of all that was of - fer'd from ev' - ry di - rec - tion, His
5. road were ap - proach - in' (The sub - ject of whis - key both think - in' of broach - in'), They

1. Bet - tin' wid him is a sin more ne - far - i - ous, Yet 'tis what Tom the Col-
2. wag - gin' his tail with an air so con - sayt - ed, Said, "Faith, I be - lieve they pre-
3. set - tle the wa - ger by all that we lay in Our wal - lets from here to the
4. bag had gone fill'd with a pur - ty col - lec - tion Of wives and re - la - tions and
5. sud - den - ly heard a voice, loud and re - proach - in', Say, "Div - il take Tom, the col-

I am indebted to my friend Mr. Frank Kidson for kindly drawing my attention to the fact that this air, which has lately gained much popularity owing to Mr. A. P. Graves' inimitable song, "Father O'Flynn," being sung to it, was popular in England as a country-dance tune during the latter half of last century, and that it occurs in the following works under the title of "The Yorkshire Lasses." A country-dance book without title in the British Museum, which Mr. Kidson considers to be one of Skillern's yearly dance books, probably for 1779. (See Appendix, No. XXVII.) One of a series of country-dances printed on single cards with directions to each dance: probably issued by Longman and Broderip between 1770 and 1780. (See Appendix, No. XXVIII.) Longman and Broderip's Collection of 200 Favourite Country Dances, vol. ii., published before 1781. Skillern's Two Hundred and Four Reels and Country Dances, this last mentioned collection is a later edition of a book with the same title, which consisted of dances from 1768 to 1775 published by Straight and Skillern; the later edition bears dates up to

1. -lec - tor did do. "Twas o - ver a bowl of pour - ty po - theen. And
2. -fer me to you." "Och, div - il a bit, thin," said Tom, get - tin' red, "You're
3. top of the road. But one con - di - tion be - fore we start. All
4. all sorts of baste. Shure, much to the Div - il that av'n - ing was sent, For
5. -lect - in' spal - peen!" The Ould Bhoy open - ed his bag in de - light, And

cres.

1. not ve - ry far from a cer - tain she - been, That Tom and the Di - vil were
2. spa - kin' on - truth, I will wa - ger my head." "Och, sure!" said the Di - vil." you're
3. gifts that come not di - rect from the heart, Tho' vex - in' to lose them, we
4. cur - sin' is ai - sy and of - ten well meant, But Nick would have none of them,
5. slip - pin' Tom in - to it, tied it up tight; And then the Ould Di - vil went

cres.   *f* >

1. hav - ing a swi - vel, And lay - in' a wa - ger that Tom would soon rue.
2. head is a thri - fle, But yet I'll say 'Done!' to be ay - ven wid you,
3. still must re - fuse them, With love - gifts or no - thin' our bags we must load."
4. sent the whole run of them Back to their own - ers in dou - ble - quick haste.
5. off for a swi - vel, And Tom the Col - lec - tor was nev - er more seen.

1780, and the "Yorkshire Lasses" seems to be among the dances for 1779. The earliest printed version of the air directly connected with Ireland which I have been able to find is in Holden's *Masonic Songs, Dublin, 1795* (see Appendix, No. XXVIII.); here the Irish flavour becomes more distinct. The setting adopted above is from Dr. Joyce's Collection, 1873, where it is entitled "The Top of Cork Road"; but it is extremely improbable that this is the original name of the tune. The second strain in Dr. Joyce's version is practically the same as that of a tune printed in Aird's *Selection*, vol. i., 1782, as "The Irish Lilt". It is impossible to decide whether "The Yorkshire Lasses" is a composition in the style of the Irish air by some English musician, or whether it is a genuine Irish air: it is certainly not older than the period about which it appeared as a country-dance tune. For the clever and humorous verses now published for the first time, I am indebted to a writer who insists upon remaining incognito. The ballad is founded upon the well-known story of "The Collector of Bantry."

v

To ladies' eyes.

THOMAS MOORE

Poco vivace.

VOICE.

1. To
2. Some
3. In

PIANO.

mf

p

1. la - dies' eyes a round, boy, We can't re - fuse, we can't re - fuse; Tho'
2. looks there are so ho - - ly, They seem but giv'n, they seem but giv'n, As
3. some, as in a mir - - ror, Love seems por-tray'd, Love seems por-tray'd; But

1. bright eyes so a - bound, boy, 'Tis hard to choose, 'tis hard to choose, For
2. splen - did bea - cons sole - - ly, To light to heav'n, to light to heav'n! While
3. shun the flat-t'ring er - - ror, 'Tis but his shade, 'tis but his shade, Him -

AIR: *Fágan Bealach* (*Faí an Bealach*, or "Clear the Way"). Although the above song was first published in the seventh number of the *Melodies*, 1818, we find on p. 54 of the *Letters of Thomas Moore to his music publisher, James Power, New York*, 1854, that as early as Sept. 1816, Moore writes, "I send you the two I promised; I have a good many more verses to 'Ladies' Eyes.' What is the real name of the tune?" *Fágan a Bailagh* bears considerable resemblance to the Scotch "Highland Laddie," a version of which is printed in Playford's *Dancing-Master*, 11th edition, 1701, as "Cockle Shells." In Lynch's *Melodies of Ireland* the tune is called "Kiss me, Lady." *Faj an Bealach* was the war-cry of the clans of Connaught and Munster.

1. thick as stars that light - en You air - y bow'rs, yon air - y bow'rs, The
2. some—oh! ne'er be - lieve them, With tempt - ing ray, with tempt - ing ray, Would
3. -self has fix'd his dwell - ing In eyes we know, in eyes we know, And

Chorus.

1. count - less eyes that bright - en This earth of ours, this earth of ours. But
2. lead us (God for - give them!) The o - ther way, the o - ther way. But
3. lips— but this is tell - ing, So here they go! so here they go! Fill

1. fill the cup wher - e'er, boy, Our choice may fall, our choice may fall, We're
2. fill the cup wher - e'er, boy, Our choice may fall, our choice may fall, We're
3. up, fill up wher - e'er, boy, Our choice may fall, our choice may fall, We're

1. sure to find Love there, boy, So drink them all! so drink them all!
2. sure to find Love there, boy, So drink them all! so drink them all!
3. sure to find Love there, boy, So drink them all! so drink them all!

u 2

'Twas early one morning.

Old ballad adapted by Dr. P. W. Joyce.

Moderato.

VOICE.

PIANO.

1. 'Twas
2. Young
3. 'Twas
4. 'Twas
5. And I

1. ear - ly	one	morn - ing	young	Wil - ly	a - rose,	And
2. Wil - ly	plung'd	in, and	he	swam the	lake round;	He
3. ear - ly	that	morn - ing	his	sis - ter	a - rose:	And
4. ear - ly	that	morn - ing	his	mo - ther	came there:	She was
5. saw a	fair	maid	stand-ing	fast by	the shore;	Her

Dr. Joyce obtained this air and one verse of the song in 1854 from the singing of a little girl of about thirteen years of age, in the county of Limerick. "In the month of September of the present year [1873] I got two complete MS. copies of the song; one from Kerry and one from Mayo; for it is well known in both the south and the west." (*Anc. Irish Music,* p. 100.) Alluding to the old ballad as he received it, Dr. Joyce mentions that although he has retained as much of the original as possible in the version given above, he has been obliged to change many of the lines and restore the rhythm where it was necessary.

1. up to his com - rade's bed - cham - ber he goes. "A
2. swain to an is - land— 'twas soft marsh - y ground: "O
3. up to her mo - ther's bed - cham - ber she goes:— "Oh! I
4. wring - ing her hands— she was tear - ing her hair, O,
5. face it was pale— she was weep - ing full sore; In deep

1. - rise, my dear com - rade, and let no one know, 'Tis a
2. com - rade, dear com - rade, do not ven - ture in, There is
3. dream'd a sad dream a - bout Wil - ly last night; He was
4. woe - ful the hour your dear Wil - ly plung'd in, There is
5. an - guish she gaz'd where young Wil - ly plung'd in:— Ah! there's

1. fine sun - ny morn - ing and a - bath - ing we'll go."
2. deep and false wa - ter in the Lake of Cool - fin!"
3. dress'd in a shroud— in a shroud of snow - white!"
4. deep and false wa - ter in the Lake of Cool - fin!
5. deep and false wa - ter in the Lake of Cool - fin!

'Twas on a windy night.

BARNEY BRALLAGHAN'S COURTSHIP.

Allegretto.

VOICE.

PIANO.

f   *p*   *f*   *p*

mf

1. 'Twas on a wind-y night At two o'-clock in the morn-ing An
2. Oh, list to what I say, It's charms you've got like Ve-nus;
3. I've got nine pigs and a sow, I've got a sty to sleep 'em; A
4. I've got an old tom cat, It's thro' one eye he's star-ing;
5. You've got a charm-ing eye, And you've some spell-ing and read-ing;
6. Then for a wife till death It's I am will-ing to take ye; But

1. Ir-ish lad so tight, All wind and wea--ther scorn-ing,
2. Own your love you may, There's on-ly the wall be-tween us;
3. calf and a brin-dled cow, And got a cab-in to keep 'em;
4. I've got a Sun-day hat, Not much the worse for wear-ing;
5. You've got, and so have I, A taste for gen--teel breed-ing.
6. och! I waste my breath, The De-v'l him-self can't wa-ken ye!

Air: "Blewitt's Jig." Regarding this air Mr. Frank Kidson writes me as follows: "The air is by Jonathan Blewitt, who, at the time of its composition, between 1811-14, was musical director of the Theatre Royal, Dublin. It was most likely first produced as a jig for stage dancing, and under the name 'Blewitt's Jig' is in *Hime's Coll ction of Country Dances for the present year, Dublin*, fol., the date of which is 1814. This is ascertained by Nos. 6 and 7 of the same collection being dated for 1810 and 1811 respectively. It must have been somewhat of a favourite in this form when Thomas Hudson, a clever London song-writer, wrote the song 'Barney Brallaghan's Courtship' to it. This was about 1825-26, and having been sung by Mr. Fitzwilliam and others at the 'Freemason's Tavern' and other convivial meetings, it was then published in sheet form with Hudson's and Blewitt's names attached, and soon after became very popular. The words of the song have been foolishly attributed to 'Father Prout,' who certainly had no hand in its creation. He, however, under the title of 'The Sabine Farmer's Serenade' produced a mock-antique Latin version of it. This, one of his 'Reliques,' was published in the first number of *Bentley's Miscellany*, Jan., 1837, and in his humorous prefatory note he refers to Hudson as the author of the 'Vulgate' version."

1. At Ju - dy Cal - lag - han's door,   Sit - ting up - on the pal - ings, His
2. You lie fast a - sleep,   Snug in bed and snor - ing,
3. Sun - day hose and coat,   An old gray mare to ride on,
4. I've got some goose-ber - ry wine—   Trees had got to ri - - per;
5. You are rich, fair and young,   As ev - 'ry - bo - dy's know - ing,
6. 'Tis just be - gin - ning to rain,   So I'll get un - der cov - er;

1. love - tale he did pour,   And this was part of his wail - ings,
2. Round the house I creep,   Your hard heart im - plor - ing.
3. Sad - dle and bri - dle to boot   Which you may ride a - stride on.
4. I've got a fid - dle fine,   That on - ly wants a pi - - er.
5. You've got a da - cent tongue   When - e'er it's set a - go - ing.
6. I'll come to - mor - row a - gain   And be your con - stant lov - - er.

f

On - - ly say   You'll have Mis - - ter Bral - lag - han,

f

Don't say nay,   charm - ing Ju - dy Cal - lag - han!

'Twas one of those dreams.

Thomas Moore.

1. 'Twas
2. The
3. He
4. Ev'n

1. one of those dreams that by mu - sic are brought Like a
2. wild notes he heard o'er the wa - ters were those To
3. lis - ten'd while, high o'er the ea - gle's rude nest, The
4. so, tho' thy mem' - - ry should now die a - way, 'Twill be

Air: "The Song of the Woods," from the ninth number of *Irish Melodies*, 1824; it is probable that this melody was one of those supplied to the poet by Crofton Croker, to which allusion is made in the preface to the seventh number of the *Melodies*.

1. bright sum - mer haze o'er the po - et's warm thought; When
2. which he had sung E - rin's bond - age and woes, And the
3. lin - ger - ing sounds on their way lov'd to rest; And the
4. caught up a - gain in some hap - pi - er day, And the

1. lost in the fu - ture his soul . . . wan-ders on, And . .
2. breath of the bu - gle now waft - ed them o'er, From . .
3. e - choes sung . . back from their full . . . moun-tain quire, As if
4. hearts and the voi - ces of E - riu pro - long Thro' the

1. all of this life, but its sweet - ness, is gone.
2. Di - na's green isle to Glen - à's wood - ed shore.
3. loth to let song so en - chant - ing ex - pire.
4. an - swer - ing fu - ture thy name and thy song.

We may roam thro' this world.

THOMAS MOORE.

Poco allegretto.

VOICE.

PIANO.

p   p poco rit.

1. We may
2. In
3. In

1. roam thro' this world like a child at a feast, Who but sips of a sweet, and then
2. Eng-land the gar-den of Beau-ty is kept By a dra-gon of pru-de-ry
3. France, when the heart of a Wo-man sets sail On the o-cean of wed-lock its

1. flies to the rest, And when plea-sure be-gins to grow dull in the east, We may
2. plac'd with-in call: But so oft this un-a-mia-ble dra-gon has slept, That the
3. for-tunes to try, Love sel-dom goes far in a ves-sel so frail, But just

poco cres.

1. or-der our wings and be off to the west. But if hearts that feel, and eyes that smile, Are the
2. garden's but care-less-ly watch'd af-ter all. Oh! they want the wild sweet-bri-ar-y fence, Which
3. pi-lots her off, and then bids her good-bye; While the daughters of E-rin keep the boy Ev-er

poco cres.

Moore's song was written for the second number of the *Melodies*, 1807, prior to which the tune "Garryowen" was printed in many collections containing Irish airs. Among these may be mentioned Gow's *Repository*, bk. ii., 1802; Holden's *Old Established Irish Airs*, vol. i., 1806; O'Farrell's *Pocket Companion*; Mackintosh's *Strathspeys, Reels, Jigs*, etc. It seems to have first come into

1. dear - est gifts that heav'n sup-plies, We nev-er need leave our own Green Isle For
2. round the flow'rs of E - rin dwells, Which warms the touch while win-ning the sense, Nor
3. smil-ing be - side his faith - ful oar, Thro' bil-lows of woe and beams of joy The

1. sen-si-tive hearts and for sun-bright eyes,
2. charms us least when it most re - pels;
3. same as he look'd when he left the shore.

Then re - member wherever your gob - let is crown'd Thro' this

world whe-ther east - ward or west-ward you roam, When a cup to the smile of dear

woman goes round, Oh! re-member the smile which a - dorns her at home.

notice through having been played in a pantomime called *Harlequin Amulet*, produced in 1800. Garryowen, which in English
means Owen's Garden, is a suburb of Limerick : an interesting account of the somewhat riotous state of matters existing there
during the latter half of last century, is given in Croker's *Popular Songs of Ireland*, 1839.

Weep no more.

SPRING SONG—TO IRELAND.

Dora Sigerson (Mrs. Clement Shorter).

Andantino.

Voice.

Piano.

p molto tranquillo.

dim.

con Ped.

p

p

1. Weep no more, heart of my heart, no more! The night has passed and the
2. Win - ter has gone with his blight - ing breath, No more to chill thee with

1. dawn is here, The cuc - koo calls from the bud - ding trees, And
2. cold or fear, The brook laughs loud in its li - ber - ty, Green

The air which I have adapted to Mrs. Shorter's charming song is from Hoffmann's *Ancient Music of Ireland*; its name is "Ballyvanchan," and I am indebted to Messrs. Pigot & Co., Dublin, for permission to print it in this work. "Weep no more" is from the volume of poems referred to on p. 48.

1. tells us that Spring is near. . . . . Sor - row no more, be -
2. buds on the hedge ap - pear. . . . . Weep no more, life of my

1. lov - ed, no more; For see, sweet em - blem of hope un - told! The
2. heart, no more! The birds are ca - rol - ling sweet and clear; The

1. tears that soft on the sham - rocks fall There turn to blos-soms of gold. .
2. warmth of Summer is in the breeze, And the Spring—the Spring is here. .

When cold in the earth.

THOMAS MOORE.

Andante molto.

VOICE.

1. When cold in the
2. From thee and thy

PIANO.

p con espress.

1. earth lies the friend thou hast lov'd, Be his faults and his fol - lies for -
2. in - no - cent beau - ty first came The re - veal - ings that taught him true

1. - got by thee then; Or, if from their slum - ber the veil be re - mov'd, Weep
2. love to a - dore, To feel the bright presence and turn him with shame From the

Thomas Duffet's song "Since Coelia's my foe," published in that author's *New Poems*, London, 1676, is marked "Song to the Irish Tune"; there is no music in this work, but in the *Lover's Opera*, 1730, we find the air designated "Since Coelia's my foe" to be the tune claimed by the Irish as "Limerick's Lament," and by the Scotch as "Lochaber no more." We may therefore fairly presume that as far back as 1676, i.e., just fifty years prior to the appearance of Ramsay's *Tea-Table Miscellany*, vol. ii., in which "Lochaber" was first printed, the air was known as an "Irish Tune." Ramsay's song and the air were published in Thomson's *Orpheus Caledonius*, vol. ii., 1733, not, as has been asserted by Stenhouse and others, in the first edition of that work in 1725. Further, Graham mentions that although the air "King James' March to Irland" in the celebrated "Leyden MS." differs from "Lochaber," it nevertheless resembles it so strongly as to point to the same family origin. A reference to this air (see Appendix, No. XXVIII.), which I have translated from the lyra-viol tablature of the "Leyden MS." will allow the reader to test for himself the accuracy of Graham's remark. The earliest printed copy of the air bearing the title "Limerick's Lamentation" which I have seen is in Daniel Wright's *Aria di Camera*. Being a choice collection of Scotch, Irish and Welsh Airs. This work is undated, but must have been issued about 1730; the version given is exceedingly good (see Appendix, No XXIX.), and is headed "Limerick's Lamentation." A much mutilated setting was also published in the twelfth edition of Playford's *Dancing Master*, 1703, as "Reeves Maggot" (Appendix, No. XXX.). A note in Bunting's handwriting which I have seen in that author's copy of Crot lis *Symmers*, mentions that the melody was sometimes call'd "Sarsfield's Lamentation." Moore's version is excellent, and in accordance with the many printed settings of the air from 1730 upward. Bunting's setting in his work of 1809 is singularly poor.

1. o'er them in si - lence and close it a - gain. And oh! if 'tis
2. i - dols he blind - ly had knelt to be - fore. O'er the waves of a

1. pain to re - mem - ber how far From the path - ways of light he was
2. life, long be - night - ed and wild, Thou canst like a soft gold - en

1. tempt - ed to roam, Be it bliss to re - mem - ber that thou wert the
2. calm o'er the sea; And if hap - pi - ness pure - ly and glow - ing - ly

1. star . . That a - rose on his dark - ness and guid - ed him home.
2. smiled On his even - ing hor - i - zon, the light was from thee.

Whene'er I see those smiling eyes.

Thomas Moore.

1. e'er I see those smil - ing eyes, All filled with hope and
2. Time will come with all its blights, The ru - ined hope, the

1. joy . . . . and light, As if no cloud could ev - er rise To
2. friend . . . un-kind, The love, that leaves wher - e'er it lights A

As "Father Quin" this air is included in Holden's *Old Established Irish Airs*, vol. ii., 1806, and again in the same author's *Periodical Irish Melodies* issued a little later. Moore's version of the air, which differs slightly from Holden's, was published with the above song in the seventh number of the *Melodies*, 1818.

1. dim a heav'n so pure - ly bright, I sigh to think how
2. chill'd or burn - ing heart . . . be - hind :— While youth, that now like

1. soon that brow In grief may lose its ev - 'ry ray, And
2. snow ap - pears, Ere sul - lied by the dark - 'ning rain, When

1. that light heart, so joy - ous now, Al - most for - get it once . . . was gay.
2. once 'tis touch'd by sor - row's tears, Will ne - ver shine so bright . . a-gain.

When first I saw sweet Peggy.

THE LOW-BACKED CAR.

SAMUEL LOVER.

Allegro vivo.

VOICE.

PIANO.

p

1. When
2. In
3. Sweet
4. I'd

1. first I saw sweet Peg - - gy, 'Twas on a mar - ket day, A
2. bat - tle's wild com - mo - - tion The proud and migh - ty Mars With
3. Peg - gy round her car, sir, Has strings of ducks and geese— But the
4. ra - ther own that car, sir, With Peg - gy by my side, Than a

1. low - back'd car she drove, and sat Up - on a truss of hay; But
2. hos - tile scythes de - mands the tithes Of death in war - like cars; While
3. scores of hearts she slaugh - ters By far out - num - bers these; While
4. coach and four, and gold ga - lore, And a la - dy for my bride; For the

mf

It is hardly necessary to remark that the above air is merely a slightly altered setting of "The Jolly Ploughman," printed in Bunting's Collection, 1840 (see p. 12). The date assigned to Lover's song in the British Museum Library is 1850, but it probably appeared a few years earlier.

1. when that hay was bloom-ing grass And deck'd with flow'rs of spring, No
2. Peg - gy, peace - ful god - dess, Has darts in her bright eye That
3. she a - mong her poul - try sits, Just like a tur - tle - dove, Well
4. la - dy would sit fore - nenst me On a cush - ion made with taste, While

1. flow'r was there that could com-pare With the bloom-ing girl I sing— As she
2. knock men down in the mar - ket town As right and left they fly:— While she
3. worth the cage, I do en - gage, Of the bloom-ing god of Love: While she
4. Peg-gy would sit be - side me with My arm a-round her waist: While we

colla voce.

1. sat in her low - back'd car, . . The man at the turn - pike bar . . . Nev-er
2. sits in her low - back'd car, . . Than Lat - tle more dangerous far, . . . For the
3. sits in her low - back'd car, . . The lov - ers come near and far. . . . And
4. drove in the low - back'd car, . . To be mar-ried by Fa - ther Maher;* . Oh, my

1. ask'd for his toll, but just rubb'd his old poll, And look'd af - ter the low-back'd car. . .
2. doc - tor's art can-not cure the heart That is hit from the low-back'd car. . .
3. en - vy the chick-en that Peg-gy is pick - ing As she sits in the low-back'd car. . .
4. heart would beat high at her glance and sigh, Tho' it beat in a low-back'd car. . .

* Pronounced Mar.

When he who adores thee.

Thomas Moore.

VOICE.

Andante.   *mf*

1. When he who a-dores thee has
2. With thee were the dreams of my

PIANO.

mf   *sf*   *rit.*   *mf*

con Ped.

1. left but the name Of his fault and his sor - row be - hind,   Oh!
2. ear - li - est love, Ev - 'ry thought of my rea - son was thine,—   In my

p

1. say, wilt thou weep when they dark - en the fame Of a life that for thee was re-
2. last hum - ble pray'r to the Spi - rit a - bove Thy name shall be min - gled with

As "The Foxes Sleep" this air is in Bunting's first Collection, 1796, in Holden's *Periodical Irish Melodies*, and in John Mulholland's *Ancient Irish Airs*, Belfast, 1810. Moore's song was printed in the *Melodies*, Bk. i., 1807. I have slightly corrected the phrasing of the air from Bunting's and Mulholland's settings.

1. - sign'd?   Yes, weep, and how-ev-er my foes may con-demn, Thy
2. mine.   Oh! blest are the lov-ers and friends who shall live The

1. tears shall ef-face their de-cree: For heav'n can witness, the'
2. days of thy glo-ry to see: But the next dear-est bless-ing that

1. guil-ty to them, I have been but too faith-ful to thee.
2. Heav-en can give Is the pride of thus dy-ing for thee.

When in death I shall calm recline.

Thomas Moore.

Allegretto.

Voice.

Piano.

mf

p

p

1. When in death I shall calm re - cline, O, bear my heart to my
2. When the light of my song is o'er, Then take my harp to your
3. Keep this cup, which is now o'er - flow - ing, To grace your re - vel when

1. mis - tress dear; Tell her it liv'd up - on smiles and wine Of the
2. an - cient hall, Hang it up at that friend - ly door Where
3. I'm at rest; Nev - er, oh! nev - er, its balm be - stow - ing On

Printed in Holden's Collection, vol. ii., 1804 as "The Bard's Legacy." Moore's song, which was evidently suggested by the title in Holden's work, was written for the second number of the *Melodies*, 1807, and a clever parody on it was introduced by H. B. Code in his play, *The Russian Sacrifice, or Burning of Moscow*, 1813; the author, however, appends a note in which he disclaims the remotest intention of derogating from the merit of the original. Captain Fraser includes the air as "How shall I

1. bright - est hue, while it lin - ger'd here. Bid her not shed one
2. wea - ry tra - vel - lers love to call. Then if some bard, who
3. lips that beau - ty hath sel - dom bless'd. But when some warm, de -

mf

1. tear of sor - row To sul - ly a heart so bril - liant and light, But
2. roams for - sa - ken, Re - vive its soft note in pass - ing a - long, Oh,
3. - vot - ed lov - er To her he a - dores shall bathe its brim, Then,

colla voce.

dim.

1. balm - y drops of the red grape bor - row, To bathe the re - lic from morn till night.
2. let one thought of its mas - ter wa - ken Your warm - est smile for the child of song.
3. then my spi - rit a - round shall hov - er, And hal - low each drop that foams for him.

f

dim.

abstain from Whiskey," in his *Airs Peculiar to the Highlands of Scotland*, 1815, with the following observation:—"The Editor has great pleasure in asserting his country's claim to this melody lately introduced as Irish, under the name of 'The Legacy,' and supposed new. Whereas it has been current in the North for sixty years as the composition of John McMurdo, of Kintail, since emigrated to America." This may be true enough, but a slight examination of the air in question will show that it is merely a pleasing version of the old Irish tune "St. Patrick's Day."

When summer comes.

DORA SIGERSON.

Andante.

VOICE.

PIANO.

1. When sum - mer
2. 'Twas such a
3. 'Twas here, I
4. O phan - tom

1. comes, then you are near to me, I feel your phan-tom pres - ence on my
2. day, as sweet a wind a - rose To kiss with per-fum'd lips your blown
3. stoop'd to pluck a droop - ing flow'r You prayed so fool - ish - ly that you might
4. love! that haunts me rest - less - ly, That from my passion-ate hands will ev - er

1. heart, In ev - 'ry wind the dead year speaks a - gain, . . . And ev - 'ry
2. hair; With brow per - plex'd and that old smile you had, . . . I won-dered
3. keep; And here you turn'd a mo-ment's space so odd, . . . I on - ly
4. fly, Fate owes me this, I will pur - sue and hold, . . . Or, find - ing

1. scene springs up to take its part.
2. what you thought of, stand - ing there.
3. laugh'd for fear that I should weep.
4. you but a sha - dow, let me die.

The air as *Domnal Og*, or, "Little Donnell," is one of these traditional airs obtained by Dr. Petrie, and published after his death by F. Hoffmann in *Ancient Music of Ireland from the Petrie Collection*, Dublin, Pigot & Co., 1876; a somewhat different version of it was printed in the Petrie Collection, 1855, as "Donnel O'Greavlh" (see p. 11). Mrs. Clement Shorter (Miss Dora Sigerson) has kindly allowed me to print her song; it is from her volume of poems entitled *Verses*, London, 1893. I am indebted to Messrs. Pigot & Co., for permission to reprint the air.

When thou art nigh.

Andante con espressione.

THOMAS MOORE.

VOICE.

PIANO.

1. When thou art nigh, It seems a new cre - a - tion round; The
2. When thou art nigh, No thought of grief comes o'er my heart; I

1. sun hath fair - er beams, The lute a soft - er sound, Tho' thee a - lone I see, And
2. on - ly think—could aught But joy be where thou art? Life seems a waste of breath When

1. hear a - lone thy sigh: 'Tis light, 'tis song to me, 'Tis all when thou art nigh.
2. far from thee I sigh; And death—aye, e - ven death, Were sweet if thou wert nigh.

Air: "'Tis a pity I don't see my Love." This graceful air was obtained by Edward Bunting from a Mrs. Fitzgerald, at Westport, in 1802, but first published in the *Ancient Music of Ireland*, 1840. In accordance with his usual belief that every so-called "traditional" tune must be old, Bunting has marked the air "Very ancient. Author and date unknown." It is possible that it is based upon some earlier melody; but in its present form the probability is that "'Tis a pity I don't see my Love" is not much older than the period in which Bunting obtained it.

When thro' life unblest we rove.

ON MUSIC.

Thomas Moore.

Andante sostenuto.

Voice.

Piano.

p leguto. *poco rit.* *con Ped.*

1. When thro' life un -
2. Like the gale that
3. Mu - sic, oh! how

1. -blest we rove, Los - ing all that made life dear,
2. sighs a - long Beds of o - ri - en - tal flow'rs,
3. faint, how weak, Lan - guage fades be - fore thy spell!

1. Should some notes we used to love In days . . . of boy - hood
2. Is the grate - ful breath of song That once . . . was heard . . . in
3. Why should Feel - ing ev - er speak When thou canst breathe . . her

Moore's song, written to "The Banks of Banna," appeared in the third number of the *Melodies*, 1810. For many years prior to that date, the air had attained great popularity, not only in Ireland, but in Scotland and England, and thus, I venture to say, was owing to the sweet little pastoral written to it by George Ogle, beginning, "Shepherds, I have lost my love." Ogle's verses are in Watson's *Musical Miscellany*, Edinburgh, 1779; the *Scots Vocal Miscellany*, Edinburgh, 1780, and, with the air, in Horsfield's *Vocal Mag.* 1775; Laurence Ding's *Favourite Songster*, 1780; *Musical Miscellany*, 1786, etc. As *Aileen, A particularly Favourite Irish*

1. meet our ear, Oh! how wel - come breathes the strain,
2. hap - pier hours; Fill'd with balm, the gale sighs on,
3. soul so well? Friend - ship's balm - y words may feign,

1. Wak'n - ing thoughts that long have slept, Kind - ling for - mer
2. Tho' the flow'rs have sunk in death; So, when plea - sure's
3. Love's are ev'n more false than they, Oh! 'tis on - ly

dim.

1. smiles a - gain . . . In fad - ed eyes . . . that long have wept.
2. dream is gone, . . Its mem - 'ry lives . . . in Mu - sic's breath.
3. Mu - sic's strain . . Can sweet - ly soothe . . and not be - tray!

dim.

Song sung by Miss Catley, both words and music were published in sheet-form by Robert Ross, the Edinburgh publisher, and although not dated, I take this sheet to be prior to any of the publications which I have quoted. Miss Catley sang in Ireland between 1763 and 1770, before which she was involved in a scandalous criminal case; she made her last public appearance in 1784, and died five years later. It is hardly necessary to point out that "The Banks of Banna," is merely an adaptation of the old air *Sin sios a rus Bonn,* or, "Down beside me," published in Daniel Wright's *Aria di Camera,* c. 1730, and many later works, and to which Moore wrote his song, "Oh, where is the slave."

While gazing on the moon's light.

THOMAS MOORE.

1. gaz - ing on the moon's light, A mo - ment from her smile I turn'd, To
2. day had sunk in dim show'rs, But mid - night now, with lus - tre meek, Il -

1. look at orbs that more bright In lone and dis - tant glo - ry burn'd: But
2. - lu - min'd all the pale flow'rs, Like hope up - on a mourn - er's cheek. I

Air: "Oonagh." Moore's song with this sweet melody was printed in the third number of the *Melodies*, 1810. Prior to that the air was included in Johnson's *Scots Musical Museum*, vol. ii., 1796, and in *The Vocal Magazine, a Selection of English, Scots, and Irish Songs*. Edinburgh, vol. ii., 1798; in both these works it is simply called "An Irish Air," and is set to Burns's song, "Sae flaxen were her ringlets." In a letter to George Thomson (Sept., 1794), Burns alludes to it as "Oonagh's Waterfall." A slightly different version of the tune is given in Abraham Mackintosh's *Collection of Strathspey Reels, Jigs, etc.*, published at Newcastle early in the century, as "A favourite Irish quick March."

1. too . . far Each proud star For me to feel its warm - ing flame; Much
2. said . . (while The moon's smile Play'd o'er a stream in dimp - ling bliss), "The

1. more dear, That mild sphere, Which near our plan - et smil - ing came: Thus,
2. moon looks On ma - ny brooks; The brook can see no moon but this." And

1. Ma - ry, be but thou mine own—While bright - er eyes un - heed - ed play, I'll
2. thus, I thought, our for - tunes run, For ma - ny a lov - er looks to thee, While

1. love these moon - light looks a - lone, That bless my home and guide my way.
2. oh! I feel there is but one, One Ma - ry in the world for me.

Why, liquor of life, do I love you so?

Translated from the Irish by JOHN D'ALTON.

1. Why, li-quor of life, do I love you so, When in all our en-coun-ters you
2. You're my soul, my trea-sure with-out and with-in, My sis-ter, my cou-sin, and
3. And ma-ny's the quar-rel and fight we've had, And ma-ny's the time you have

1. lay me low? More stu-pid and sense-less I ev'-ry day grow, What a
2. all my kin; Tis un-luck-y to wed such a pro-di-gal sin, But all
3. made me mad, But while I've a heart it can nev-er be sad While you

This air, set to D'Alton's translation, is printed in Horncastle's *Music of Ireland*, pt. iii., 1844. The original Irish song, which is attributed to Carolan, is given with D'Alton's translation in Hardiman's *Irish Minstrelsy*, vol. i., 1831; another translation by Edward Walsh is in that writer's *Irish Popular Songs*, 1847.

1. hint if I'd mend by the warn - ing! 'Tis tat - tered and torn, you've
2. oth - er en - joy - ments are vain, love, My bar - ley ricks all
3. smile at me full on the ta - ble. For sure - ly you are my

1. left my coat, I've not a cra - vat to save my throat, Yet I'll
2. turn to you, My till - age, my plough, my hor - ses too, My
3. wife and bro - ther, My on - ly child— my fa - ther and mo - ther—My

1. par - don you all, my spark - ling coat, If you'll cheer me a - gain in the
2. cows and my sheep, I have bade them a - dieu: For I care not while you re -
3. out - side coat— I have no o - ther, Och, I'll stand by you while I'm

1. morn - ing.
2. - main, love.
3. a - ble.

Widow Machree, it's no wonder you frown.

Samuel Lover.

Spiritoso.

VOICE.

PIANO.

mf cres.

1. Wi - dow Ma - chree, it's no won - der you frown, Och hone!
2. Wi - dow Ma - chree, now the win - ter's come in, Och hone!
3. Take my ad - vice, dar - ling Wi - dow Ma - chree, Och hone!

rit.   *mf cres.*

1. Wi - dow Ma - chree, Faith, it ru - ins your looks, that same dir - ty black gown,
2. Wi - dow Ma - chree, To be pok - ing the fire all a - lone is a sin,
3. Wi - dow Ma - chree, And with my ad - vice, faith, I wish you'd take me,

Samuel Lover composed both the words and music of the above song, which was first published by Duff and Hodgson, London, as No. 8 of the "Songs of Handy Andy."

1. Och hone! Wi - dow Ma - chree. How al - ter'd your air With that
2. Och hone! Wi - dow Ma - chree. Sure sho - vel and tongs To each
3. Och hone! Wi - dow Ma - chree. You'd have me to de - sire Then to

1. close cap you wear—"Tis de - stroy - ing your hair Which should be flow - ing free; Be no
2. oth - er be - longs And the ket - tle sings songs Full of fam - i - ly glee; Yet a -
3. stir up the fire, And sure Hope is no li - ar In whis - p'ring to me That the

1. lon - ger a churl Of its black silk - en curl, Och hone! Wi - dow Ma-chree.
2. -lone with your cup Like a her - mit you sup, Och hone! Wi - dow Ma-chree.
3. ghosts would de - part When you'd me next your heart, Och hone! Wi - dow Ma-chree.

Y

With cheeks as bright as roses.

SWEET KITTY MAGEE.

BASIL O'BRIEN.

Poco vivace.

VOICE.

PIANO.

mf

mf

1. With cheeks as bright as ro - ses And
2. Since then I've of - ten told her That
3. I've land and sheep and cat - tle,— I've

1. air - y steps so light and free, 'Twas com - ing from the
2. she's my love, and on - ly she, But all I get is
3. wealth,— but all is nought to me Un - til I win my

Air: "Kitty Magee," preserved in the Petrie Collection ; it was obtained from a MS. book of dance music noted down about the middle of last century. Dr. Petrie does not consider it anterior in age to that of the MS. from which it came. An entirely different tune bearing the same title is printed in Mulholland's *Ancient Irish Airs, Belfast,* 1810. In kindly supplying me with verses for the graceful melody, Mr. O'Brien has taken the original name for his subject and heroine.

1. mar - ket That first I met sweet Kit - ty Ma - gee. Such
2. laugh - ter, And sau - cy looks from Kit - ty Ma - gee. And
3. sweet - heart,— My laugh - ing, blue - ey'd Kit - ty Ma - gee. 'Twas

1. cur - ly hair of nut - brown hue, Ro - guish eyes of spark - ling blue,
2. when the lit - tle hand I press, It's "Now, be good!" and "Let me be!"
3. yes - ter - eve she shy - ly said She's still too young to wed - ded be;

1. Glanc - ing with - al so laugh - ing - ly, Blythe - some, charm - ing Kit - ty Ma - gee.
2. Then with a bound she springs a - way, 'Witch - ing, smi - ling Kit - ty Ma - gee.
3. "Wait till the spring re - turns a - gain," Blushing - ly whis - per'd Kit - ty Ma - gee.

With deep affection.

THE BELLS OF SHANDON.

Rev. Francis Mahony.

p con espress.

Andante.

VOICE.

1. With deep af-
2. I've heard bells
3. I've heard bells

Ullogaun.

PIANO.

p Adagio. ad lib. e con espress. *molto rit.*

1. -fec - tion and re - col - lec - tion I of - ten think of those Shan - don
2. chim - ing full man - y a clime in, Toll-ing sub - lime in ca - the - dral
3. toll - ing "Old A - drian's mole" in, Their thun-ders roll - ing from the Vat - i -

p

con Ped.

1. Bells, Whose sounds so wild would in days of child - hood Fling round my
2. shrine; While at a glibe rate brass tongues would vi - brate, But all their
3. - can, And cym - bals glo - rious, swing - ing up - roar - ious In the gor - geous

Air: "The Groves of Blarney." I have already traced the history of this melody on p. 257. The author of the song was Francis Sylvester Mahony, better known by the pseudonym of "Father Prout." The above setting of the air, with its fine *Ullogaun* or Lament, is from Holden's *Irish Tunes*, vol. i., 1806, in which collection the melody, as "The Groves of Blarney," was first printed. Richard Millikin, the author of the humorous old song, "The Groves of Blarney," was born in 1767, and died in 1815.

1. cra - dle their ma - gic spells. On this I pon - der wher - e'er I
2. mu - sic spoke nought like thine; For mem - 'ry dwell - ing on each proud
3. tur - rets of Nô - tre Dame; Thy sounds were sweet - er than the dome of

1. wan - der And then grow fond - er, sweet Cork, of thee, With thy bells of
2. swell - ing Of thy bel - fry knell - ing its bold notes free Made the bells of
3. Pe - ter Flings o'er the Ti - ber, peal - ing so - lemn - ly. Oh! the bells of

poco rit.

1. Shan - don that sound so grand on The pleasant wa - ters of the ri - ver Lee.
2. Shan - don sound far more grand on The pleasant wa - ters of the ri - ver Lee.
3. Shan - don sound far more grand on The pleasant wa - ters of the ri - ver Lee.

colla voce.

p rit.

Would God I were the tender apple blossom.

IRISH LOVE SONG.

KATHARINE TYNAN.

1. were the ten-der ap-ple blos-som That floats and falls from off the twist-ed
2. God I were a-mong the ros-es That lean to kiss you as you float be-

1. lough, To lie and faint with-in your silk-en bo-som, With-in your silk-en
2. -tween, While on the low-est branch a bud un-clos-es, A bud un-

This air is preserved in the Petrie Collection; it was obtained in the county of Londonderry, but its name was not ascertained. Mrs. Hinkson has kindly allowed me to use her song, which, with the air, is printed in A. P. Graves's *Irish Song Book*, 1895.

poco rit.

1. bo - - som, as that does now! Or would I were a lit - tle bur-nish'd
2. clos - - es to touch you, Queen. Nay, since you will not love, would I were

poco rit.　> *sf* >

cres.　*f*

1. ap - ple For you to pluck me, glid - ing by so cold, While sun and
2. grow - ing A hap - py dai - sy in the gar - den path; That so your

cres.　*f*

rit. e dim.

1. shade your robe of lawn will dap - ple, Your robe of lawn, and your hair's spun gold. . . .
2. sil - ver foot might press me go - ing, Might press me go - ing ev - en un - to death! . .

rit. e dim.

Wreathe the bowl.

THOMAS MOORE.

Spiritoso.

VOICE.

PIANO.

1.
2. 'Twas
3. Say,

1. Wreathe the bowl With flow'rs of soul The bright - est Wit can find us; We'll
2. nec - tar fed Of old, 'tis said, Their Ju - nos, Joves, A - pol - los; And
3. why did Time His glass sub-lime Fill up with sands un - sight - ly, When

1. take a flight Tow'rds heav'n to - night, And leave dull earth be - hind us. Should
2. Man may brew His nec - tar too, The rich re - ceipt's as fol - lows: Take
3. wine, he knew, Runs brisk - er through, And spar - kles far more bright - ly? Oh,

Air: Nora Kista." The earliest printed copy of this tune which I have seen is in Thompson's *Country Dances for 1770*; it is there named "The Wild Irishman." And included it in his *Selection of Scotch, English, Irish, and Foreign Airs*, vol. i., 1782, as "Norickystie, or the Wild Irish Man." It is also in Holden's Collection, vol. i., as "Noreen Keesta," and in O'Farrell's *Pocket Companion*, vol. ii., as "Noran Kishta"; Bunting names it "Nora with the Purse" in his Third Collection, 1840. Moore's song was written in October, 1817, and appeared in the following year in the seventh number of the *Melodies*.

1. Love a - mid The wreaths be hid That Joy, th'en-chant - er, brings us, No
2. wine like this, Let looks of bliss A - round it well be blend - ed, Then
3. lend it us, And, smi - ling thus, The glass in two we'll sev - er, Make

1. dan - ger fear, While wine is near, We'll drown him if he stings us.
2. bring Wit's beam To warm the stream, And there's your nec - tar, splen - did! } Then
3. plea - sure glide In dou - ble tide, And fill both ends for ev - er! }

wreathe the bowl With flow'rs of soul The bright - est Wit can find us; We'll

ten.

take a flight Tow'rds heav'n to - night, And leave dull earth be - hind us!

Ye dark-hair'd youths.

EDWARD WALSH.

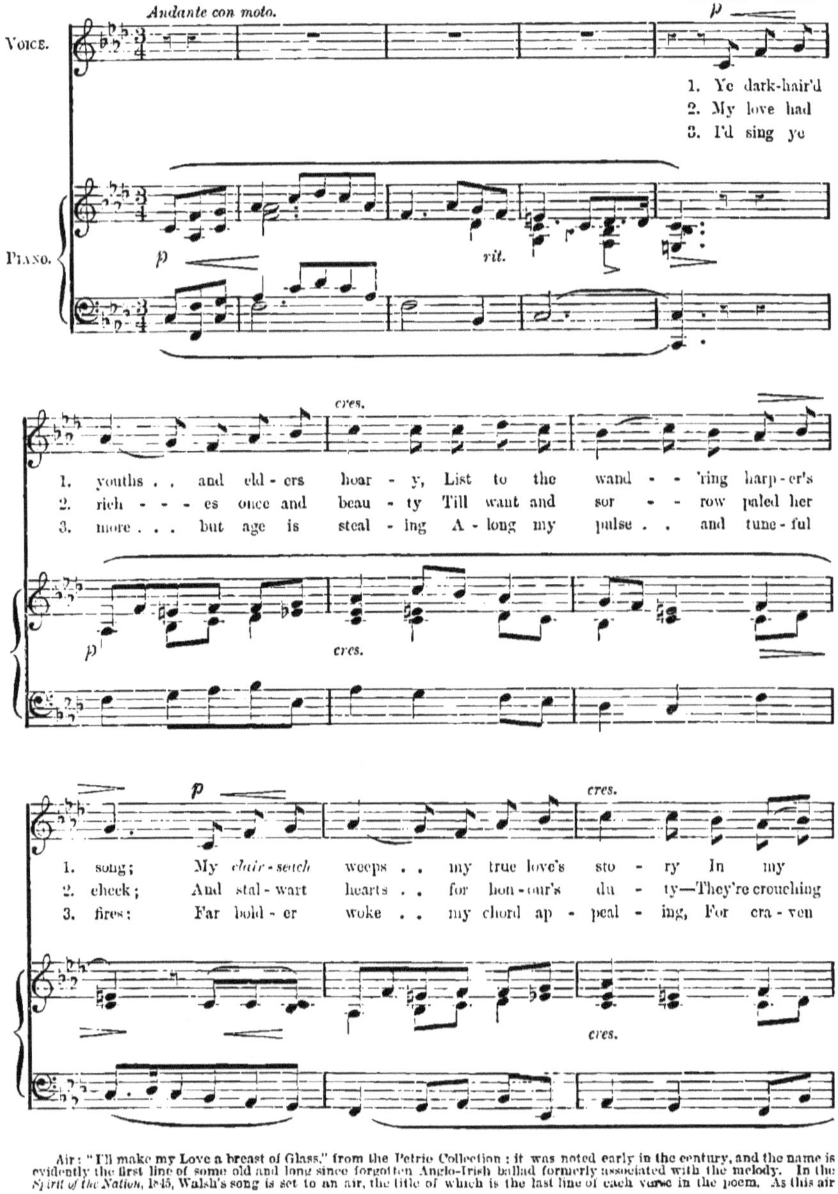
Andante con moto.
Voice.
Piano.
p
rit.
cres.
1. Ye dark-hair'd
2. My love had
3. I'd sing ye
1. youths . . and eld - ers hoar - y, List to the wand - - 'ring harp - er's
2. rich - - - es once and beau - ty Till want and sor - - row paled her
3. more . . . but age is steal - ing A - long my pulse . . and tune - ful
1. song; My clair - seach weeps . . my true love's sto - ry In my
2. cheek; And stal - wart hearts . . for hon - our's du - ty—They're crouching
3. fires; Far bold - er woke . . my chord ap - peal - ing, For cra - ven

Air: "I'll make my Love a breast of Glass," from the Petrie Collection; it was noted early in the century, and the name is evidently the first line of some old and long since forgotten Anglo-Irish ballad formerly associated with the melody. In the *Spirit of the Nation*, 1845, Walsh's song is set to an air, the title of which is the last line of each verse in the poem. As this air

1. true   love's na-tive tongue: She's bound and bleed - ing 'neath th'op - pres - sor, Few her
2. now,   like cra-vens sleek.   O, Heav'n! that ere   this   day   of   ri - gour Saw sons of
3. *Sheamus,* to your sires.   A - rouse to ven - geance, men of   brav-'ry For brok-en

1. friends   and fierce her   foe,   And brave hearts cold . . who would re - dress her, *Mo chroevin*
2. he - roes ab-ject,   low—   And blood and   tears . . thy face dis - fig - ure, *Mo chroevin*
3. oaths— for al - tars   low—   For bonds that bind . . in bit - ter   slav-'ry *Mo chroevin*

1. e - vin   al - ga,   O!
2. e - vin   al - ga,   O!
3. e - vin   al - ga,   O!

appears to me to be somewhat unsuitable, I have given the preference to the above one from Petrie's volume. "Mo chroevin evin alga" (*Mo chraoibhin aoibhinn aluinn og*) means "My fair noble maid." It is hardly necessary to observe that the ill-used maiden, whose misfortunes the bard so passionately laments, is fair Erin herself.

Ye good fellows all.

BUMPERS, SQUIRE JONES.

Attributed to ARTHUR DAWSON.

Spiritoso.

VOICE.

1. Ye good fel-lows all, Ye
2. Ye lov-ers who pine, Ye
3. Ye sol-diers so stout, Ye
4. Ye fox hun-ters eke, Ye

PIANO.

mf

1. good fel-lows all, Who love to be told where good clar-et's in store, At-
2. lov-ers who pine For lass-es that oft prove as cru-el as fair, Who
3. sol-diers so stout, With plen-ty of oaths tho' not plen-ty of coin, Who
4. fox hun-ters eke, That fol-low the call of the horn and the hound, Who your

cres.

1. -tend to the call Of one who's ne'er fright-ed, But great-ly de-light-ed With
2. whim-per and whine For li-lies and ros-es, With eyes, lips or nos-es, Or
3. make such a rout Of all your com-mand-ers Who serv'd us in Flan-ders, And
4. la-dies for-sake Be-fore they're a-wake, To beat up the brake Where the

cres.

The following extract from the *Dublin University Magazine*, January, 1841, describes the incident in connection with the above song and air. "Respecting the origin of Carolan's fine air of 'Bumper Squire Jones,' we have heard a different account from that given on O'Neill's authority. It was told by our lamented friend, the late Dean of St. Patrick's as the tradition preserved in his family and was to the following effect. Carolan, and Baron Dawson, the grand, or great grand-uncle to the Dean, happened to be enjoying, together with others, the hospitalities of Squire Jones at Moneyglass, and slept in rooms adjacent to each other. The bard, being called upon by the company to compose a song or tune in honour of their host, undertook to comply with their request, and, on retiring to his apartment, took his harp with him, and under the inspiration of copious libations of his favourite liquor, not only produced the melody now known as 'Bumper Squire Jones,' but also very indifferent English words to it. While the bard was thus employed, however, the Judge was not idle. Being possessed of a fine musical ear, as well as of considerable poetical talents, he not only fixed the melody on his memory, but actually wrote the

1. six bot-tles more. Be sure you don't pass The good house Mon-ey-glass, Which the
2. tip of an ear: Come hi-ther, I'll show ye How Phyl-lis and Chlo-e No
3. eke at the Boyne. Come leave off your rat-tling Of sie-ging and bat-tling And
4. ver-min is found: Leave Pi-per and Blue-man, Shrill Duch-ess and True-man—No

1. jol-ly red god so pe-cu-liar-ly owns; 'Twill well suit your hu-mour, For
2. more shall oc-ca-sion such sighs and such groans; What mor-tal so stu-pid As
3. know you'd much bet-ter to sleep with whole bones; Were you at Gib-ral-tar Your
4. mu-sic is found in such dis-so-nant tones: Would you rav-ish your ears With the

1. pray what would you more Than mirth with good claret, and bumpers, Squire Jones?
2. not to quit Cu-pid, When call'd by good claret, and bumpers, Squire Jones?
3. notes you'd soon al-ter, And wish for good claret, and bumpers, Squire Jones!
4. songs of the spheres? Hark a-way to the claret—a bumper, Squire Jones!

noble song now incorporated with it, before he retired to rest. The result may be anticipated. At breakfast on the following morning, when Carolan sang and played his composition, Baron Dawson, to the astonishment of all present, and of the bard in particular, stoutly denied the claim of Carolan to the melody, and charged him with audacious piracy, both musical and poetical, and to prove the fact, sung the melody to his own words amidst the joyous shouts of approbation of all his hearers— the enraged bard excepted, who vented his execrations in curses on the Judge both loud and deep." Alluding to English tunes being incorporated as Irish in Irish musical collections, the author of a series of valuable articles on folk-airs which have lately appeared in the *Musical Times*, asserts that John Playford published the tune of "Bumper Squire Jones" at an early date in the *Dancing-Master* as the "Rummer," and that most probably the tune is the composition of a London dancing-master. That this statement is based upon an error of judgment will be seen by a reference to the Appendix, Nos. XXXI., XXXII., and XXXIII., where I have printed Playford's "Rummer" alongside of the settings of "Bumper Squire Jones," given by Thumoth and John Lee; the version adopted above is from Bunting's Collection of 1809, but with the first bar repeated to complete the form of the eight-barred period. The reader will perceive that apart from the termination, where the tune descends the octave, the two airs have little in common beyond both being in six-eight rhythm. I see no reason to doubt the tradition that Carolan composed the air. "Bumper Squire Jones" was sung in Henry Brooke's Opera, *Jack the Giant Queller*, performed in Dublin in 1748, to verses beginning :—

Since, Sir, you require
Me with Freedom the Price I desire.

You know I'm your priest.

BALLINAMONA ORO.

JOHN O'KEEFE.

The above song, with the tune "Ballinamona," is from O'Keefe's *Poor Soldier*, 1783; it is sung by the character Father Luke in the second act of that opera. As "Balin a mone" the air is in Burk Thumoth's *Twelve English and Twelve Irish Airs*, c. 1745, and as "Ballina mona" in Johnson's *Choice Collection of Two Hundred Favourite Country Dances*, vol. iv., 1748.

1. mar - ry a wife, And then, my dear Dar - by, you're set - tled for life; With your
2. sheep - ish your look, You out with your ring, and I pull out the book, With my
3. love and to hold; I put up my book, and I poc - ket the gold, Sing - ing
4. joy to each face; The pi - per plays up, and my - self says the grace, With my

1. Bal - li - na - mo - na o - ro,   Bal - li - na - mo - na o - ro,
2. Bal - li - na - mo - na o - ro,   Bal - li - na - mo - na o - ro,
3. Bal - li - na - mo - na o - ro,   Bal - li - na - mo - na o - ro,
4. Bal - li - na - mo - na o - ro,   Bal - li - na - mo - na o - ro,

1. Bal - li - na - mo - na o - ro! A snug lit - tle wed - ding for me! . . .
2. Bal - li - na - mo - na o - ro! A snug lit - tle wed - ding for me! . . .
3. Bal - li - na - mo - na o - ro! That snug lit - tle gui - nea for me! . . .
4. Bal - li - na - mo - na o - ro! A good wed - ding din - ner for me! . . .

1. A snug lit - tle wed - ding for me! . . .
2. A snug lit - tle wed - ding for me! . . .
3. That snug lit - tle gui - nea for me! . . .
4. A good wed - ding din - ner for me! . . .

You remember Ellen.

THOMAS MOORE.

Andante con espressione.

VOICE.

1. You re -
2. They
3. "Now,

PIANO.

p   *sf*   *rit.*

1. -mem - ber El - len, our ham - let's pride, How meek - ly she bless'd her
2. roam'd a long and wea - ry way, Nor much was the maid - en's
3. wel - come, la - dy!" ex - claim'd the youth, "This cas - tle is thine, and these

p

1. hum - ble lot, When the stran - ger, Wil - liam, had made her his bride And
2. heart at ease, When now, at close of one storm - y day, They
3. dark woods all!" She be - liev'd him craz'd, but his words were truth, For

This air, which is called "Were I a clerk," was sent to Moore through his Irish publisher, William Power, by Dr. George Petrie. Moore inserted it with his song, in the fifth number of the *Melodies*, 1813 ; the subject of the ballad is to be found in many old Scotch and English ballads.

1. Love was the light of their low - ly cot. To - geth - er they toil'd thro'
2. see a proud cas - tle a - mong the trees. "To - night," said the youth, "we'll
3. El - len is La - dy of Ros - na Hall! And dear - ly the Lord of

poco rit.   *mf*

1. winds and rains, 'Till Wil - liam at length, in sad - ness, said, "We must
2. shel - ter here, The wind blows cold, the hour is late;" So he
3. Ros - na loves What Wil - liam the stran - ger woo'd and wed; And the

colla voce.

dim.

1. seek our for-tune on oth - er plains"—Then, sigh-ing, she left her low - ly shed.
2. blew the horn with a chief - tain's air, And the por-ter bow'd as they pass'd the gate.
3. light of bliss in these lord - ly groves Shines pure as it did in the low - ly shed.

mf

dim.

2

Young Rory O'More.

RORY O'MORE.

Samuel Lover.

Spiritoso.

VOICE. / **PIANO.**

mf / *p* / *ff* / *mf*

1. Young Ro - ry O'-More court - ed
2. "In - deed, then," says Kathleen, "don't
3. "Ar-rah, Kath-leen, my dar-lint, you've

1. Kath - leen bawn, He was bold as a hawk, — she as soft as the dawn; He
2. think of the like, For I half gave a pro - mise to sooth-er - ing Mike. The
3. teased me e - nough, Since I've thrash'd for your sake Din - ny Grimes and Jim Duff, And I've

cres. / *ten.* f

1. wished in his heart pret - ty Kath-leen to please, And he thought the best way to do
2. ground that I walk on, he loves I'll be bound." "Faith," says Ro - ry, "I'd ra - ther love
3. made my - self dhrink-ing your health quite a baste, So I think af - ter that I may

cres. / *f*

mf / *ten.*

1. that was to tease. "Now, Ro - ry, be ai - sy," sweet Kath-leen would cry— Re -
2. you than the ground." "Now, Ro - ry, I'll cry, if you don't let me go, Sure I
3. talk to the priest." Then Ro - ry, the rogue, stole his arm round her neck, So

mf

The composition of this melody has been attributed to Robert Owenson, but upon what authority I know not. I have also seen it stated that Lover was its composer; but this is apparently incorrect. Lover's ballad, with the music, was issued as a sheet-song by Duff and Hodgson, London, about 1840, and the wording on it is: "Written and *arranged* by S. L." In his note to "Rory O'More" in the *Lyrics of Ireland*, 1858, Lover throws no light on the authorship of the tune; he merely relates that being

1. - proof on her lip but a smile on her eye,—"With your tricks I don't know, in troth, what I'm about, Faith you've
2. dhrame ev-'ry night that I'm hat-ing you so." "Och," says Ro-ry, "that same I'm de-light-ed to hear For
3. soft, and so white, without free-kle, or speck, And he look'd in her eyes that were beaming with light, And he

colla voce.   *colla voce.*

poco rit.   *a tempo.*

1. teas'd till I've put on my coat in-side out;" "Och, jew-el," says Ro-ry, "that same is the way You've
2. dhrames always go con-thra-ries, my dear; So, jew-el, keep dhramin' that same till you die, Bright
3. kiss'd her sweet lips—Don't you think he was right?" "Now, Ro-ry, leave off, sir, you'll hug me no more, That's

colla voce.

cres.

1. thrat-ed my heart for this man-y a day, And 'tis pleased that I am, and why not, to be sure? For 'tis
2. morn-in' will give dirt-y night the black lie: And 'tis pleased that I am, and why not, to be sure? Since 'tis
3. eight times to-day that you've kiss'd me before!" "Then here goes an-o-ther," says he, "to make sure, For there's

cres.

1. all for good luck," says bold Ro-ry O'More.
2. all for good luck," says bold Ro-ry O'More.
3. luck in old num-bers," says Ro-ry O'More.

called upon to write a novel, he availed himself of the popularity attached to the name of the ballad, and entitled the story "Rory O'More." The success of the novel induced our author to dramatise it, and in its third form, "Rory O'More" was again received by the public with such approbation, that it was played one hundred and eight nights during the first season, in London, and afterwards universally throughout the Kingdom. This was in 1837, and the piece was produced at the Adelphi Theatre. The tune was certainly very popular, and it seems to have been much played by the military bands on the day of Her Majesty Queen Victoria's Coronation. Bunting prints a lively air in his second collection, which he entitles "Rory O'More: King of Leix's March"; but it has nothing in common with the above melody.

APPENDIX.

I.
BLACK-EYED SUSAN.
Composed by LEVERIDGE.

II.
AILEEN AROON.
(An Irish Ballad. Sung by Mrs. Clive at y^e Theatre Royal.)
A Sheet-song, c. 1740–5.

III.
ELLEN A ROON.
The Beggar's Wedding, 1729. Act iii., Air xviii.

IV.
AILEN AROON.
Burk Thumoth's *Twelve Scotch and Twelve Irish Airs*, c. 1745, p. 26.

My friend Mr. F. Kidson has kindly pointed out to me that the song "Your welcome to Paxton, Robin Adair," was published as early as 1763 in an Edinburgh song-book entitled *The Lark*. Braham introduced his version of the air with the verses beginning "What's this dull town to me, Robin Adair," probably about 1812–13. Both words and music are printed in *The Cabinet of Harmony*, 1814, *The English Minstrel*, 1815, and in an American publication called *The Passionate Minstrel*, 1816. Contemporary issues of the song in sheet form bear "Sung by Mr. Braham at the Lyceum and at Bath."

V.
TO RODNEY WE WILL GO.
Aird's *Scotch, English, Irish and Foreign Airs*, vol. iii., 1788, p. 160.

NOTE.—The version of the air used by Moore was printed in O'Farrell's *Pocket Companion*, bk. iv., c. 1810, under the title of "The Drop of Dram." Moore's song appeared three years later in bk. v. of the *Melodies*.

THE TULIP.
(March.)

VI.   James Oswald's *Airs for the Spring, c.* 1757.

THE IRISH LADY, OR ANNISEED-WATER ROBIN.

VII.   Playford's *English Dancing Master*, 1651, p. 48.

NARRAMORE.

VIII.   Holden's *Old Established Irish Tunes*, vol. ii., 1806, p. 33.

WE'LL ALL TAKE COACH AND TRIP IT AWAY.

IX.   O'Farrell's *National Irish Music, c.* 1797-1800, p. 38.

JACK'S HEALTH.

X.   Playford's *Dancing Master*, 7th edit., 1686.

A SONG.

XI.   D'Urfey's *Pills to Purge Melancholy*, vol. v., 1719, p. 112.

XII.

From a MS. of circa, 1730-5.

THE WATTER OF BOYNE.

XII b.

From the Leyden MS., c. 1690-2.

PUT IN ALL.

XIII.

Dancing Master, 17th edit., vol. ii., 1728, p. 121.

THERE WAS A PRETTY GIRL.

XIV.

The Beggar's Wedding, 1729. Act iii., Air iii.

CHA MI MA CHATTLE.

XV.

Musick for Allan Ramsay's Collection of Scots Songs, bk. iii., c. 1725.

PAST ONE A CLOCK IN A COLD FROSTY MORNING.

XVI.

The Beggar's Wedding, 1729. Act ii., Air x.

AT PAST TWELVE O'CLOCK ON A FINE SUMMER'S MORNING.

XVII.

Flora, 1732.

PAST ONE O'CLOCK.

XVIII.

Burk Thumoth's *Twelve Scotch and Twelve Irish Airs*, c. 1745, p. 30.

THAMMA HULLA. (The varied repetition of the second strain omitted.)

XIX.

Holden's *Old Established Irish Tunes*, bk. ii., 1806, p. 34.

AN IRISH SONG. SET BY MR. LEVERIDGE.

XX.

D'Urfey's *Pills to Purge Melancholy*, vol. iv., 1719, p. 278.

ARAH, MY DEAR EVLEEN.

XXI.

Holden's *Irish Tunes*, bk. i., 1806, p. 21.

ABIGAIL JUDGE.

XXII.

George Thomson's *Original Irish Airs*, vol. ii., 1816, p. 101.

WILL YOU GO TO FLANDERS.

XXII.   McGibbon's *Scots Tunes*, bk. ii., 1746, p. 2.

ISBEL FALSEY.

XXIII.   C. St. George's *Manx Melodies*, 1820.

O JENNY, YOU HAVE BORNE AWAY THE PALM.

XXIV.   Petrie Collection, 1855, p. 33.

THE WINTER IT IS PAST.

XXV.   Oswald's *Caledonian Pocket Companion*, bk. x., c. 1758-60, p. 9.
Slow.

THE PRIEST IN HIS BOOTS.

XXVa.   C. & S. Thompson's *Compleat Collection of 120 Favourite Hornpipes*, c. 1765-77, No. 23.

THE YOUNG MAN'S DREAM.

XXVI.   Bunting's *Ancient Irish Music*, 1796, p. 19.

NOTE.—It is improbable that Thomson's settings of this air were in any way influenced by the version printed in Moore's *Irish Melodies.* Although not published until two-and-a-half years after the appearance of the "Last Rose of Summer," it is evident from the following remark, extracted from the preface to George Thomson's *Irish Airs,* that the tunes were forwarded for musical arrangement to Beethoven long before the fifth number of the *Melodies* was issued. "After years of anxious suspense and teasing disappointment, owing to the unprecedented difficulty of communication between England and Vienna, the long expected symphonies and accompaniments at last reached the Editor, three other copies having previously been lost on the road." It will be remembered that Moore's "Last Rose of Summer" was issued in the fifth number of the *Melodies,* December, 1813, and that Thomson's *Irish Airs,* vol. ii., appeared May, 1816. Thomson projected the idea of forming an Irish collection as early as 1793.

APPENDIX.   343

YORKSHIRE LASSIE.

From a titleless country-dance book in the British Museum Library, c. 1770.
From Longman and Broderip's 200 Favourite Country Dances, vol. ii., prior to 1781.
XXVII.   From Skillern's Compleat Collection of Two Hundred and Four Reels and Country Dances, c. 1779.

YORKSHIRE LASSES.
XXVIIᵃ.   From a Country-Dance Card, c. 1770-80.

SONG AND CHORUS, NEVER BEFORE PRINTED.
("That Masonry is a Devine Institution.")
XXVIIᵇ.   Holden's Masonic Songs, 1798.

CHORUS.

KING JAMES'S MARCH TO IRLAND.
                                                        Leyden M.S., c. 1690-2.
XXVIII.

LIMBRICK'S LAMENTATION.
XXIX.   Daniel Wright's Aria di Camera, c. 1730, p. 36.

REEVES MAGGOT.
XXX.   Dancing Master, 12th edit., 1703.

NOTE.—The air entitled "Sarsfield's Lamentation" in the Hibernian Muse, c 1786, is entirely different from "Limerick's Lamentation."

XXXI.

THE RUMMER.

Playford's *Dancing Master*, 7th edit., 1686, p. 180.

XXXII.

BUMPERS ESQUIRE JONES (transposed from D).

Burk Thumoth's *Twelve English and Twelve Irish Airs, c.* 1745, No. 33.

XXXIII.

BUMPER 'SQUIRE JONES (transposed from D).

Carolan's Collection, 1780, p. 12.

ADDENDA.

FLY NOT YET. AIR: "PLANXTY KELLY," p. 62.—An early version of the tune was sung in Shield's Opera, *Robin Hood*, 1784, to verses beginning "When the chill sirocco blows." Almost the same setting of the air as that adopted by Moore was used in *The Siege of St. Quintin*, 1808, an opera, the text of which was written by Theodore Hook.

HAVE YOU BEEN AT CARRICK, p. 70.—The poor version of the melody alluded to in the note is in the first series of the *Poets and Poetry of Munster*, 1849, p. 72.

HOW DEAR TO ME THE HOUR. AIR: "THE TWISTING OF THE ROPE," p. 82. George Thomson's setting of this air is in two-four time; it is printed in vol. ii. of his *Irish Airs*, 1816.

I'VE COME UNTO MY HOME AGAIN, p. 101.—O'Farrell prints a version of this air in his *Pocket Companion*, bk. ii., p. 150, *c.* 1805, as "The Maid of Calligan."

OH, BREATHE NOT HIS NAME. AIR: "THE BROWN MAID," p. 174. Another setting of this air is known as "The Brown Irish Maid," and to it Moore wrote his song. "By that lake whose gloomy shore," for the fourth number of the *Melodies*. It was sung in *Rosina*, 1783, to verses beginning, "By that fountain's flow'ry side." In the *Hibernian Muse, c.* 1789, it is entitled "The Irish Girl."

'TIS BELIEVED THAT THIS HARP. AIR: "GAGE FANE," p. 282. This air is preserved in the *Hibernian Muse, c.* 1789; it is there simply headed "Irish Air."

AS I WENT A-WALKING ONE MORNING IN SPRING (See page 10).

Air and words from Dr. Joyce's Collection, 1873. The following is the first verse of a London broadside ballad printed early in the century ; it will be seen that it is practically the same as the first few lines of the ballad obtained in Ireland :
The Green Bushes. Hodges (from Pitt's), 31, Dudley Street, Seven Dials.

As I was a walking one morning in May
To hear the birds whistle and the nightingales sing,
I heard a young damsel, so sweetly sung she
Down by the green bushes where he thinks to mee.

The third line of the Irish song is evidently derived from "The Blackbird," preserved in Ramsay's *Tea-Table Miscellany*, Bk. i. of the later editions, but *not*, as has been so often stated, in the first edition of 1724.

Upon a fair morning for soft recreation
I heard a fair lady was making her moan.

The same expression is found in "The Lady's Lamentation for the loss of Senisino" printed in Robert's *Calliope*, 1737, Pt. v., and in *Universal Harmony*, 1745.

As musing I rang'd in ye meads all alone,
A beautiful creature was making her moan.

DID YOU HEAR OF THE WIDOW MALONE? (See page 46).

Lever's song occurs in his novel *Charles O'Malley*, 1841 ; it is supposed to be sung with great applause by the character Miss Macan. Versions of the air are given in Holden's *Old Established Irish Tunes*, vol. i., 1806, as "Whacker awanl awee," and in O'Farrell's *Pocket Companion for the Irish Pipes*, as "Why should we part so soon." In various collections of Irish songs the air has been erroneously named "Captain Magan" from the first line of Colman's song printed with the melody in Crosby's *Irish Minstrel*, London, 1808. An equally erroneous name is "The gap in the hedge," taken from a modern song written to the tune in Messrs. Boosey's Album. About 1844, Lever's poem was published as a sheet song by J. Chalmers, Dundee, set to an Irish air with pianoforte accompaniment by John Daniel : but this air, although good, has been entirely superseded by the one given above. The originality of Lever's composition has been challenged, and the assertion made that it is founded on an old Irish folk-song.

FAIREST! PUT ON AWHILE (See p. 52).

In "restoring" Moore's song to what he considers the correct version of "Cummilium," Professor Stanford has made a singular mistake ; he has stripped the song of its Irish melody to deck it out anew in an English garb. There are countless versions of the air under different titles. "Mad Moll" in Playford's *Dancing Master*, 10th edition, 1698, is probably the earliest in print, and after that we have the melody varied under such titles as "The Virgin Queen," "Yellow Stockings," "Hey my Kitten" (from Dean Swift's nursery song), "Shall I be Sick of Love," and many other names. But the version called "Cummilium" deserves a distinctive position, not only on account of its beauty, but because it is in this form that Ireland has a right to put forth a claim for the tune. Why then throw it aside in favour of the English setting ? "Cummilium" was first printed in a somewhat rare little collection of Irish airs entitled "*Jackson's Celebrated Irish Tunes, Dublin, c. 1775,* and it is possible that Jackson gave the air the name by which it is now known in Ireland. Want of space prevents me from dealing with Mr. Chappell's English claims for the tune ; I must refer the reader to that author's *Popular Music of the Olden Time*, p. 604. I need hardly draw attention to the name "Mad Moll," being in itself suspiciously Irish.

FOR GET NOT THE FIELD (See p. 53).

From Moore's *Melodies*, no. vii., 1818. This lovely air, known as "The Lamentation of Aughrim," probably dates from the terrible battle of Aughrim, about which Count Plunket, editor of O'Kelly's *Jacobite War in Ireland*, has kindly supplied me with the following: In the battle of Aughrim (12th July, O.S., 1691), the Irish—fighting for James II.—were cut to pieces, losing between three and four thousand men, "the flower of their army and nation." So well had they fought until the death of their commander, St. Ruth, and the consequent confusion, that the Willamite loss was almost as great. The English gave no quarter. Aughrim is still a synonym for lamentation with the Irish peasantry.

HOW SWEET THE ANSWER ECHO MAKES (See p. 77).

As *Dnolicu*, or, "The Wren," a somewhat different setting of this air occurs in Bunting's *Ancient Music of Ireland*, 1809. Alluding to Moore's song, which was published in the eighth number of the *Melodies*, 1821, Mr. T. W. Lyster remarks in his book of *Select Poetry, Dublin*, third edition, 1896 :—" Perhaps we may discover in it a reminiscence of the delightful evenings spent by Moore at Sevres, with his Spanish friend, Villamil, when he listened to Madame Villamil playing the guitar ; while ' lawns and lakes' may be a memory of his wanderings by day in the forest of St. Cloud. The harmonious little song has the line distinction of unity and logical sequence ; it goes direct to its aim with a skilful economy in words. Stanza follows stanza *necessarily ;* the order could not be altered without destroying the sense. The touch of cynicism in lines 11-12 is very harmless ; merry little Tom Moore was a devotedly loving husband, and a genial friend to the end of his days."

HOW DIMM'D IS THE GLORY THAT CIRCLED THE GAEL (See p. 88).

This is one of that most ancient and peculiarly Irish class of airs called Caoines, or Lamentations for the dead ; it is from the Petrie Collection, and "was noted from the playing of Frank Keane, a native of the southern part of the county of Clare, in which secluded district he had learnt it from the singing of the women. Of the words sung to it, however, he had no recollection" (Petrie Coll., p. 107). I have adapted Callanan's line "Lament for Ireland" to the melody, which seems to suit it admirably.

I'D MOURN THE HOPES THAT LEAVE ME (See p. 90).

It has been the fate of this melody to receive a great variety of titles. Through O'Keefe having introduced it in *The Poor Soldier*, 1783, with verses beginning,—

A rosetree in full bearing
Had sweet flowers fair to see.

it became known as "The Rose Tree," and under this title Moore inserted it in the *Melodies*, no. v., 1813. O'Daly (*Poets and Poetry of Munster*, 1849) calls it *Moirin Ni Chuilliouain*, or, "Little Mary Cullenan." From a song written to it by John O'Tuomy (1706—1775) ; this does not prove, however, that *Moirin Ni Chuilliouain* was the original name of the air ; the Tipperary name, "The Rosetree of Paddy's Land," is obviously derived from O'Keefe's song. Prior to its appearance in *The Poor Soldier*, we find it in Oswald's *Pocket Companion*, book x., c. 1760, as "The Gimlet " ; in Thompson's *Country Dances for 1764* as "The Irish Lilt," and in Aird's *Scotch, English, Irish and Foreign Airs*, vol. i., 1782, as " The Dainty Besom Maker." In Gow's Second Collection, 1788, it is named "Old Lee Rigg—or Rose Tree," and in Mulhollan's *Irish Tunes*, 1804, "Killeavy." As already mentioned on p. 14, "The Rosetree" belongs to the same family of Irish melodies as "The girl I left behind me," with which air it bears much affinity.

I'VE COME UNTO MY HOME AGAIN (See p. 101).

This air is one of the many versions of "Lough Sheelin" (see p. 28); it resembles the setting called "Kildroughalt Fair," to which Moore wrote "Oh, Arranmore, lov'd Arranmore" (see p. 171). As "My lodging is uncertain," it is to be found in O'Farrell's *Pocket Companion*, vol. iii. and in Horncastle's Collection, pt. i. Griffin's song, which I have adapted to the melody, is from his *Poetical and Dramatic Works*, Dublin, 1857. It will be seen that the first verse is founded on the fragment of the old song published in Horncastle's work—

> I come unto my home again and find myself alone,
> The friends I left in quiet there are perished all, and gone.
> My father's house is tenantless, my early love lies low,
> And my lodging is uncertain, I know not where to go.

LONG, LONG HAVE I WANDERED IN SEARCH OF MY LOVE (See p. 140).

Dr. Petrie gives two versions of this air as "Nora of the Amber Hair," in his *Ancient Music of Ireland*, 1855; the first setting, and the one which I have adopted here, seems to have been associated with an Irish song, a translation of which, by Walsh, will be found on p. 170 set to an air from Dr. Joyce's Collection. In adapting the song "Long, long have I wandered," which Petrie states was written to the *second* version of "Nora of the Amber Hair," I have been guided by the fact that, while Mangan's translation sings excellently to Petrie's *first* version of the air, Walsh's verses do not seem to suit them so well. Of George Roberts, to whom the authorship of "The Fairy Rath" is attributed, nothing seems to be known; the song, which appears in O'Daly's *Poets and Poetry of Munster*, 1849, with a translation by James Clarence Mangan, shows clearly the danger of falling in love with a Fairy. (For Petrie's second version of the above air see p. 206 of the present work.)

OH! ARRANMORE (See p. 171).

As "Kildroughalt Fair" this melody was printed in Holden's Collection, vol. ii., 1806; it is merely one of the many settings of "Lough Sheeling" (see p. 40). Moore's song was written for the tenth and concluding number of the *Melodies*, 1834. Another setting of "Kildroughalt Fair" is given in Bunting's second Collection, 1809, as "Bridget O'Neill," and I may be permitted to observe that this tune is evidently the original of the air known in Scotland as "My only jo and dearie O," and printed with Richard Gall's beautiful poem, "Thy cheek is like the rose's hue" in the *Scots Museum*, vol. vi., 1803. The air was one of those sung in the pantomime of *Harlequin Highlander* performed at the circus in Edinburgh. It must be admitted, however, that "My only jo and dearie O" is an infinitely more beautiful form of the air, although perhaps more modern, than either "Kildroughalt Fair" or "Bridget O'Neill."

OH! MY SWEET LITTLE ROSE (See p. 179).

Dr. Joyce has kindly allowed me to use this setting of the air *Rois geal Dubh*, or, "The Fair Black-hair'd little Rose." Different settings of it are given by Petrie, Bunting and O'Daly. Regarding his version, which I believe was printed for the first time in *Irish Music and Song*, 1888, Dr. Joyce makes the following comment: "I have been familiar with the air since my childhood, and I always heard it played and sung in minor; and I believe that it is only the minor mode that brings out the true character. I give the simple and, as I believe, the most ancient vocal version, as I heard it sung by the best singers among the old people of Munster forty years ago." I have taken Furlong's translation of the Irish song from Hardiman's *Irish Minstrelsy*, vol. i., 1831

ONE CLEAR SUMMER MORNING, NEAR BLUE AVONREE (See p. 204).

This characteristic air from the Petrie Collection is considered by the author of that work to be of northern origin, as he had never heard it sung in the provinces of Munster or Connaught. It was noted down about 1810, from the singing of a gentleman who had learned it in his childhood. Dr. Petrie designates it as "Coola Shore; or, When I rise in the morning with my heart full of woe." Walsh's translation is published in his *Irish Popular Songs*, 1847, and the following note is appended to the song in that work, "*Abhan-an Righe*, a river of the county of Kilkenny. It is called *Avonree*, or the *King's River*, from the death of the monarch, Niall, who, about the middle of the ninth century, was drowned in its waters during a flood, while he was endeavouring to preserve the life of a soldier of his train, who had been swept into the current of the river." It is hardly necessary to observe that the stately maiden of the poem, for love of whom so many thousands had died, is meant to represent fair Erin herself.

REMEMBER THEE (See p. 220).

I have not observed this melody, entitled "Castle Tirowen" in the seventh number of the *Melodies*, 1818, in any book of Irish tunes printed prior to that date. From Moore's correspondence we know that he was supplied on various occasions with MS. collections of airs by people residing in Ireland, whose attention was drawn to Power's handsome publication; it is possible that "Castle Tirowen" was one of those unpublished melodies. The gentleman alluded to in the preface to the seventh number of the *Melodies*, as having supplied Moore with nearly forty ancient airs and fragments of Irish poetry, was Crofton Croker, the well-known writer. In a letter of May, 1818, to his music publisher, Power, we find the poet writing: "I have got a most valuable correspondent and contributor for our future Melodies—a Mr. Croker, near Cork, who has just sent me thirty-four airs, and a very pretty drawing of a celebrated spot in the neighbourhood. He promises me various traditions too, and sketches of the scenery connected with them. All which will be of the greatest service to us." (Suppressed Letters of Moore to Power. 1854, p. 65.)

THERE IS NOT IN THE WIDE WORLD (See p. 265).

From the *Melodies* No. I, 1807; the air is there designated "The Old Head of Denis." On p. 36 of the *Ancient Music of Ireland*, Dr. Petrie gives an air in 3-8 time obtained from the singing of a peasant woman in 1837, in the county of Sligo, and which he considers to be the original form of Moore's air. I cannot see the slightest reason to agree with Dr. Petrie; "The Head of Old Denis" is a setting of probably the oldest of our folk-tunes which has been common to Ireland and Scotland for many centuries; these versions are countless, and those who are fortunate enough to possess James Oswald's *Caledonian Pocket Companion*, 12 bks., 1743-1764, may turn up the following tunes, all of which are different forms of the air in question: "Earl Douglas' Lament," bk. vii., "Corronside," bk. viii., "Ludo's Lament" and "Armstrong's Farewell," bk. ix., "Bennet's Dream," bk. x. Also "Robi donna gorach" in Neil Gow's *Collection of Strathspeys*, 1848, "Todlen Hame" in Johnson's *Scots Museum*, vol. iii., 1790, "My name is Dick Kelly" in Murphy's *Irish Airs*, 1809, and "The Lame Yellow Beggar" (erroneously stated to be the composition of O'Cahen) in Bunting's Collection, 1840, are all forms of the same tune.

LONDON : WILLIAM CLOWES AND SONS, LIMITED, TYPE-MUSIC AND GENERAL PRINTERS, STAMFORD STREET AND CHARING CROSS.

www.ingramcontent.com/pod-product-compliance
Lightning Source LLC
Chambersburg PA
CBHW021109270326
41929CB00009B/797